PRACTICE IN CONTEXT

Practice in Context
Situating the Work of Writing Teachers

Edited by

CINDY MOORE
St. Cloud State University

PEGGY O'NEILL
Loyola College

National Council of Teachers of English
1111 W. Kenyon Road, Urbana, Illinois 61801-1096

Staff Editor: Bonny Graham
Interior Design: Jenny Jensen Greenleaf
Cover Design: Carlton Bruett

NCTE Stock Number: 36613-3050

Library of Congress Cataloging-in-Publication Data

Practice in context : situating the work of writing teachers / edited
   by Cindy Moore, Peggy O'Neill.
      p. cm.
   Includes bibliographical references and index.
   ISBN 0-8141-3661-3
   1. English language—Composition and exercises—Study and
teaching. 2. English language—Rhetoric—Study and teaching.
3. Report writing—Study and teaching. I. Moore, Cindy, 1963– .
II. O'Neill, Peggy, 1963– . III. National Council of Teachers of
English.
PE1404 . P63 2002
808' .042071—dc21

2002010989

CONTENTS

Contents

III Supporting Practices

Contents

FOREWORD

Only Connect

KATHLEEN BLAKE YANCEY
Clemson University

What coherent whole can I make of snow on a beach?
RICHARD ROSENBLATT

E arlier this year, Paula Gillespie, a gifted teacher and writing center director at Marquette University, invited me to give a talk to beginning teachers on reflective teaching. How to define it, I wondered. The phrase *reflective teaching* is itself vague, still in search of a definition. We need a place to begin. Perhaps we could start with teaching itself, I think, one dimension of which is reflectiveness. Key to that, I continue reasoning, is *connecting*—students with our curriculum; students with students and faculty with students; and faculty with our curriculum and theirs.

Put more coherently, reflective teaching is (I decide)

the art
of bringing together in a self-aware way
the teacher's intent,
the disciplinary and institutional curricula, and
the students' experiences.

I share this definition with the participants at the beginning of the workshop, but I understand the term through the voices of Bakhtin. The graduate-students-who-are-becoming-teachers amplify, animate, and give life to the definition. When asked what it might mean to them, they query:

What is reflective teaching?

How can I connect it with peer tutoring?

What's the relationship between reflective teaching and leadership?

Will reflective teaching help me with the challenges I am facing as a teacher?

How can I encourage students to be connected?

How can I encourage students to take reflection outside the classroom?

And not least,

Do I already do it? (Am I already a reflective teacher? What would that mean? How would I know?)

———————

Reflective teaching:
change by design as a mechanism of agency—and hope.

Reflective teaching isn't new. No doubt we've all had teachers who were reflective. These teachers knew both curriculum and students. They observed where and when their curriculum "worked," and they knew how to talk about it and how to change it. They knew theory, but they didn't worship it; they used it to inform practice. They often found that practice was a best source for theory. They encouraged their students to theorize from practice. They observed their own teaching performances, noting there too what worked, what didn't, what might. They didn't need our word-du-jour critical-fronting their reflectiveness, although they *were* critically reflective. For them, the point wasn't critique. Rather, critique was a vehicle leading to understanding and to action. Unvoiced, invisible, unnamed, and untheorized (at least until recently), reflective teaching has nonetheless enriched our learning lives for as long as we can remember.

In the workshop at Marquette, as here, I understood that in defining teaching as reflective, I am also constructing it and, in so doing, beginning a process of demystification. I'm suggesting, in other words, that we *can* define reflective teaching, that we can nurture and foster it. Before we defined it and began talking about it explicitly, such teaching seemed a mystery, not the result of process or development, but rather a gift, an instinct or a talent. The teaching variant of the originary genius, reflective teaching seemed "available" only to those so born. You either had it—or (more likely) you didn't. And if you want to be a good teacher and suspect you aren't quite there, it's not very helpful to discover, after the fact, that you should have arranged to be a member of the teaching elect. Even if you're "born" to reflective teaching (as to good writing), your work is done once you're born. Constructed the "elected" way, then, reflective teaching isn't amenable to change—designed or accidental, it matters not.

Reflective teaching is located in the nexus of teacher, student, curriculum, and life: it assumes change by design as a mechanism of agency—and hope.

———————

Like writers, teachers also are reflective practitioners; for them, reflection is key to understanding performance.

Key to reflective teaching are the construct, the intellectual frameworks, and the language. With these, we can think both more systematically and more coherently about what it is that we do when we try to help students learn, in part because reflective teaching is more about learning than it is about teaching. And that is what we see in this volume of essays—efforts to put into dialogue and coherence the various dimensions of the teaching enterprise so that it becomes a learning enterprise for both teachers and students.

Such teaching is informed by four assumptions:

1. Reflective teaching is a theoretical enterprise.
2. Reflective teaching is purposeful.
3. Reflective teaching is informed by data.
4. Reflective teaching is oriented to change; its outcome is student learning.

———————

Reflective teaching uses the past to make sense of the future.

Today we have theorists and discourse to help us think about what reflective teaching is. Perhaps most influential among the former is the philosopher Donald Schön, who comes to reflective teaching through his definition of the reflective practitioner. Central to his definition is the concept of patterns. Schön argues that it is by reflecting on our own work—by knowing it, by reviewing it, by discerning patterns in it, by projecting appropriately from those patterns, and by using such projections to hypothesize a new way of thinking about a situation—that we come to know and understand our work and perhaps thus improve it. And Schön's work suggests that reflective teaching, in its understanding of the relationship of individual iteration to generalizations, is a deliberate art.

Within the last decade particularly, we've come to understand that reflective teaching involves the kinds of activities outlined by Schön. As in composing, the processes of reflective teaching are often recursive; not every reflective teacher will engage in all of them. But together they make reflective teaching visible, as we see in the essays collected here.

More specifically, we can identify five processes that reflective teachers engage in:

◆ *Reflective teachers focus.* Often that focus is planned, as when we intend to try something new. We craft a new assignment; we attempt a new response. Other times, a focus emerges from a student comment, a class listserv discussion, a session reading and responding to student texts. That focus, however, becomes a point of learning for both teacher and students. The question "What if?" becomes concurrently a way of seeing and a way of contributing to students' composing.

◆ *Reflective teachers record their practices and those of their students in texts of multiple kinds.* Such records—observational logs, student interviews, planned interventions and actual activities, student texts—permit a reviewer to answer the question "What happened?" from multiple perspectives and on the basis of several forms of evidence.

◆ *Reflective teachers perform multiple kinds of analysis on the records of teaching and learning.* Sometimes texts are analyzed for repetition or for change. Sometimes the perceptions of a teacher are compared with those of students. Sometimes a prototypical student helps us understand how what we ask of students connects with earlier experiences, conflicts with other curricula, or constructs students in ways intended and not. In all these records, patterns are traced; repetitions noted, counted, and categorized; themes discerned.

◆ *Reflective teachers create plural interpretations through the use of many frameworks, with the aid of multiple theories, within various contexts.* The analysis itself only signifies within a specified context, and explicating that context—and often more than one—brings meaning to the analysis. This allows us to say that, seen through one lens, the data suggest one interpretation; seen through a different lens, they may mean something different. Interpretation is thus multiple and rich.

◆ *Reflective teachers are committed to change.* The point of interpretation isn't only to understand what was; it is also to suggest what might be in another iteration. Reflective teaching relies on the past to point us in appropriate directions.

———————————

Reflective teaching is a communal activity.

According to Lee Shulman (1996), reflective teachers perform two tasks in particular that contribute to their ability to help students learn:

◆ First, they *interrupt their practice;* they stop what they are doing in order to gain perspective as they examine what has happened.

◆ Second, they *prepare to share* their observations with others. In that preparation and in that sharing, reflective teachers create knowledge about their teaching and their students' learning.

What's included in this volume, then, is reflective teaching made visible: teachers bringing practice to life, analyzing what seemed to happen, and making sense from the available data as informed by useful theory. As the editors observe, individual chapters are the local versions of global concerns: course design, assignments, supporting activities, and teacher response and assessment. Put differently, our master narratives of the teaching of writing are rewritten through these individual accounts.

As I've thought about the key moves that Shulman recommends and the kinds of teaching lives most of us inhabit, however, I've understood Shulman's tasks in another way, one seemingly more mundane but perhaps more important. What struck me when I first heard Shulman talk about reflective teaching and about the two tasks that enable teachers to make knowledge was how formal they seemed. For him, sharing seems to be the decidedly public act that we see in this volume, an interruption of teaching that is luxurious in its infrequency, typically at predetermined points on a school calendar. But most of us teach most of the time; we just can't stop all that often, and when we do, we aren't necessarily preparing book chapters or conference presentations.

There is, however, another way to understand cessation of activity and to define the sharing that follows. It's true that we stop practice during the summer (most of us) for extended periods, but I can also suspend practice, at least temporarily, at moments: after reading a set of essays, after my last class of the day, when I'm jogging. In fact, we do have opportunities to stop practice, as we do to share what we think we have learned. I share with my teaching friends, of course—the new approach that really seemed to work and I'm so excited about that I wander down the hall in search of a friend to tell; the student I can't seem to reach and I worry over when I should be focusing elsewhere. Given the ubiquity of electronic conversation, I share with colleagues around the country, and they share with me. While it's not formal in Shulman's sense, this sharing is productive and illuminating; it is, I think now, sometimes only within some of those shared, informal observations that we find the stuff of reflective teaching. And today I wonder as well if sharing, in this sense, also means sharing with students, bringing our observations and hypotheses to them. Perhaps in making this knowledge—for that too is what reflective teaching is about—we will find in students our best audience and our best collaborators both.

What would it mean to think of reflective teaching as an art?

At the beginning of this foreword, I defined reflective teaching as an art. "Put more coherently," I said, "reflective teaching is . . .

> the art
>> of bringing together in a self-aware way
>>> the teacher's intent,
>>> the disciplinary and institutional curricula, and
>>> the students' experiences."

In this definition, I assume—as do the writers included in this volume—that each teaching act is both unique and not; that there are certain patterns in the way we learn to write; and that if we are reflective about our teaching, we can identify those patterns in a useful way, for ourselves and for others. In other words, teaching and learning can be systematic and predictable.

A quarter of a century ago Richard Young made much the same argument about writing. In opposition to those who understood writing as a solitary and random act subject only to muse and prayer, Young argued the reverse: that writing is not mysterious, that it is more than a gift or a talent, and that it can be taught and learned. "The imaginative act," he said, "is not absolutely beyond the writer's control; it can be nourished and encouraged" (1980, 57). Young's favored technique to help the writer was the heuristic, a set of questions intended to bring a writer to insight. In describing the value of the heuristic, Young also suggested the value of any technique that can be used to structure a creative act such as writing or teaching:

> For to use a heuristic appropriately the writer must see the situation he is confronting at the moment as a specific variant of the kind of situation for which the procedure was designed; he must behave in some sense as though he has been there before. If he regards each situation as unique, he has no reason to believe that a technique that was useful once will be useful again. (57)

The writer, like the teacher, needs to understand each individual act more generally, as *a specific variant of the kind of situation for which the procedure was designed.* If, then, the situation and its more general features can be identified, we can employ those again to good effect—as writers, and by implication, as teachers.

And, not surprisingly, Young ties his argument about teaching qua art to Aristotle's conception of art and to teaching explicitly. The teacher, in Young's interpretation of Aristotle, is an artist precisely because she or he is a theorist who can assign causality and in so doing help others. The *Metaphysics,* according to Young, is the text

> where he [Aristotle] argues that art comes to men [sic] through experience, emerging as they become aware of the causes of success in carrying out a particular activity. Both the man of experience, i.e., the man who has a knack, and the man who has an art can carry out that activity, but, he says, we view artists "as being wiser in virtue not of being able to act, but of having the theory for themselves and knowing the causes" (1941, 690). One crucially important implication of this difference, he maintains, is that the artist can teach others to carry out the activity, while those who merely have a knack cannot. (1980, 56)

The teacher-as-artist, then, is purposeful because in assigning causality—in order to explain why something "works"—she or he moves beyond explanations such as "the good teacher" and "the able student." Rather, the teacher-as-artist talks in terms of the "fit" between an assignment and the processes leading to it and the development it intends. Or she speaks in terms of context, for instance, about the placement of an assignment *within* a curriculum. Or in terms of a responding strategy that goes beyond conventional understanding, widely held beliefs, or published research. In other words, reflective teachers assign causality to the stuff of teaching—tasks and processes and outcomes—as well as to the match between that stuff and the particular students who are themselves creating the stuff of learning. In Aristotle's world, then, what a teacher does matters: the teacher as artist has both *theory* and *causes.*

Teachers can theorize about successful practice precisely because they can link causally that practice with students and with outcomes. Moreover, reflective teaching, in its understanding of the relationship of individual iteration to generalizations, is a deliberate art.

Reflective teaching, as I've defined it, brings theory and practice together. It relies on four assumptions that link theory, practice, and data—that link teaching and learning. It entails five processes that, like the processes of composing, are recursive and generalizable. It creates knowledge through a two-step sequence: occlusion of practice and a sharing of what is in order to understand what can be. And what can be will be better than what was: that is the promise of reflective teaching.

Reflective teaching is more than useful, however, and more than important, although it is both of those. It is profound, and it is an art.

Reflective teaching changes the world we inhabit precisely because it changes all of us.

Works Cited

Shulman, Lee. 1996. "Course Anatomy: The Dissection and Transformation of Knowledge." Paper given at the American Association of Higher Education Conference on Faculty Roles and Rewards in Atlanta.

Young, Richard. 1980. "Arts, Crafts, Gifts, and Knacks. Some Disharmonies in the New Rhetoric." Pp. 53–60 in *Reinventing the Rhetorical Tradition,* ed. Aviva Freedman and Ian Pringle. Ontario: Canadian Council of Teachers of English; Conway, AR: L & S Books, University of Central Arkansas.

INTRODUCTION

Like many books, this collection was conceived out of personal need. When the idea for the book presented itself, both of us were in the midst of either preparing new writing teachers for the classroom or designing workshops for experienced writing teachers. As we talked long distance about our respective faculty-development projects, we suddenly discovered that both of us were confronting the same problem: how to introduce teachers to effective classroom practices while at the same time stressing the importance of disciplinary and institutional contexts. As experienced teachers, we understood the necessity of situating a particular teaching method within the context of current research and theory on teaching, learning, and writing. We also understood how crucial it is to think about where one is teaching, who one's students are, and who one is as a teacher.

Although there are many resources available for preparing writing teachers, none seemed to fit our complex needs. Not only did we want to emphasize the importance of context and reflection, but also we wanted our students to see how real teachers think through various aspects of classroom practice. And because neither of us was employed by a state university with a large graduate program and the accompanying numbers of graduate teaching assistants to prepare, we needed something that would work for the assortment of graduate students and instructors we encountered: secondary English teachers pursuing an M.A., new teaching assistants preparing to teach college composition for the first time, graduate students taking the TA prep course only because it fit within their schedule, adjunct instructors with no previous course work in composition, and experienced instructors who wanted to rejuvenate their practice.

Realizing that we couldn't write the book we needed by ourselves, we sought the help of experienced teachers from across the country. From the responses we received, we have compiled a collection of essays composed by writing teachers that describe a particular aspect of instruction (e.g., course design, writing assignment, supporting activity, or assessment) and situate that practice within specific institutional and disciplinary contexts. Because we believe that the theoretical underpinnings of teaching writing cross contexts, we have included contributors who represent a variety of teaching locations, including high schools, community colleges, Research I universities, and regional university campuses. Equally important, these contributors are positioned in diverse ways within their institutions. With respect to the college-level faculty, for example, many are professors at various stages in their academic careers; others are full-time instructors or graduate students. Some dedicate most of their time to teaching, while others combine teaching with administrative work. (Like both of us, most of the authors have taught in a variety of contexts at different points in their careers.) Such diversity demonstrates not only that all writing teachers can (and do) engage in reflective practice, but also that, regardless of particular career circumstances, we have much in common when it comes to considering how to best help students grow as writers.

Besides representing an assortment of institutions, theoretical positions, and instructors, the essays describe a variety of writing courses, not just first-year composition. Although many instructors begin their careers teaching this course, some, if not most, will eventually teach a range of writing courses, from basic writing to advanced composition and even graduate workshops. For many instructors, adjusting to new courses can be difficult because the support structure surrounding first-year composition often isn't available for other courses. We see this book, then, not only as a collection that meets the needs of new teachers but also as one that can grow with teachers as they encounter new courses, move to new institutions, and collect more experience.

Perhaps the most difficult aspect of this project was clarifying theoretical contexts. The tension between theory and practice is long established in writing studies (as in other disciplines), and the call for connecting theory and practice is a common one. In many colleges and universities, however, theory—or theoretical work—is still privileged over teaching, while in other contexts, such as community colleges and secondary schools, theory is downplayed or disparaged in favor of practical techniques. In writing studies, attempts to bridge this gap and reconfigure the relationship between theory and practice has been an ongoing enterprise. George Hillocks (1995) highlights the connection by referring to reflective practice, or "theory-driven teaching," that requires teachers not only to develop knowledge about learning, discourse, and teaching, but also to "reason about choices, plan in light of those reasons, implement those plans, examine their impact on students and revise and reformulate reasons and plans in light of that experience" (36–37). Like Hillocks and the many others who strive to unite theory and practice, we are convinced that writing teachers need to perceive a dynamic relationship between the two. But as professionals who prepare teachers, we find it difficult to make this relationship clear for veteran instructors, let alone new or preservice writing teachers. While many of us (especially those of us who are experienced teachers) often have a strong sense of what we want to do in the classroom, we aren't often called on to articulate *why* we do what we do. By making visible these connections, this book contributes to "demonstrating how reflection and action interact" (Roskelly and Ronald 1998, 26), enabling the pairing of theory and practice in response to particular situations, a move that is critical for all teachers but often difficult for inexperienced ones. As Pat Hinchey explains, "When the theoretical underpinnings of a practice are not clear—when the only rationale for a practice is that others say it 'works'—there are no clear guidelines to help implementers adapt a practice soundly to local conditions" (qtd. in Dobrin 1997, 26).

The contributors to this collection have taken time to both think through the theoretical warrants for a particular assignment or activity and assess how the practice actually works for their students, thus demonstrating how other teachers might adapt practices for local needs. While most invoke names of scholars and researchers whose work supports what they do in their classrooms, they are careful to present their rationales in language that is accessible to teachers with varying levels of experience. Much of the theoretical work drawn on falls into familiar categories, those delineated in taxonomies of the discipline by scholars such as James Berlin (1987) and Richard Fulkerson (1990). These categories include expressivism, social constructionism, cognitivism, feminism, and cultural studies. Yet, as we know from our own experience—and then rediscovered by reading the contributions we received—many people draw from various theoretical conversations. After all, in practice theoretical taxonomies rarely if ever exist in their pure form but rather tend to blur along the edges. In addition to formal theory (what we usually term Theory), contributors consider more personal beliefs about teaching and learning. In this way, we are using theory to mean what Louise Phelps (1989) calls the "deep structure" for teaching practice (37), or, as James Zebroski (1994), Sidney Dobrin (1997), and others explain it, theory with a small *t*. Particularly compelling are the essays that successfully bridge formal and informal theory, public and private knowing—that make theoretical justifications appear highly important but deeply personal. As they consider the theoretical discussions included in each essay, readers should think about theory in two ways: as both a scholarly conversation carried on among prominent academics in journals and books and as more of an everyday intuitive endeavor carried on by teachers in their classrooms.

Of course, as new teachers learn about theory and practice, they also must find their own voices among the many that participate in professional discussions about teaching. As Hephzibah Roskelly and Kate Ronald (1998) have recently argued: "[T]eachers, especially student-teachers, are often frustrated by their attempts to make someone else's experience their own" (16). Learning how to incorporate the ideas or practices one encounters in a text on teaching into one's own classroom approach can be especially frustrating when a new teacher finds herself or himself in a different type of institution, teaching different students, or teaching a different curriculum than that described in the text. By considering explanations of what teachers do in their classrooms and why, as well as how they have tailored their instruction to the particulars of their situations, readers should begin to see the dynamics involved in teaching writing and the importance of adapting methods to fit individual needs.

Contents

Each of our contributors offers a description of an approach, assignment, or activity that he or she has identified as particularly effective. We use *effective* to mean that through the activity students learn something about writing or being a writer and that what they learn coincides with the teacher's goals and the goals of the program or department. Sample classroom materials and student responses are provided throughout to help readers design their own activities and consider how students might benefit from them. To give readers an idea of how institutional histories and values shape classroom practice, contributors have also included discussions of their specific teaching sites and students. These discussions provide both demographic information and a sense of the character of individual classrooms and/or schools—those qualities that distinguish them from other contexts and have influenced the particular approach or practice featured in the essay.

Because this collection is also a guide meant to provide teachers with examples of useful classroom methods, the contents have been arranged in terms of practice, with sections on course design, assignments, supporting activities, and response and assessment. Each of the sections includes seven to nine essays or chapters written by different teachers and highlighting different teaching ideas.

Part I: Course Design

This section offers seven illustrations of how a writing course might be designed to meet the needs of a particular group of students and to reflect current trends in writing research and theory. Following a typical sequence of writing instruction, the section moves from first-year composition through advanced undergraduate courses and ends with a discussion of a graduate-level writing workshop course. The main principle guiding our selection process was that the course design and rationale be clear and well integrated, demonstrating to others the crucial connections between theory, practice, and location. Readers should note that although many of the courses described here are informed by multiple theories, they reflect a deliberate attempt to achieve internal coherence: a noticeable alignment between assignments, supporting activities, and assessment methods that helps students succeed. It is this sense of coherence, more than a particular theory or theme, that readers can apply to their particular teaching situations.

The section opens with Suellynn Duffey's essay on basic writing. Duffey explains how she and her colleagues at Ohio State University revised the basic writing curriculum as part of a proactive response to the institution's changing commitment to "remediation." By building on what they knew about literacy, their student population, and their institution, program administrators were able to create courses rich in reading and writing that not only benefited at-risk students but also addressed the concerns of university administrators. Following Duffey's discussion of basic writing is Catherine Latterell's presentation of a first-year composition course that requires students to think critically about technology. Drawing on the work of critical theorists such as Ira Shor and Anthony Giddens, Latterell describes how her course "desocializes" students, encouraging them to experience "habits or routines" in new and important ways. The next selection, Pavel Zemliansky's "Writing about Growing Up behind the Iron Curtain," depicts another theme-based course. Informed by Zemliansky's experience growing up in the former Soviet Union, the course offers students opportunities to consider their own lives in relation to those described by authors from former Soviet bloc countries. By the end of the semester, students understand how personal beliefs are shaped by social circumstances. Like Zemliansky's course, Katie Stahlnecker's builds on her interests as well as the students' own experiences, but this time more explicitly since the focus is on autobiography. Although Stahlnecker's course appears to be informed more by expressivist theories than social construction, it still requires that students think in terms of the larger culture as they explore personal topics such as family heritage.

Following these discussions of composition courses are essays that focus on two upper-level writing-in-the-disciplines courses. Hildy Miller's course incorporates service-learning as a means for preparing English majors for writing beyond the academy, thus highlighting the relevance of English degrees for undergraduate majors. Students in Miller's course spent nine hours a week in writing internships, where they experienced firsthand the difference between academic discourse forms and the various workplace genres they would encounter after graduation. Though Mark Schaub's writing-in-the-disciplines course focuses on many of the same concepts as Miller's, it places greater emphasis on academic genres and depends on a more traditional structure. Students learn how "discursive systems" operate by completing a series of assignments asking them to identify, analyze, and evaluate genres specific to both the world of work and their academic disciplines. The section closes with a discussion of a graduate-level nonfiction writing workshop that, like Miller's and Schaub's courses, emphasizes genre. Designed by Stephen Wilhoit to reflect his learner-centered teaching philosophy and address his students' particular needs, the course requires class members to compile their own "reader-rhetoric," which they use as a reference for class discussions and major writing assignments.

Part II: *Writing Assignments*

Writing assignments are the fundamental elements of a writing course, as demonstrated in Part I. Because they provide the focal points around which all other class activities revolve, assignments bear much of the burden for enacting an instructor's theories and pedagogy. They also make up the largest portion of a student's course grade. In this section, contributors offer a detailed description of an assignment (or assignment sequence) that has proven successful in helping students improve as writers, thinkers, and readers. They also discuss the theoretical and institutional contexts that inform the tasks they present. While readers may not be able to import these assignments directly into their own courses, the detailed explanations and rationales provide direction for adapting them to meet individual needs.

Reflecting the common classroom progression from personal to more objective forms of writing, the section opens with Tonya Stremlau's discussion of an autobiography assignment used in the beginning of her "accelerated" first-year course. Informed by expressivist theories that emphasize the development of a sense of personal "voice" or authority, this assignment, argues Stremlau, is beneficial for students like hers who have been traditionally marginalized. Stremlau shows how hearing-impaired students in particular can benefit from both writing about their own struggles within a hearing-centered society and examining their stories in the light of published narratives about deaf culture. The next assignment, designed by Heather Bruce, also emphasizes students' personal experience but this time in relation to academic ways of knowing. Drawing on the work of critical and feminist theorists, Bruce outlines a synthesis project that invites students to consider how they have come to know what they know about a topic of personal interest and then to compare their personal episte-mologies with those revealed in scholarly discussions of the topic. The assignment helps students recognize the constructed nature of both personal and public knowledge.

From these explicitly personal assignments, the section moves to an argument assignment that requires students to consider their beliefs and values through a more objective, critical lens. Draw-ing on feminist notions of argument as well as traditional rhe-torical concepts such as *kairos,* Margaret Strain explains how she complicates and deconstructs the adversarial, two-sided ar-gument form by requiring students to create polylogues on con-troversial topics. According to Strain, the assignment helps students understand not only the complexity of most social is-sues but also the highly constructed nature of personal opinions. Approaching argument from another angle, Mary Mulder shows how critical and liberal-humanist pedagogies can be successfully mingled to promote thoughtful analysis, meaningful research, and compelling persuasive writing. By examining an issue of personal importance to them from both traditional and poststructuralist perspectives, the community college students in Mulder's class are encouraged to embrace the idea of a shared American experi-ence while at the same time recognizing the history and contin-gency of that experience.

The section continues with three essays that explicitly chal-lenge conventional notions of research writing. Addressing her students' discomfort with academic discourse in general and per-suasive forms in particular, Margrethe Ahlschwede offers a sequence of activities that helps students realize the power of language and their own powers as language users. Through her Save the World project, which encourages students to use a variety of research methods and persuasive forms, Ahlschwede makes the point that anyone can inspire change. Eve Gerken's discussion of her recent move to a flexible research-writing process and assignment, which replaces the traditional research paper required of high school seniors, confirms many of the points made by Ahlschwede. Yet, while they both emphasize the benefits of uniting form with function, Gerken focuses more on how experimenting with nontraditional research forms can help students express their own voices and develop a sense of themselves as writers. Like Ahlschwede and Gerken, David Seitz is interested in nontraditional forms. His ethnographic research assignment, which requires four to five weeks of observations and interviews, offers students an important alternative to traditional library research and prompts them to investigate innovative reporting methods. Because of its emphasis on the connections between culture and individuals—an emphasis supported by social constructionist theories—students in Seitz's class (like those in Bruce's and Mulder's) gain important insights about the nature of knowledge, language, and community.

The section closes with Dan Melzer's description of a semester-long online newspaper project. The collaborative project, which prompts multiple forms of writing, gives students a chance to imagine audiences outside of the immediate classroom. Because they compare their work to that of traditional print newspapers, students learn much about the different rhetorical challenges that accompany different discourse forms.

Part III: Supporting Practices

Since the process movement took hold in the1980s, invention, drafting, responding, revising, and editing have been accepted as important aspects of the writer's work. Teachers, therefore, are expected to incorporate these activities into the classroom while allowing for the recursiveness and uniqueness that accompany individual writing efforts. At the same time, teachers must include a range of other activities that encourage student development but may not lead explicitly to the production of a final, polished text—activities that improve critical reading, research, or discussion skills. Besides illustrating numerous practices that directly support the completion of major writing assignments, then, contributors to this section describe a variety of ancillary activities, including dialogic reading responses and journal writing. They also demonstrate how seemingly universal methods are shaped by local needs and values.

The section opens with veteran high school teacher P. L. Thomas sharing his struggle to get students "to practice a writing process that is open-ended and chaotic." Influenced by traditional, conservative, small-town values, Thomas's students tend to see writing in terms of rigid formulas and inflexible rules. They resist, at first, his unconventional approach but eventually come to understand that the key to good writing is making effective rhetorical choices—choices that may or may not conform to traditional conventions. Following Thomas's essay, which emphasizes development of authorial identity or agency, Annette Powell describes how she revised her classroom practices to emphasize the social forces that shape attitudes and beliefs. Through reading and reflection, Powell realized how her own subject position as a woman of color at a predominantly white university contributed to classroom dynamics, but, instead of blaming the students, she adjusted her methods, incorporating student-centered discussions, informal response papers, and rhetorical analysis to help students grapple with contested topics.

From Thomas's and Powell's comprehensive approaches to supporting writing assignments, the section moves to illustrations of more self-contained activities. Margaret McLaughlin's "The Focused Reading Response," for example, illustrates how brief dialogic reading responses foster comprehension while generating potential topics for future writing assignments. This technique, which McLaughlin adapted from Ann Berthoff's depictions of the double-entry journal, requires students to select and copy a quote from the text, explain its significance, and then make a personal connection to it. While McLaughlin's discussion centers on assigned reading, the next essay, by Janis Haswell, describes a research journal that students complete as they read and select sources for a research-based essay. In "Locating Students in Academic Dialogue," Haswell shows how such a journal helps students develop their abilities to evaluate sources and synthesize ideas.

The journals that Haswell and McLaughlin describe function as prewriting or invention strategies because they help students generate ideas before they draft more formal texts. With the next essay, the section turns toward strategies that can be used after students complete a draft. In "Moving beyond 'This is good' in Peer Response," Peggy Woods explains how she encourages students to provide useful comments for one another during peer review sessions. By drawing on the students' previous experiences with feedback, Woods helps them distinguish between discouraging comments and the types of comments that encourage revision and foster a sense of community among writers. Paul Johnson's essay takes a different approach to facilitating effective peer response: he advocates using an electronic bulletin board for anonymous draft workshops. According to Johnson, his students "are subject to the prevailing cultural condition known as Minnesota Nice, which requires politeness in all exchanges, even at the expense of honesty or critique." Because the aliases are assigned by Johnson, students are accountable for their work but don't feel pressured to build social relationships as they might when responding face to face.

Wendy Bishop's essay shifts the discussion from response to revision. For her "radical revision" assignment, students not only have to substantially revise an essay but also write a meta-essay that focuses on what they have learned through the process of revision. Bishop attests to the success of this activity for a variety of writing students; it is fun yet theoretically informed, it requires rule following as well as rule breaking, it places conventions in dialogue with experimentation, and, finally, "it teaches writing as a writer experiences it." The next essay, by Brian Huot, offers numerous strategies for teaching students how to proofread and edit their texts. Most students, Huot contends, don't have a systematic approach to proofreading because they have had little if any formal instruction in it. He offers a set of practices that are situated "within a rich understanding of the process of writing" to illustrate how teachers can emphasize correctness in more productive ways.

The section closes with Janice McIntire-Strasburg's "Reading the Writing Process on the Web," which addresses process within the context of an end-of-semester hypertext portfolio. Like a traditional hard-copy collection, a hypertext portfolio demands that students bring together everything they have learned throughout the semester. Yet, as McIntire-Strasburg explains, because Web portfolios require different reading strategies, they can provide unique opportunities to emphasize rhetorical principles such as audience.

Part IV: Teacher Response and Evaluation

Responding to and evaluating student writing are critical components of the work of writing teachers. Activities such as commenting on drafts in progress, grading final papers, evaluating portfolios, and assigning course grades not only absorb much of a teacher's time and energy, but also help students gauge their development as writers. Because writing teachers always seem to be looking for ways to make their evaluations more useful and meaningful, there is a long and rich history of advice on how to respond and evaluate—from using checklists and rubrics, to conferencing, to employing holistic grading. Contributors to this section discuss these methods and other, more recent trends, such as reflection and self-evaluation, which offer important opportunities for students to become critical readers of their own texts and to participate more fully in the assessment process.

While it is tempting, and perhaps all too typical, to regard writing assessment as something added on to the end of an assignment or semester, the contributors see their response and evaluation methods as fully integrated into their course designs. Although the assessment methods presented here may not be radically new, each essay offers a unique glimpse into how particular methods can be adapted to meet specific needs and goals.

The first essay, "Taking Out the Guesswork: Using Checklists in the Composition Classroom" by Lee Nickoson-Massey, offers a structured response and evaluation technique that incorporates student reflection. Using checklists for response, argues Nickoson-Massey, helps make criteria explicit because it guides both the feedback students receive and the discussions they have about writing and revising. In addition to the response checklist, Nickoson-Massey uses a list of grading criteria that students develop collaboratively for the final course portfolios. Through this collaborative activity, "learning about assessment practices is integrated into the students' learning experience."

In the next essay, which also highlights reflective writing, Kate Freeland shows how she uses student conferencing as an effective response strategy for her basic writing students. By requiring pre- and postconference reflections, asking open-ended questions, learning to listen, allowing for silence, and mirroring students' ideas, Freeland has been able to make fifteen- to twenty-minute conferences more productive. Carl Gerriets's essay, "Building Relationships through Written Dialogue," incorporates some of the same strategies and rationales that Freeland uses, but the focus here is on written communication. With the help of student Jennifer Lowe, Gerriets explains how he employs reflective cover letters to establish a written dialogue with students at his community and technical college who "are on campus only long enough to attend class before rushing off to a part- or full-time job or to relieve the babysitter."

Following Gerriets and Lowe is a chapter by Jeff Sommers, who teaches at a two-year branch campus. In "A Comprehensive Plan to Respond to Student Writing," Sommers explains how he responds to students' reflective memos and drafts by tape-recording his comments. As students listen to Sommers's comments, they annotate their drafts. This approach allows him to cover more ground in less time and encourages students to be active participants in the response process. All of this fits within a portfolio system of assessment that requires students to include reflective, metacognitive letters with all of their revised work.

Up to this point, the contributors have been college writing teachers discussing college classrooms. The section moves into the secondary classroom with Steven Smith's essay, "Why Use Portfolios? One Teacher's Response," in which Smith explains a curriculum for ninth- through twelfth-grade students based on year-long portfolios. According to Smith, his students, most of whom "are working class, will be the first in their families to attend college, and have rarely been encouraged to make connections between education and an improved life," respond favorably to the recursive process of collection, reflection, and selection emphasized in his approach.

The section closes with an essay that demonstrates how teachers' writing assignments can be incorporated into the evaluation process. "Criteria for Measuring Authentic Intellectual Achievements in Writing," by Kendra Sisserson, Carmen K. Manning, Annie Knepler, and David Jolliffe, reports on the results of a collaboration between the authors and Chicago public school teachers. The authors discuss a comprehensive rubric that, unlike other assessment methods, does not focus exclusively on student writing. One part of the rubric "evaluates the extent to which writing assignments ask students to construct knowledge, elaborate, and relate their writing to their own lives," while the other part "examines the extent to which students demonstrate these skills." The rubric allows teachers to gauge both the success of students' writing and the quality of their own assignments.

Final Note

Although this collection addresses both theory and practice, suggesting that it can stand alone, we see it as being most usefully placed in dialogue with other texts and with teachers' own experiences. A teacher preparation course, for example, might successfully use this book as a way to illustrate ideas developed in a collection of theoretical essays. Similarly, because it shows how pedagogical trends actually play out in classrooms, this collection also could be used to complement a practice-oriented instructional guide. Teachers not enrolled in a theory and pedagogy course but eager to learn more about good teaching might use the book as a guide for drawing connections between practice, theory, and institutional location. However readers use the book, we hope it offers a way to think about what writing teachers do—and how disciplinary and institutional contexts shape instruction and students' responses to it.

Works Cited

Berlin, James. 1987. *Rhetoric and Reality: Writing Instruction in American Colleges, 1900–1985.* Carbondale: Southern Illinois University Press.

Dobrin, Sidney I. 1997. *Constructing Knowledges: The Politics of Theory-Building and Pedagogy in Composition.* Albany: State University of New York Press.

Fulkerson, Richard. 1990. "Composition Theory in the Eighties: Axiological Consensus and Paradigmatic Diversity." *College Composition and Communication* 41: 409–29.

Hillocks, George Jr. 1995. *Teaching Writing as Reflective Practice.* New York: Teachers College Press.

Phelps, Louise Wetherbee. 1989. "Images of Student Writing: The Deep Structure of Teacher Response." Pp. 37–67 in *Writing and Response: Theory, Practice, and Research,* ed. C. M. Anson. Urbana, IL: National Council of Teachers of English.

Roskelly, Hephzibah, and Kate Ronald. 1998. *Reason to Believe: Romanticism, Pragmatism, and the Teaching of Writing.* Albany: State University of New York Press.

Zebroski, James. 1994. *Thinking through Theory: Vygotskian Perspectives on the Teaching of Writing.* Portsmouth, NH: Boynton/Cook.

I

Course Design

CHAPTER ONE

Teaching and Literacy in Basic Writing Courses

SUELLYNN DUFFEY

Georgia Southern University

Institutional Context

For many years, the basic writing program I directed at Ohio State University worked toward three main goals. First, it studied ways to resist the intellectual and other stratification that basic writing courses often entail (see McNenny and Fitzgerald 2001). Second, the program consistently intensified its curricula in order to resist perpetuating the academic castes that result from offering only watered down college work to basic writers, denying them access to and practice in the real intellectual work of the academy. Third, the program positioned its courses strategically in order to continue offering extra instruction to students we believed would need it. Working toward these goals allowed the program to withstand the winds of change carrying politicians' arguments that "remedial" education at the college level "covered" what students should have already learned in high school. According to this argument, funding remedial education required the state to pay a second time for what had already been paid for (in dollars to high school education). Although our program was not in crisis, it was easy to see that the further our university (and the national current) moved away from open admission policies, the more vulnerable basic writing programs were.[1] To us at OSU, it seemed reasonable that just as babies who learn to speak at widely different ages are still considered "normal," our first-year college students would continue to develop as writers at different paces, no matter how selective the admissions criteria. Thus, we took a proactive approach to our program, continually revising it to avoid vulnerability to economic demise.

Before I go further, I want to describe the students in our courses, since the population of basic writers at any given institution is in large measure locally defined (see Jensen 1986; Troyka 1987a; Bartholomae 1987; Horner and Lu 1999). Ohio State, a very large research university, drew its students mainly from Ohio. Although it had greater ethnic and racial diversity than might a regional campus in the upper Midwest, its diversity paled in comparison to what might be expected in New York or Texas, for example. Nearly all of the basic writing students were of traditional age and native speakers of English. They were a mix of residential and commuter students. A combination of criteria placed them into basic writing courses, College Board scores providing the first screening. All incoming students with ACT verbal scores of 17 and below were required to write a placement essay during summer orientation. On the basis of the writing samples, students were placed into one of three course levels: (1) a two-quarter basic writing series, (2) a one-quarter enhanced basic writing and first-year composition course, or (3) the first-year "nonremedial" course. The course I will describe was for students in the middle placement level, those who needed more support than the five-credit first-year nonremedial course afforded but whose writing was closer to "standard" school prose than the weakest of students. Over the years, this middle course had changed so that, among other things, its catalog number was not remedial—i.e., "precollege"—but the course still served the same student population. This numbering change is one of the strategies we used to decrease our program's vulnerability to economic arguments to disband it.

Along with the renumbering, the credit load change (from three hours to seven) allowed us to argue that we were reducing costs. Because such an argument may seem counterintuitive, let me explain. Previously, students at this middle placement level took three hours of basic writing followed by five hours of nonremedial composition in a subsequent quarter (for a total of eight credit hours). After our changes, however, students at this level took seven credit hours, so overall the university paid for fewer hours of instruction. In addition, we used our scholarly knowledge and banked on the value of collaborative learning. While students met each week (for five credit hours) with an instructor, they also met (for two credit hours) with peer groups led by trained undergraduates in the Writing Center. With this restructuring, we had turned the three-hour basic writing course into the intensive, nonremedial, five-hour course—plus two— and we put current theory into our program structure as well as into our pedagogical practices.

Thus, the basic writing students received almost the same number of credit hours as before and the university saved money. Because the peer group leaders were compensated with course credit and professionalizing experiences, the university also got added value in what it offered undergraduate tutors. By arguing that our proposed change would reduce costs, we had guaranteed students continued specialized instruction:

1. more experienced instructors than were available in the nonremedial courses (a local phenomenon that might not be replicated at other institutions)

2. an intensified credit-load for the course

3. a challenging curriculum

True, by choosing concentrated instruction in one quarter versus instruction spread out over a longer period, we had opted for more intensive as opposed to extensive writing instruction. While we did not know for certain that intensive instruction would be equivalent to extensive, we gambled that it was better than placing students directly into the nonremedial course with no extra support at all.

Pedagogical Aims

So what kind of a course did we design? We had learned from research that tracking tended to perpetuate itself because students placed into lower tracks usually stayed there (Loban 1976). One of the reasons, we suspected, was that students received "watered down" curricula (Lunsford 1987). We had also learned from teaching experience that if we expected more from our students and created strong learning contexts, they were able to do more. As a result, we gradually created more intellectually demanding courses.

Early in the basic writing program's history, students did not write anything longer than a paragraph. At that time, the program subscribed more closely to what's often called a "building block" theory of learning—that learners start with the small components of language and learn them in isolation (i.e., separate from rich linguistic and cultural contexts) before they are ready to move on to more complex tasks. Over time, though, practices changed as teachers saw that writing short paragraphs in some ways impeded students' ability to write longer, well-developed, sustained pieces in their subsequent courses. The program thus ceased to limit students to writing short paragraphs.

Lynn Troyka helped us articulate problems with the building block theory of writing instruction. In "Perspectives on Legacies and Literacy in the 1980s," for example, Troyka (1987b) describes her basic writing students as "holistic," "field-dependent thinkers" who "perceive the world as a whole, not as a combination of separate parts" (23). Troyka continues, "Such students learn best with a 'top-down' model of language processing. They move easily from seeing the whole of a paragraph or an essay to then seeing the sentence and finally downsliding to consider the word" (23). While Troyka taught nontraditional community college students in New York City and not all student populations are like hers, Troyka's insights translate easily into what I've found to be good writing pedagogy for many students at all placement levels: Use a top-down model of instruction. Supply students with a context for their tasks. And help students separate part from whole, particularly in our comments on their texts.

After longer writing tasks were in place, we began to integrate reading into the courses, because we saw reading and writing as parallel acts of composing. Mariolina Salvatori in "Reading and Writing a Text" (1987) articulates theoretically and demonstrates with student examples the kind of integration we sought. She explains, for example, that "the improvement in writers' ability to manipulate syntactic structures—their maturity as writers—*is the result, rather than the cause,* of their increased ability to engage in, and to be reflexive about, the reading of highly complex texts" (178; emphasis added). We wanted students to engage in practices of meaning making, *negotiated* meaning making—through both reading and writing, even if the written texts they produced were not necessarily conventional replicas of standard academic prose.

Course Content

To accomplish our pedagogical aims, all the basic writing courses engaged students in quarter-long inquiries and constant reading and writing. The subjects for inquiry varied, but the course I discuss here focused on literacy, language, and community. This frequently used theme seems particularly appropriate for basic writing classes because it addresses how language both excludes people from and includes them in cultural, social, and academic groups. While giving students practical tools to succeed in the university (such as reading and writing skills), the course also gave them conceptual tools (through the course content) with which to reflect on the academic caste systems that designated them as basic writers. This metaknowledge, I believe, is as important as any practical skills students may gain from a writing class.[2]

The array of texts offered critiques of academic literacy (e.g., Paulo Freire's "The Banking Concept of Education"), readings about language and literacy (e.g., Barbara Mellix's often anthologized essay "From Outside, In" and excerpts from Deborah Tannen's *You Just Don't Understand*), and examples of literacies not privileged by the academy, such as student writing used authoritatively instead of just as models. Students also read Mike Rose's *Lives on the Boundary,* in keeping with our long-standing practice of assigning entire books. The practice began when we first adapted the curriculum that David Bartholomae and Anthony Petrosky lay out in *Facts, Artifacts, and Counterfacts: Theory and Method for a Reading and Writing Course* (1986).

In addition to the reasons Bartholomae and Petrosky offer (e.g., the importance of engaging students in a seminarlike environment), we had others. We wanted students simply to read, since many had read very little. But, more significant, we believed that the extended discourse in a book offered students a *qualitatively* different reading experience than did a series of short essays. Among other things, it offered more complexity, the opportunity to return to passages and ideas and reconsider them, and the sense of sustained attention. (We also knew some students would feel a sense of accomplishment when they could say, "I read a whole book!")

Writing Assignments

Like reading an entire book and returning students' attention to it over a sustained period of time, the writing assignments also called for recursive attention to the same topics. This recursivity was enacted in many ways, most notably through sets of paired assignments. The first in each pair set the stage for the second, each in a different way. Instructors in the basic writing program were expected, for example, to assign a "diagnostic" essay on the first day or so of class as a double check on students' placement. I used this requirement to serve both programmatic needs (placement accuracy) and to focus students' attention immediately on literacy. The first-day essay asked students to "consider an attitude you have toward reading, writing, speaking, or listening and write an essay in which you relate an incident that shows how an event or person helped shape the attitude you now hold." Since students would later write a personal literacy history, they were, on the first day, generating material they could use later. No class time was "wasted" by meeting the program's needs, and this assignment brought into the structure of the class an interval of time between students' first production of a text and its revision, a good pedagogical tactic.

We often say that such preliminary assignments "get students ready" to do upcoming tasks, and I would agree. A second pair of assignments bore a similar relationship. For one task, students interviewed a classmate about his or her literacy in preparation for a later interview, a more substantial assignment that required more research and asked students to investigate the literacy of someone in their family. While the first assignment in both sets "got students ready" for the later assignment, I would like to draw attention here to our terminology because it too easily obscures the truly diverse heuristic and other functions that such a sequencing of assignments can and should perform.

The first interview and write-up clearly offered students practice with the processes and techniques of interviewing and representing information. But the two interview assignments are in fact such different tasks that teachers should hesitate to see too great a transfer from one assignment to the next. I originally noticed this potential problem with transfer because the first interview write-ups were weak whereas the subsequent literacy biographies often resulted in stronger writing and strongly positive student perceptions of doing the assignment. With a little reflection, I realized that interviewing a stranger and interviewing one's mother, for example, occur within such radically different contexts that in some ways it's accurate to say they are not the same task at all. Certainly the form of the tasks—generating questions, asking them, probing for additional information, culling and sorting information, interpreting it, and reconstructing it into an essay—is the same for both assignments. But the rhetorical situations and the content the interviews generated make the two assignments so different that to say the first assignment "got students ready" for the second seems accurate only at a high level of abstraction, maybe that of a teacher's view or an on-paper rationale, not at the level of students performing the tasks.

The students' success with the second interview assignment suggests the positive potential of sequencing. This assignment built on the familiarity students already had with literacy because they had written about their own histories and read about others' literacy histories (their peers' drafts and class-assigned readings). In other words, the students had developed knowledge about literacy that became "prior knowledge" on which they built "new" knowledge in the subsequent assignment. The sequence also offered the opportunity for students to deepen their knowledge of literacy by conversing about it with someone they knew well—that is, by using it in a new but familiar rhetorical and emotional context. (The assignment directed them to consider what significant influences shaped the person's literacy and how and why the person's literacy was different from or similar to theirs.) This assignment sequence exemplifies principles on which I build courses: reading and writing that cycle between the familiar and the not-so-familiar, the personal and the distant, the specific and the general, "received knowledge" and challenges to it, and the organic development of concepts in students' thinking and writing. This sequence also exemplifies a cycle—or a spiral—of interrelated tasks. The spiral—or, more accurately, *intersecting spirals*—continued into the final course project, which asked students to consider causes and effects of people's literacy experiences by synthesizing information from the readings and from their own and classmates' writings. The goal was for them to write a "definition of literacy," a culminating project of synthesis, analysis, and theory building that I try to design into every class I teach.

Thus, the title of this essay, "Teaching and Literacy in Basic Writing Courses," intentionally carries a double meaning. First, the course taught literacy (as a content) by teaching *about* the subject. Some of the readings, for example, explored race, class, and gender in relation to literacy. But the course also asked students to *enact* literate processes at the same time they were asked to become more consciously aware of them. Most obviously, it asked them to undertake recursive reading and writing tasks. More specifically, it led them through language-based inquiry, meaning-making processes based on the concrete data the class generated, interpretation in the context of competing interpretations, and more. In such ways, we can offer basic writing students the opportunity to succeed in the academy by doing its real work, not watered-down versions of it. We can also responsibly balance our commitment to basic writers against fiscal pressures.

Notes

1. This trend toward what is often called "excellence" subsequently gained strength and has continued. Georgia Southern, for example, the university where I now teach, disbanded its developmental writing program last year in concert with rising admission requirements.

2. I should note that this particular course is one I team-taught with Kay Halasek. Kay and I adapted a generic, collaboratively developed course.

Works Cited

Bartholomae, David. 1987. "Writing on the Margins: The Concept of Literacy in Higher Education." Pp. 66–83 in *A Sourcebook for Basic Writing Teachers,* ed. Theresa Enos. New York: Random House.

Bartholomae, David, and Anthony Petrosky. 1986. *Facts, Artifacts, and Counterfacts: Theory and Method for a Reading and Writing Course.* Upper Montclair, NJ: Boynton/Cook.

Horner, Bruce, and Min-Zhan Lu. 1999. *Representing the "Other": Basic Writers and the Teaching of Basic Writing.* Urbana, IL: National Council of Teachers of English.

Jensen, George H. 1986. "The Reification of the Basic Writer." *Journal of Basic Writing* 5: 52–64.

Loban, Walter. 1976. *Language Development: Kindergarten through Grade Twelve.* Research Report No. 18. Urbana, IL: National Council of Teachers of English.

Lunsford, Andrea. 1987. "Politics and Practices in Basic Writing." Pp. 246–58 in *A Sourcebook for Basic Writing Teachers,* ed. Theresa Enos. New York: Random House.

McNenny, Gerri, and Sallyanne H. Fitzgerald, eds. 2001. *Mainstreaming Basic Writers: Politics and Pedagogies of Access.* Mahwah, NJ: Lawrence Erlbaum.

Salvatori, Mariolina. 1987. "Reading and Writing a Text: Correlations between Reading and Writing Patterns." Pp. 176–86 in *A Sourcebook for Basic Writing Teachers,* ed. Theresa Enos. New York: Random House.

Troyka, Lynn Quitman. 1987a. "Defining Basic Writing in Context." Pp. 2–15 in *A Sourcebook for Basic Writing Teachers,* ed. Theresa Enos. New York: Random House.

Troyka, Lynn Quitman. 1987b. "Perspectives on Legacies and Literacy in the 1980s." Pp. 16–26 in *A Sourcebook for Basic Writing Teachers,* ed. Theresa Enos. New York: Random House.

CHAPTER TWO

Reexperiencing the Ordinary: Mapping Technology's Impact on Everyday Life

CATHERINE G. LATTERELL
Penn State Altoona

Among other attributes, I inherited from my dad (who was a chemistry professor) a sensitivity to suggestions that school is somehow separate from "the real world." At family picnics when I was a kid, I remember him suppressing a wince when someone would ask, not unkindly, "So, are you teaching this summer or working?" Perhaps this is why an underlying assumption of my composition teaching is that language is central to how we experience and understand ourselves and the world we live in.

Put another way, to teach people to read and write is to teach them a way of experiencing the world, and this is the guiding principle of the course and assignments described here. By teaching reading and writing as acts of knowledge making about themselves and everyday life, we engage students in critical reflection of the social, cultural, and material forces influencing who they are and how they live. And we promote in students the possibility of shaping, instead of always being shaped by, these multiple influences.

The world where I teach is the branch campus of the Pennsylvania State University in Altoona, and the assignments I describe here are from my syllabi for English 15, titled Rhetoric and Composition, which is the writing requirement for all incoming Penn State students. Penn State Altoona, previously a two-year campus, became a four-year college in 1997 and currently enrolls approximately four thousand students. The school grants nine associate degrees and ten baccalaureate degrees in electromechanical engineering, business administration, integrative arts, and English, to name a few. The school also serves students earning the first two years of their university education on a small campus before they transfer to Penn State's University Park campus to complete degrees in a wide range of disciplines.

While students come from all over the state as well as other parts of the country, the majority of our students come from towns in western Pennsylvania designated as part of Appalachia—towns with manufacturing and agricultural income bases and low percentages of college graduates. Like students attending many community colleges or other small public two- and four-year schools, the young people in my classes possess markers of both the margin and the center of modern U.S. cultural life. Like everyone else in the country, they take their cultural cues from popular mass media, yet their lived experiences, rooted in small towns, also condition their perspectives. This dual perspective provides most students with remarkable rhetorical skills as cultural critics, giving us a ready-made starting point for the class. That students don't come to my first-year composition class expecting to connect what we do in the classroom to their everyday lives (to "the real world") is my challenge.

Course Description and Rationale

Many teachers sharing my views about teaching writing have chosen to focus on topics revolving around popular culture, the media, or issues of gender, race, and class in U.S. society. I have chosen to focus my first-year composition course on the impact of technology on our everyday lives. Although the course and assignments continue to evolve, my goal for the class has been to increase students' critical awareness and use of technology in their daily lives. The class does not focus on being critical of technology's impact, meaning finding fault. Rather, it is about generating an increased consciousness among students of the ways in which they use and are used by the technologies surrounding us all. As one of the goals of my first-year composition course states, by the end of the course, students will have developed a keener understanding of the role of technology in many aspects of their lives so that they can become more responsible technology consumers *and* technology critics.

To succeed at this goal, I must help students step back from, or desocialize, their everyday experiences with technology; in doing so, we open up these experiences for reflection, critical analysis, and, possibly, change. Developed by Ira Shor and promoted by James Berlin (cf. 1988, 1996), desocialization is a practice of critical dialogue in which "students extraordinarily re-experience the ordinary" (Shor 1992, 122). Similar to this practice is Anthony Giddens's concept of deroutinization—which I believe is a more fitting term. As Giddens defines it, deroutinization "refer[s] to any influence that acts to counter the grip of the taken-for-granted character of day-to-day interaction" (1979, 220; see also 1984). Why should we care so much about examining the habits or routines we barely notice in our daily lives? Giddens argues that it is routines that help us maintain a continuity of social action between individuals because they speak to our human need for connection to others. Consequently, by deroutinizing social behaviors, we uncover the values undergirding them and can begin reflecting on what these values mean—how they shape our sense of self and our conceptions of the communities of which we are a part. Particularly in this course, we focus on going beneath the surface of, or deroutinizing, our technology use in order to uncover those values and their influences on us. The course I have developed over the past five years is based on these assumptions, drawn from critical pedagogy and Giddens's social theories.

The course is organized around an examination of the rhetorical codes surrounding technology use in our lives. It consists of four units and one final self-evaluation essay, which introduces a final portfolio representing the students' work during the semester (see the appendix for an outline of course reading/writing assignments). Each unit begins with readings dealing with competing notions about the topic of the unit. Additionally in each unit, students' personal experiences of technology use are located within specific social contexts to which they belong. The first unit introduces the theme of technology's impact on everyday life; the second unit asks students to analyze student life on campus as it is influenced by a particular technology or technological practice; the third unit highlights and questions the impact of the Internet and culminates with students drafting a Web site review; and the fourth unit asks students, within the context of our theme, to develop a researched proposal in which they identify a problem or challenge involving a local community to which they belong and propose possible solutions. During each unit, students typically write a couple of one- to two-page mini-essays or short responses and three drafts of an essay assignment. I grade using a portfolio system, in which students submit their work at the end of each unit as well as at the end of the semester.

The Assignments

The following descriptions outline three assignments from the course just described. The first is a short writing assignment from the first unit. Though short, it is vital for setting the context from which the class will operate throughout the semester. The next two assignments are both formal essays, from the second and third units. Throughout the discussion that follows, I have tried to go beyond summarizing a particular assignment in order to situate each one within my course goals, and I reflect on challenges I have faced with each of them.

Assignment 1: Keeping a Technology Journal

The purpose of the first writing assignment is to use writing to help students deroutinize their daily technology use. As a class, the students must begin making visible the taken-for-granted impact of technology on everyday life. During initial class discussions, students hear the word *technology* and think of their cars or of the computers in dorm rooms and labs. Without this journal assignment and the subsequent class discussion, it can be difficult to broaden students' thinking about technology.

The assignment has a simple design. Students must carry a notebook with them for two separate two-hour periods over a weekend. In this notebook, they must record every incident or act in which they use a technology and the time of that use. As the assignment states, "To keep this journal, you will need to decide what counts as a technology, and you will need to figure out a way to be descriptive without going overboard." Although it does not dawn on students at first, I am fully aware this is an unrealistic, even impossible, task. Students need to be told that we do not expect completeness with this journal, but rather that they use their judgment about the level of descriptive detail. I do suggest an approximate number of pages for the two time periods, but beyond that each student has to figure out his or her own way to keep such a journal.

Upon reflection, I believe the class period following this assignment is vitally important for making this course's theme real to the students. During the follow-up class, students begin for the first time to deal with the question of how to define what counts as technology and how to make technologies visible in their daily routines. To begin, students break into groups, share their technology journals, and draft a working definition of what it means to identify something as a technology. As a whole class, we use the board (or a text-sharing software program if we are in a computer classroom) to create a mega-list. The process of making the taken-for-granted more visible begins as we list items from the more obvious, such as cars, dorm keycards, computer systems, and stereos, to the less obvious, such as walking paths, toothbrushes, shoelaces, aspirin, and buttons.

As a result of keeping a journal and the culminating class dialogue, two related points about the impact of technology on everyday routines come to light for the students. After creating our mega-list, students drafting a working definition of technology start asking, "What does *not* count as a technology?" A ripple of engagement spreads through the room as students debate this question. This is the second point of realization: what comes to light are the ways in which technologies are not just objects but processes or practices. Once, for example, a student had me add social security numbers to our list of technologies, but there was a mumble of disapproval among his classmates. The student then explained that in the first weeks of college he was asked for this number many times, but before coming to college he hadn't memorized it. This number identified him to admissions, registration, and financial aid people; it had become his student identification number. Now it is with him daily, allowing him access to the library, dorms, the gym, food service and so on. Through this kind of class discussion, students come to their own understanding of the Foucauldian concept that technologies and their power in our daily routines are not centered on objects but in the ways those objects are used and in the actions of people and institutions. Such discussion leads us to the subsequent writing assignments.

Assignment 2: Mapping Technology's Impact on Campus

Building on the technology journal assignment, the purpose of the major writing assignment in unit two is for students to identify and describe how the use of a particular technology or technological practice helps define what it means to be a student on our campus. The assignment reads:

> For this essay, you will need to choose a particular technological object or practice of college life and define its purpose and use as well as explore how your experience as a student has been influenced by this object or practice. Your audience for this essay will be future first-year students, people who have not attended college or been on the Penn State Altoona campus before.

This assignment is ultimately an act of analysis of the cultural codes that operate to define their experiences as college students on our campus. The objects or practices that students have chosen to write about have included student ID cards, bus routes, parking regulations, e-mail accounts, phones, registration procedures, campus coffeehouses, the clock tower, pizza delivery, study lounges, and the duck pond that was built in the center of our campus.

I should note that as this assignment has evolved, I have learned that it doesn't work well when students choose to write about computers. The main problem I've encountered is that students writing about computers have tended to produce the least reflective analyses of the class. As a result, I have decided that, while students can write about a specific software application such as e-mail or a specific online Web site such as the advising site, they cannot write about computers in a generic way. Why the problem? The prevalence of popular narratives in which computers, like a fairy godmother, act as a force of good are so powerful that it is a rare first-year student who can resist using them as the beginning and ending of their analysis. It isn't that students shouldn't be allowed to write about the positive impacts of computers (or any technology); the problem occurs when pat sound bites (such as "Computers help me do research") are offered with little or no concrete description or detail of how the student actually did research using a computer. Such popular "analysis" replaces actual or in-depth explanations.

The most important lessons in rhetorical analysis with this assignment occur for students as they deal with distinctions between the intended purposes of particular technological objects or practices and the actual uses of them. This assignment challenges students to be descriptive, of course, but it also asks them to analyze the intended purpose of a pond or a library or a bus, as well as the ways these technologies contribute to students' definitions of "campus life" or "the college experience." These unsanctioned definitions can reveal much about power relations: between other things, between students, and between students and various administrative structures.

Assignment 3: A Rhetorical Analysis of the Internet

The third major writing assignment, part of unit three, departs from the essay structure but maintains the course's emphasis by asking students to reflect on how one particular technology, the Internet, influences their lives. This assignment is a Web site review. In just a few short years, the Internet has become a part of students' everyday lives. This assignment specifies the Internet as the focus of analysis because of its currency and because it will increasingly play larger roles in our lives. The demands of this kind of assignment are familiar enough that I won't go into detail. In fact, my Web site review assignment grows out of a now

common assignment asking students to develop a rhetorical analysis of visual media such as advertising images. Like those assignments, this one asks students to consider visual as well as textual
content and the meanings implied by them. (Versions of this kind
of assignment, as well as primers for helping students develop
analysis of visual images, can be found in a number of first-year
composition textbooks.)

The connection I ask students to make to their everyday lives
in this assignment is in linking a particular individual interest to
specific Web sites that allow them to experience their interest
from new perspectives. In the past, students have used garden-
ing, poetry, music, wrestling, day trading, and politics, to name a
few, as the starting points for their Web site reviews. The lens of
the Internet encourages new levels of reflection on these topics of
their own choosing. For a generation of young people who feel
they have been pegged as Internet savvy, students definitely ex-
ude an increased level of critical engagement with this assignment—a kind of "This could be good for me" attitude. With this
assignment, they play out some of their very real questions about
how the Internet will shape their futures.

Final Thoughts on the Challenges of This Course

Because the course focuses on how technology and technological
practices influence our everyday routines, a major challenge is to
raise students' critical consciousness of the historical contexts
out of which knowledge has emerged and the relationship of this
knowledge to students' current social contexts. In the process,
students are also challenged because the course is about breaking
educational routines. Desocializing our everyday practices demands a participatory classroom in which students and teachers
expel social behavior, language, and commonsense attitudes from
their "unexamined nests in consciousness" (Shor 1992) and make
them available for critical study through dialogue. Such a prob-
lem-posing course design intentionally works to deroutinize what
it means to be a student or a teacher. It requires power sharing
between students and teachers, thus increasing students' stake in

the course content and the shape of their writing. Consequently, it is important, I have learned, to begin the semester talking about students' expectations for themselves and of me and to return to this discussion periodically during the semester. A pedagogy of critical reflection is demanding, and yet the rewards, as students develop critically reflective lenses for reading and acting in the world around them, keep me coming back.

Appendix

Sample Course Units

Unit 1—Reflecting on technologies and technological practices in our everyday lives.

Types of reading: "Urban Spaceman" from *Consuming Passions: The Dynamics of Popular Culture* by Judith Williamson; "Invisible Technologies" from *Technopoly: The Surrender of Culture to Technology* by Neil Postman.

Culminating assignment: Write a narrative focusing on how a particular technology or technological practice impacted you in the past. For this essay, choose an event or incident from your past in which the presence of some technological device or practice had a significant impact on not only your behavior but also your *outlook*.

Unit 2—Reading the cultural codes embedded in our technology use.

Types of reading: Excerpts from *The Saturated Self: Dilemmas of Identity in Contemporary Life* by Kenneth Gergen; "Technological Somnambulism" from *The Whale and the Reactor: A Search for Limits in an Age of High Technology* by Langdon Winner.

Culminating assignment: Write an essay in which you define student life on campus as it is influenced by a particular technology or technological practice. (See Assignment 2: Mapping Technology's Impact on Campus.)

Unit 3—A rhetorical analysis of the Internet.

Types of reading: "In the Shadow of the Image" from *Channels of Desire: Mass Images and the Shaping of American Consciousness* by Stuart and Elizabeth Ewen; "Analyzing Signs and Sign Systems" from *Media Analysis Techniques* by Arthur Asa Berger.

Culminating assignment: Write a descriptive and evaluative review of an Internet Web site (or series of related Web sites). Your goal is to review the content and design of this Web site for a specific group of readers that you identify. (See Assignment 3: A Rhetorical Analysis of the Internet.)

Unit 4—Defining a problem and proposing a solution.

Types of reading: "Attacking Youth Violence" by Joseph R. Biden, published in *Criminal Justice Ethics*, 1998; "Making Single Motherhood Normal" by Iris Marion Young, published in *Dissent*, 1994.

Culminating assignment: Write a proposal that formulates a problem, considers the alternatives, and offers a possible solution(s) for a particular group or community of which you are a part.

Works Cited

Berlin, James A. 1988. "Rhetoric and Ideology in the Writing Class." *College English* 50: 477–94.

———. 1996. *Rhetorics, Poetics, and Cultures: Refiguring College English Studies*. Urbana, IL: National Council of Teachers of English.

Giddens, Anthony. 1979. *Central Problems in Social Theory: Action, Structure and Contradiction in Social Analysis*. Berkeley: University of California Press.

———. 1984. *The Constitution of Society: Outline of the Theory of Structuration*. Berkeley: University of California Press.

Shor, Ira. 1992. *Empowering Education: Critical Teaching for Social Change*. Chicago: University of Chicago Press.

CHAPTER THREE

Writing about Growing Up behind the Iron Curtain

PAVEL ZEMLIANSKY
James Madison University

Setting and Institutional Context

Florida State University is a four-year public institution located in Tallahassee. According to the FSU mission statement (2000), the school's "primary role is to serve as a center for advanced graduate and professional studies while emphasizing research and providing excellence in undergraduate programs." More than thirty thousand students attend FSU. While many students come from Florida, the university also has a significant out-of-state and international student contingent.

In their first year, all Florida State students are required to take a two-semester sequence of writing courses. The first course, ENC-1101, in which students are usually not required to use external sources for their writing, teaches basics of invention, revision, writing workshops, and so forth. During the second course, students are asked to incorporate the voices and opinions of others into their writing. While it is somewhat restrictive to say that ENC-1102 teaches only academic writing, since the genre is difficult to define in broad terms, the course certainly encourages students to analyze texts for both content and style, to conduct research, and to produce mainly analytical writing, although with a personal voice. These goals are achieved through the use of a reader (currently the program uses *The Presence of Others* edited by Andrea Lunsford and John Ruszkiewicz [2000]); extensive class discussions, which often cover political and social issues; and, as in many writing programs across the country, a research paper. To teach research, we use Bruce Ballenger's *The Curious Researcher* (1998).

ENC-1102 is not the only option for those students who successfully complete ENC-1101. Instead of ENC-1102, they can take ENC-1145, Writing about Topics. It's an umbrella title because different sections of ENC-1145 write about different topics. Recent sections of ENC-1145 have ranged in subject from Writing about Tallahassee to Writing about *Star Trek* to Writing about Issues in Sports. Class sizes in all first-year writing courses are generally twenty to twenty-five students. The course I discuss here, Writing about Growing Up behind the Iron Curtain, I taught in the spring of 2000. It was a section of ENC-1145, with an enrollment of twenty-three writers, most of them from Florida.

Course Description

In designing the course, I hoped to engage students in a dialogue about growing up in a different culture and social system and to invite them to compare their own experiences in the United States with those of their peers abroad. To produce engaging prose, writers must be able to use ideas and notions other than their own while carefully weaving their own life experiences and memories into the text. Thus, I hoped to achieve a balance between personal stories and analysis of the class readings. For all writing assignments, the students were invited to use personal examples as well as the material from the texts. I encouraged the class to think and write about concrete individuals (including themselves) rather than make broad generalizations.

I wanted the students to "stay personal" with their topics for one main reason: for inexperienced writers, the task of analyzing and incorporating into their texts large amounts of information from sources usually seems daunting. At the outset of the project, they get the impression they are being asked to use every bit of information available about their topics, and they simply don't know where to begin. Their resulting texts lack focus and voice, functioning instead as summaries of available sources. By asking my students to connect the readings with episodes in their own lives, I hoped to help them stay focused on selecting and using only the material that related to their own life stories.

We used two texts, *The "Children of Perestroika" Come of Age* by Deborah Adelman (1994) and *On the Golden Porch* by Tatyana Tolstaya (1990). Adelman's book consists of interviews with young Russian adults recorded in the early 1990s, while Tolstaya's work is a collection of autobiographically based short stories about life in the former Soviet Union. To learn principles of research, we also used Ballenger's *The Curious Researcher* (1998). Students were required to write weekly response journals and were also encouraged to use the ideas from those journals in their essays.

In addition to journals, the course required four larger writing assignments—three traditional papers and one multimedia group project, for which each individual group was free to choose the format. After reading several chapters of Adelman's book (topics include education, work, family life, and military service) and comparing those chapters to their own experiences growing up in the United States, students were asked to draft the first essay:

Essay # 1

Recall an event or experience that has in some way influenced your life. Describe it and show your readers (interested, friendly peers) why you consider it important. Compare your experience with those of the people in Adelman's book. What was similar and what was different? What people, events, and social circumstances influenced you and them? Were the outcomes similar or different for them and for you? Remember that this writing is exploratory and is meant to help you learn about yourself and others rather than prove a point or develop a thesis.

As could be expected, many students wrote about getting a driver's license, getting their first summer job, going to college, serving in the military, and other events typical in the lives of young adults. I constantly encouraged the writers to draw connections between their own lives and the lives of the people in the class texts. Following are some examples of writing and discussion prompts I used to achieve this connection:

- ◆ What family/social backgrounds do the three people in Adelman's book come from? How are these backgrounds similar or different from your own?

- ◆ What events or actions do you think these people identify as important in their lives and why? Do they in any way explain their actions or the importance of these events? Please point to specific places in the texts.

- ◆ Is there any connection between their present positions in society and their family or social backgrounds or actions and choices?

By having students combine personal experiences with the readings, I wanted them to arrive at concepts such as value of education, value of work, and value of family in their own lives and in the lives of the people in the book and to consider how these values might have been shaped and influenced by their respective cultures and societies.

The second essay built on students' previous work with the sources:

Essay #2
For this essay, you need to select two or three representative interviews from Adelman's book and, possibly, one or two stories by Tolstaya and explain how they enlighten/illustrate what life is like in the former Eastern bloc. You are writing for an audience that is less familiar with the topic than you are. This audience is also likely to understand you better if you use your own personal experiences here in the United States. You are expected to make some generalizations about the issues under discussion here, but remember that every time you make such generalizations you need to use examples and specific details.

By assigning this essay, I wanted the students to have some practice in reading the texts closely and at the same time learn that close reading can and should be personal and interested.

Perhaps predictably, the most popular topics of the second essay were education, work, relationships, and military service. Some students compared and contrasted their own ideas on the subjects with those expressed by Adelman's interviewees and Tolstaya's characters; others tried to make broader generalizations by doing some external research in addition to the required readings.

The next project focused on the same sources but used them in very different ways:

Multimedia Group Project

For this project, you will work in groups to produce a representation of a problem or aspect related to the subject of this class that interests you, in a medium of your choice. Some possible media include Web sites, posters, brochures, and zines. Please remember that you are writing for a general audience of your peers that is less knowledgeable about the subject than you are.

Some of the more successful projects included a Web site whose authors wrote fictionalized diaries of the people in *The "Children of Perestroika" Come of Age,* basing them on the real events described in the book; a zine for teenagers describing life of young people in Russia; and a mock TV news program about Russia with a full transcript. Besides simply providing much needed variety, this project helped the students see how personal vision and "hard facts" can be combined to create interesting writing. I also invited the students to use the topics of their multimedia projects as starting points for the final paper of the semester—the research essay:

The Research Assignment

Your task for this project is to become an authority through research on one of the aspects of the culture at the center of this class. Assume you are writing for an audience with knowledge of the subject that is inferior to yours. At the same time, be aware that your job is not to report what you already know about young people in the Eastern bloc but to find out more through research. You are free to choose between an argumentative or an exploratory paper. Consider using personal experiences and stories in your projects.

For this assignment, as for all other course projects, I invited the class to explore rather than to argue, to complicate instead of asserting a fixed position. Ballenger's book, with its excellent set of essay-writing activities, was a great help here. I constantly had to look for ways to counter two problems: first, some students relied too heavily on what they previously knew about the subject of the course, reading and writing hastily and without close attention, probably thinking of research mostly in terms of finding only information that agreed with their position; second, many students tended to choose broad sociopolitical topics for research, perhaps defaulting to an understanding of school writing as something that requires general topics.

As I continue to reflect on what I learned from teaching this course, I realize that most students enjoyed the ability to connect book material with their own life stories. Some did not expect to be given this opportunity, especially with the research paper. The flip side of this was the students' willingness to close down the topic too soon, to assume they had explored and written about all important and interesting aspects of the subject. Too often writers in the class assumed that the lives of their foreign counterparts were similar, if not identical, to theirs; this led to insufficient examination of the readings. The students figured that since they knew their own lives best and were allowed to write about them, they could base their writing almost exclusively on their own life experiences and marginalize analysis of the texts. To counter these assumptions, I found it useful to keep reminding the class that analyzing and researching is not always about providing final answers and "closing the case" but about complicating topics, looking at them from multiple angles, and questioning established notions.

Assessment

I assessed the students' progress by using a modified portfolio system. Rather than submitting one large portfolio with all their work at the end of the semester, students were required to put together miniportfolios containing the work done in the process of writing a specific essay. In a pocket folder, they submitted the preliminary and final drafts of the essay, all the response journals, and some in-class writings done in the process of writing a specific essay. I also required a one-page process memo in which students were asked to describe how they wrote the essay and to evaluate their own success and growth as writers.

Benefits of portfolio assessment have been discussed elsewhere, and it is not my purpose here to contribute to the discussion. In relation to my course, though, it is worth pointing out that portfolios allowed students to see their work of the previous several weeks as a whole and trace their own progress. Including reading responses and in-class writings in the portfolios helped students see the connection between the drafting of an essay and the smaller writing assignments that were often used for invention purposes. I consider process memos important because awareness of writing processes, strengths and weaknesses, and successes and failures is a sign of a mature writer. Typically, students described their drafting and revision habits, identified and discussed strong and weak points, and offered comments and evaluations of their participation in the revision workshops.

Rationale and Reflection

In the epilogue to Richard Straub and Ron Lunsford's book *Twelve Readers Reading: Responding to College Student Writing* (1995), Richard Larson urges teachers to assign papers that "will leave students knowing much more after completing them than they did before" (384). Larson contends that the function of student writing should not be mere transmission of knowledge that is already available but generation of new knowledge.

But where will such new knowledge come from? Obviously, reading is a powerful way to generate it. When combined with each individual reader's own experiences, discussion of texts may help produce interesting and invested writing. As Doug Brent (1992) notes, readers are able to understand new texts because they bring in "the familiar: the convention of discourse, the world knowledge, the linguistic knowledge, the personal associations" (31). Following Brent's reasoning, then, the students in my class tried to connect their previous knowledge about the topic and the class readings to create new texts combining both elements.

The FSU first-year writing program envisions the multiple sections of Writing about Topics as a collection of courses from which almost any student can select something she or he is already interested in. But sometimes, when schedules or other constraints do not permit students to sign up for the section of their choice, they end up in a course that focuses on a topic that looks unfamiliar to them. On the first day of my Iron Curtain course, several students were worried about their ability to do well in the class given their lack of knowledge about its subject. With reading, discussion, and writing, however, many of these students were able to generate new knowledge on the basis of existing knowledge. Some were even surprised by their ability to write about a topic that only several weeks before appeared unfamiliar. My encouragement to use personal experiences in learning probably helped many students become interested in the reading and the writing for the class.

The approach to reading and writing I used in my course aimed at achieving several goals. I wanted to help the students see that new knowledge does not appear out of a vacuum but is usually based on existing knowledge. I also wanted them to become better readers by bringing their views of the world into their interpretations of texts. Finally, I wanted them to treat writing not merely as a way to transmit information but also as a means of generating new knowledge.

The next time I teach ENC-1145, I would like to take a broader approach, calling the course Writing about Culture and Identity. I want the class to look at how our environments and communities shape our lives and ideals, without necessarily focusing on one culture only. While I still plan to use Adelman's book because it provides an excellent glimpse of a culture so different from the students', I will include texts that focus on other ways of life. But the overall purpose of the course will largely remain the same—to promote students' growth as writers by helping them create texts that incorporate the personal and the public, the writers' own memories and other people's stories, and the students' own cultural ideas and assumptions and those of others. I expect students to generate many descriptions and evaluations of cultures, subcultures, and societies they call their own. Next time I teach this course, I will also be sure to emphasize continually to the students that this is first and foremost a writing class and not a course in history or sociology. Such an emphasis is useful because it focuses students' attention on the writing process and not on acquiring information about the topic only.

Works Cited

Adelman, Deborah. 1994. *The "Children of Perestroika" Come of Age: Young People of Moscow Talk about Life in the New Russia.* Armonk, NY: M. E. Sharpe.

Ballenger, Bruce. 1998. *The Curious Researcher: A Guide to Writing Research Papers.* Boston: Allyn & Bacon.

Brent, Doug. 1992. *Reading as Rhetorical Invention: Knowledge, Persuasion, and the Teaching of Research-Based Writing.* Urbana, IL: National Council of Teachers of English.

Florida State University. 2000. *Mission Statement of the Florida State University.* <www.fsu.edu/~rsect/Factbook/General/mission.html>. (28 May, 2000)

Larson, Richard. 1995. Epilogue. Pp. 375–86 in *Twelve Readers Reading: Responding to College Student Writing*, Richard Straub and Ronald Lunsford. Cresskill, NJ: Hampton Press.

Lunsford, Andrea A., and John J. Ruszkiewicz, eds. 2000. *The Presence of Others: Voices and Images That Call for Response.* 3rd ed. Boston: Bedford/St. Martin.

Tolstaya [Tolstaia], Tatyana. 1990. *On the Golden Porch.* New York: Vintage International.

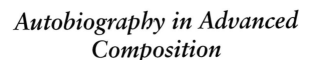

CHAPTER FOUR

Autobiography in Advanced Composition

KATIE HUPP STAHLNECKER
University of Nebraska at Omaha

Teaching Context

I have been teaching English for twelve years at the University of Nebraska at Omaha, an urban commuter college with a student population of approximately fourteen thousand. The university, which sits in the heart of Nebraska's largest city, attracts a diverse crowd, including students of all races and backgrounds. While most of the students are traditional in terms of age, a high percentage consists of older, returning students. The course I primarily teach—English 2400: Advanced Composition—fulfills a university-wide third writing course requirement and is one of four choices offered by the English department. Other choices include Critical Approaches to Literature, Technical Writing, and Modern Familiar Essay. Because most of the other colleges on campus also offer advanced writing courses related to their majors, Advanced Composition usually attracts arts and sciences majors who choose this course over the other three, perhaps because it provides the most direct extension of their first-year composition courses.

The course description of Advanced Composition as listed in our undergraduate catalog is as follows: "A study in the principles of rhetoric, expository modes, research techniques, consistency in grammatical structure, and variety of usage with attention to audience adaptation and writer's style" (University of Nebraska 2000, 201). English Composition 1150 and English Composition 1160—the courses that fulfill the first two writing requirements for all majors—focus on narrative and investigative writing, respectively. Advanced Composition fits into the writing program as it aims to bring together the personal and the academic writing with heightened attention to "audience adaptation and writer's style" (201).

My Approach

In my sections of Advanced Composition, students learn to focus on all of the composition course elements by writing four personal but researched essays that they then compile in their final projects as bound autobiographies. I designed this particular approach for Advanced Composition, which is constantly shaped and reshaped according to my students' interests and needs, specifically to reach the student population at UNO. From my several years of experience teaching the two prerequisite writing courses, I had an idea of what worked for first-year students—and what didn't.

Students generally enjoy English 1150 because it involves personal-based writing, but some feel stifled by the guidelines. In other words, students in this first writing course usually feel comfortable with the subject matter, but they find it difficult to express themselves within the rules and expectations of the assigned modes such as narration, observation, and description. Students of English 1160, the second writing course, typically enjoy learning new strategies of investigation, but they too often struggle with the artificiality of not only imposed modes such as persuasion and evaluation but also the subject matter of traditional academic research papers. I designed Advanced Composition to encompass the best of both courses—personal subject matter and investigation—while focusing more on personal style.

Although my assignments all have certain parameters, they allow for what nearly all of my first-year students crave: freedom. I designed the class, therefore, not to teach students how to conform to a certain style but to encourage them to develop a style that works for them when composing nonfiction. I encourage them to experiment with everything from point of view to visual aids. In addition, I promote the kinds of research that do not necessarily take place in a library, such as digging through the family files or talking with a relative over coffee. As a result, what I initially imagined as a course driven by narrative writing with some research included has grown into one that produces fascinating and original multimedia autobiographies by each student.

The four formal writing assignments are as follows:

Heritage: Describe your family ancestry as it is in some way relevant to your life today. Consider how your background has shaped or influenced you.

Family: Extend a metaphor to describe your family and the roles that each member plays. In depth, discuss the roles and what it means to fill them.

Mentor: Select someone who has had a positive impact on your life and write an essay explaining the significance. Use a popular text of some sort (a poem, a song, a movie, etc.) to help illustrate the relationship.

Self: Use your experiences to explore the organizing/guiding principle in your life.

These assignments serve merely as springboards from which the writers may dive. Although I do hope to see students, for instance, speak of their families metaphorically, I neither offer nor expect any particular format or page length. In fact, if anything, I expect the unexpected. Given these relatively loose parameters, my approach to the teaching of each assignment relies heavily on workshop activities rather than lecture. Since I do not rely on textbooklike writing conventions, such as the principles of argumentation, to teach style and technique, I run the course essentially as a workshop in which students learn by trial and error with my help and that of one another. All along the way, we share our ideas and our writing, providing praise, suggestions, and constructive criticism.

This writing process, which I describe in detail in the following paragraphs, works well with students because it capitalizes more on their intellect and common sense than on their ability to memorize or follow rules. As a result, students seem to become personally invested in the tasks of the course, engaging themselves more than they might with more traditional or textbook exercises. Although I facilitate this multistep writing process, its success or failure rests largely on the students' shoulders. Fortunately, the personal subject matter and relative freedom afforded to them creates engaged and productive participation practically without fail.

After I introduce the general parameters of the assignment, as a class we analyze several finished versions of the assignment essay from previous classes. I present essays with the widest available range of styles and formats on overhead transparencies and invite the class to discuss the strengths and weaknesses of each one. For each assignment, I usually read one or two sample essays in the traditional prose format. Then I present some of the other unique creations students have produced for that particular assignment. For the heritage essay, for instance, I often illustrate using a piece by a young man who provides full-page color photos along with prose to make the written connection between ancient Hispanic warriors and his own child. For the mentor assignment, I show a young woman's essay about her basketball coach that she presented on round sheets of paper inside of a real (flattened) basketball.

This spectrum of formats and styles, which demonstrates a mere sampling of the possibilities, serves as an invention exercise, as it usually prompts students to imagine the directions they can take in their own essays. Furthermore, in the discussions that ensue from these exercises students inevitably discover for themselves whether the various approaches are effective and whether the alternative formats complement or distract from the prose. In essence, we brainstorm as a class about creative and effective ways to address the issues presented in the assignment. Holly, a former student, once described the exercise like this: "Listening to the originality in her previous students' writings got me excited and helped me to be more creative with my own" (2000).

Next, I randomly assign peer editing groups comprising three or four students each, and they verbally discuss their written responses to prewriting questions such as "What do you like and not like about this assignment?"; "What approaches to engaging your audience are you considering?"; "How do you plan to incorporate research?" I briefly join and participate in each group as they continue to brainstorm and bounce ideas off one another. I also introduce each group to the text for the course, *The Book of Questions* by Gregory Stock (1987). I invite them to page through this collection of rhetorical questions about values, beliefs, and life and encourage them to answer a few of their choice. This exercise, aside from helping the students focus their ideas for the essay, provides an opportunity for them to get to know the classmates with whom they will soon share their personal stories.

At the next class meeting, I ask the students to more closely scrutinize *The Book of Questions* for an intriguing question that relates to the essay assignment at hand and respond to it in one to two pages. For the family essay, for instance, they might choose to respond to question 102, which reads, "How close and warm is your family? Do you feel your childhood was happier than most other people's?" (Stock 1987, 91). This step in the process produces prewriting that in most cases serves as a platform for the first draft.

For each essay, before a first draft is due we also engage in various other invention exercises. For the family essay, for example, students bring to class several examples of metaphors they find in published essays, poems, novels, articles, and so forth. In their small groups, they choose the best one of each student's metaphors, write them on a transparency, and explain their choices to the class. Spending time analyzing and explaining the effectiveness of other writers' metaphors gives them a better understanding of the purpose of metaphorical writing as they attempt to compose their own.

Once the students have first drafts in hand, they participate in peer editing sessions during which they read and respond to the essays of two classmates. For each essay, I prompt their responses with general questions. In the case of the heritage essay, for example, students consider questions such as "Does the essay include an appropriate amount of history (names, dates, etc.)?"; "Does it tell an interesting story? If so, point out what works particularly well. If not, explain what's missing and/or ineffective"; "Has the writer clearly specified the significance of his or her heritage? In other words, is the common thread that has influenced or shaped the writer obvious?" During these workshop sessions, I also take a glance at each student's essay and provide brief comments. Having read two other essays and received three opinions regarding their own writing, students leave the workshops with plenty of food for thought as they approach the revision stage. According to my former student Holly, "The best part about the class was being grouped up to critique each other's rough drafts. This was a ground breaking lesson for me to actually 'listen' to someone else's ideas on my work, someone who was my peer and not just my professor" (2000).

Between the due dates for the first and the final drafts, I meet with students in ten- to fifteen-minute individual conferences, during which I address any concerns they have about their essays, the workshops, or the class in general. I also use the conferences to establish a personal relationship with these students. I consider this a significant step in the process since I ask them to entrust me with their life stories. Students then hand in final revisions of their essays along with written self-evaluations in which they assess the strengths and weaknesses of their texts, discuss revisions, list concerns for me to comment on, and describe what they might do differently if they had more time.

The final phase of the writing process is my evaluation of the student essays. As a student myself, I know how frustrating and misleading short, pithy comments from a teacher can be. I appreciate the advice of Robert Connors and Andrea Lunsford (1993), who encourage teachers to assess our methods of evaluation so that "we can begin to learn how our students 'read' these teacherly tropes, which seem so obvious and helpful to us but may not be so easily deciphered by those still striving to enter the community we take for granted" (219). Furthermore, I realize that more than just words are on the line, particularly in the kind of writing students do for my Advanced Composition course—writing that often bares the writers' souls. Thus, I write detailed in-text and end comments. Then I return student papers one week later in five-minute individual conferences, which provide a space in which students can discuss the evaluation of their essays. I agree with Peggy O'Neill and Jane Mathison-Fife (1999), who contend that teachers "need to create opportunities for students to respond, to engage in real conversations, not just metaphorical ones, about their writing and our teaching" (49). Through these conferences and my participation in the process in general, I aim to do just that and to demonstrate to my students the levels of commitment and investment I expect from them.

Reflection and Rationale

From day one, I encourage students to dialogue with me and with one another about the course as a means to negotiate, challenge, and revise it when needed. Some students initially (and inevitably) resist or misinterpret this personal format for a writing course. They most commonly voice concern about revealing too much, so we talk at length about what Steven M. Strang (1995) terms "personal vs. private" writing. His distinction helps the students see that they need only write about what they are both ready and willing to reveal in this academic setting and that they are in complete control over what is shared. Other students fret about having nothing worthy to say about themselves and their lives. When we read the sample student essays from past semesters, however, we discuss the ways these writers craft even seemingly boring or meaningless events or occurrences into engaging stories. Still others take these writing tasks as an opportunity, finally, to have a captive audience for their all-important stories. As Elliot W. Eisner (1991) confirms, "when one writes, the public character of the form demands organization, and when autobiographical, the problems of appearing egoistic or saying too much or seeming self-promoting are constant threats" (34). To minimize such problems, I prompt discussions about the value of adding outside sources as a way of projecting our experiences for an audience so that writer and reader can connect in the shared human experience. Thus, although these and other concerns arise over the course of a semester, through dialogue, they are manageable.

Ultimately, despite some hesitancy and overzealousness on the part of some students, I continue to rely on this personal involvement in my Advanced Composition course because in theory it makes sense and because in practice it works. This approach, theoretically, allows students to trace their past, sort out the present, and clarify the values and convictions they are developing for the future. The essays themselves, although personal, engage writers in both reader- and writer-oriented goals. In other words, they provide an excellent forum for students to examine themselves, but they also lead to the examined life in relation to cultural and societal knowledge and the formulation of values and convictions. As Mary Kay Jackman (1999) asserts, "The importance of personal, lived experience in adult education cannot be ignored . . . in established theories of how learning happens" (65). The more personally involved students are with a subject, the more they will learn about it. Personal-based writing engages the students because it draws on what they know and what they perceive as relevant in life rather than on what they do *not* know and what *someone else* perceives as relevant, as is the case with much academic writing.

In addition to the personal involvement it encourages, I appreciate the way my course helps students see themselves more as writers than as students writing. Like Peter Elbow (1991), I feel strongly that "life is long and college is short" and that "the best test of a writing course is whether it makes students more likely to use writing in their lives" (136). Though academic writing skills are valuable and should serve students well in college, the kind of writing I promote in my Advanced Composition course is more likely to be revisited later in life—when writing a letter to the editor or an entry in a learning journal, for instance. In addition, particularly at a university such as UNO, which is made up largely of older, nontraditional students, drawing on students' life experiences is crucial. As Malcolm Knowles (1990) contends,

> To children, experience is something that happens to them; to adults, their experience is *who they are.* . . . The implication of this fact for adult education is that in any situation in which adults' experience is ignored or devalued, they perceive this as not rejecting just their experience, but rejecting them as persons. (60)

My course design for Advanced Composition aims to do just the opposite—celebrate and focus on my students' life experiences.

The beauty of this approach is that it serves not only the writer but also the reader. When the subject matter engages the writer, he or she not only learns more but also provides a more enriching experience for the reader. "A story about personal experience" explains Linda Brodkey, "invites listeners to join the teller in reflecting on troubling events—a child's behavior, a parent's or in-law's criticism, infidelity, pregnancy, unemployment, low wages, high prices, ill health" (1996, 150). The writer benefits from a newfound audience and sense of authority, and the reader welcomes an opportunity to provide insight or advice.

The reader also appreciates any attempts by the writer to make the piece pleasing to the eye. According to scholars such as Michael Hassett and Rachel Lott (2000), traditional essay forms can undermine the "potential rhetorical effect of what students write" (33). Such forms also can give students a false sense of what works for real-world writers and their readers. "We would not expect our students to pick up, rely on for research, or read for personal information documents that look like the essays our students create" (33). Thus, it makes sense to promote any attempts at a multimedia presentation. Moreover, according to Louis, a former student in Advanced Composition, students typically do not expect anyone outside of the classroom setting to read their conventional essays. "The 'project' format also allows individuality to flower. Across a crowded room, one could pick out his/her work, no stack of manila binders in this class! Very seldom does a college course produce anything that you would want to show to a parent, child, or grandchild" (2000).

Visual or not, there's just something about autobiographical writing that raises the bar of involvement and pride for students. Last semester, for instance, in a class of fifteen, ten students voluntarily presented something to the class that was related to their heritage. One young woman performed a voodoo dance she had learned in Haiti, her native land. Another, from Japan, sang Japanese songs for the class. Yet another performed an American Revolution reenactment. These and other presentations, though related to the students' writing, were done just in the spirit of sharing. Students were not assigned such projects, and I did not offer extra credit for them. Each presentation, however, concluded with a question-and-answer session during which we discussed, oftentimes at length, how these performances sprang from their writing for the class. Thus, the personal nature of the assignments prompted students to share and explain their writing in a way that was real and meaningful to them, which is not always the result in such workshop-driven situations.

Furthermore, when working with personal writing, students seem to pay more attention to discussions about certain conventions such as transitions or grammar. When using their sentences about cousin Ron and best friend Susie as examples, I manage to sneak in the lessons, and before I know it, students have learned something. While the class is working on the family essay, for instance, I ask for a few volunteers to illustrate their preliminary drafts on the overhead. Together as a class, we then scrutinize the transitions throughout, and if they don't flow smoothly, we try to guess the relationships between one family member and the next. Inevitably, our guesses are wildly inaccurate, so as the writer clarifies the connections, we begin to imagine and articulate ways he or she might make them clearer in print. Suddenly, the need for transitions makes a sense it never has in most students' previous English classes; it appears to students, for perhaps the first time, as a *real* need, not just another rule imposed by grammarians. According to my former student Louis, "The transition concept is probably the most important of your 'tricks.' I have gone back over the first few essays and examined the 'island' paragraphs I have created. [The transition exercise] will help me greatly from now on" (2000). In a spreadsheet analysis of his papers completed in the class, Louis further notes that the technique category, which includes spelling, typos, and grammatical errors, showed remarkable improvement, from nineteen errors in the first essay to zero errors in the fourth essay. This student's experience in Advanced Composition, although an isolated example, demonstrates the vast potential for improving writing skills and learning stylistic techniques.

Perhaps teaching writing as more a matter of personal than academic concern is unconventional, but from the writer's and the reader's and the instructor's perspectives, it works. This approach may produce these favorable responses precisely because it steps outside the conventional boundaries of academic writing. It is human nature to be compelled by issues relevant to us and to one another. Hence, this course design for Advanced Composition capitalizes on a trait that comes naturally to most students, a reassuring element in the sometimes mystifying experience of learning how to write.

Works Cited

Brodkey, Linda. 1996. *Writing Permitted in Designated Areas Only.* Minneapolis: University of Minnesota Press.

Connors, Robert J., and Andrea A. Lunsford. 1993. "Teachers' Rhetorical Comments on Student Papers." *College Composition and Communication* 44: 200–23.

Eisner, Elliot W. 1991. "What the Arts Taught Me about Education." Pp. 34–48 in *Reflections from the Heart of Educational Inquiry: Understanding Curriculum and Teaching through the Arts,* ed. G. Willis and W. H. Schubert. Albany: State University of New York Press.

Elbow, Peter. 1991. "Reflections on Academic Discourse: How It Relates to Freshmen and Colleagues." *College English* 53: 135–55.

Hassett, Michael, and Rachel W. Lott. 2000. "Seeing Student Texts." *Composition Studies* 28: 29–47.

Holly. 2000. E-mail interview by author. Omaha, Nebraska, 1 August.

Jackman, Mary Kay. 1999. "When the Personal Becomes Professional: Stories from Reentry Adult Women Learners about Family, Work, and School." *Composition Studies* 27: 53–67.

Knowles, Malcolm Shepherd. 1990. *The Adult Learner: A Neglected Species.* 4th ed. Houston: Gulf.

Louis. 2000. E-mail interview by author and spreadsheet analysis. Omaha, Nebraska, 1 August.

O'Neill, Peggy, and Jane Mathison Fife. 1999. "Listening to Students: Contextualizing Response to Student Writing." *Composition Studies* 27: 39–51.

Stock, Gregory. 1987. *The Book of Questions.* New York: Workman.

Strang, Steven M. 1995. *Writing Exploratory Essays.* Mountain View, CA: Mayfield.

University of Nebraska at Omaha. 2000. *UNOmaha: University of Nebraska at Omaha Undergraduate Catalog 2000–2001.* Vol. LVI.

Chapter Five

Writing beyond the Academy: Using Service-Learning for Professional Preparation

Hildy Miller
Portland State University

When I worked in the English department at the University of Minnesota, I found that, like many others around the country, the department had been undergoing the challenging process of updating itself by revising its curriculum and rethinking its purposes for undergraduates. In the past, the department had largely addressed the question of how undergraduates could apply their English degrees to their professional goals by assuming most would use them to teach English somewhere in the K–college levels. But the department's undergraduate adviser was aware from the surveys, focus groups, and interviews she had conducted with students that the picture was far less straightforward than that. Only a small number would actually go on to teach. Most majors were drawn to the field quite simply by their love of language. They loved to read literature and often wanted to be creative writers. Many hoped to use their rhetorical abilities to effect meaningful social action in some way. Yet there was a stubborn gap between these things they cared about and the realities of the twenty-first-century marketplace. In fact, many students were unaware of the range of professional possibilities open to them. In my work helping to direct writing across the curriculum there, I was concerned with how departments taught both disciplinary writing and the writing students would do on the jobs for which the disciplines were preparing them after graduation. Though the English department had carefully thought through which courses would be writing intensive, and thus serve as sites for students to focus on writing in the discipline of English studies, it had not addressed the problem of professional preparation.

With these common concerns in mind, the undergraduate adviser and I designed and co-taught a service-learning writing course focused expressly on providing career exploration and preparation for those students who wanted and needed it. In making the idea of professional preparation a primary focus, we were deviating a bit from the usual emphasis in composition and service-learning on using this pedagogy mainly to help students develop a social conscience or to increase their cultural awareness (Herzberg 1994; Jacoby 1996; Schutz and Gere 1998; Brown 1998; Deans 2000). Rather, we were following, at least partly, models more often used by disciplines such as business, in which service-learning is regarded more as an internship—that is, as a sort of apprenticeship in which students develop preemployment skills (Silcox 1995). We hoped students would learn not only from their own experiences of writing on the job, but also, given the collaborative nature of the class, from other students and from the special speakers we brought in to talk about the varieties of writing jobs they might investigate once they graduated. To get to this practical end, we did have students reflect on the nature of community literacy and how this literacy differed from academic literacy (Peck, Flower, and Higgins 1995; Flower 1998; Ervin 2000), but we never lost sight of our concrete goals. What follows is a description of and rationale for a version of an upper-division writing course entitled Writing beyond the Academy.

Course Overview

Although we envisioned the course primarily as a chance for students to learn about writing in the workplace, it was secondarily an opportunity to give something back to the community. Minneapolis-St. Paul is a large first-tier city with a social conscience made manifest in a vast array of nonprofit organizations focused on a variety of social issues and serving a variety of constituencies in need. So we had no shortage of agencies seeking help with writing newsletters, brochures, annual reports, news releases, and Web sites. Since many jobs that English graduates typically secure are with nonprofit agencies, the students would be able to see firsthand what this workplace setting is like. These organizations in turn are often underfunded, so they would benefit from the tangible help our student writers could provide. In order to prepare students for this kind of writing in these kinds of work settings, we planned to study the many forms of public relations writing in class by having students read chapters from our textbook and bring in examples of writing from their internships. Through discussion, we hoped that students could bring some of their workplace experiences into the classroom to share with others. They could talk not only about actual writing formats, but also about the rhetorical contexts of their particular workplaces. Brochure writing at an understaffed and overworked rape crisis center was vastly different for our twenty-year-old male student than it was at a convivial and well-staffed ESL tutorial center for our sixty-year-old female student. In class, students could reflect on these differences with one another. So the course was structured to have students allocate ten internship hours a week to both their work at their sites (nine hours) and to our class meetings (one hour, on average).

Course Requirements

Since we envisioned the course as both highly participatory and highly reflective, we established course requirements that we thought would reinforce both goals. To encourage participation, students were asked to be active and responsible in their internships, to attend class well prepared by doing the required readings and writings, and to collaborate with classmates by contributing commentary on their work and ideas. These participatory requirements counted a full 25 percent of their final grade. To encourage reflection, students were given multiple opportunities to reflect on their writing, their work experiences, and how their thoughts about future employment might be changing. Informally, students kept a thirty-page course log throughout the course. The log was included in a portfolio of writing along with several other pieces, including reflective memos on two or three samples of writing for their workplaces and a formal reflective paper in which they considered what they had learned from their internships.

Special Features of the Course

Since our purpose was primarily for students to explore English-related writing careers, we included several special elements that proved key to focusing the students.

Relevant Writing Internships

We arranged for internships mainly in nonprofit agencies, which could provide students with opportunities to practice genres of writing they might encounter in jobs after graduation. Brochures, newsletters, feature writing, and news releases were typical of the public relations writing most students were asked to do on the job. Annual reports, instruction manuals, and Web site pages were typical of the business and technical writing they were asked to do. Each internship site was, of course, unique, but most were variants of the sorts of nonprofit agencies for which many English graduates eventually work. So, for example, two students worked at a sexual violence center, one at Planned Parenthood, and another for a library tutoring service. In other cases, students lined up their own internships. One English major who was interested in trying out sportswriting found a job writing about sports events in the community. By meeting with each student ahead of time, we were able to match everyone with a job that pertained somehow to his or her interests.

One-on-One Consultations

Key to the success of the course were several consultations we held with students before the course began, at midterm, and after the course was over. Students were asked on written questionnaires and through informal conversations what they hoped to accomplish in the course, what kinds of writing experience they had, and what career possibilities they were interested in exploring. Through these sessions, we were able to give class members individualized attention and ensure that they would move forward in their plans. These plans varied considerably, from students vitally interested in grant writing or sportswriting to those who had virtually no idea what they might do upon graduation. Class discussions in which students traded stories about their internship experiences also gave them insight into the discovery processes of their classmates.

Speakers on Various Writing Careers

Throughout the course, we scheduled many outside speakers from a variety of writing careers, including a technical writer, a proposal writer, a campus publications writer, and several writers for nonprofit agencies. These speakers were themselves former English majors, many of whom had graduated from our department. They spoke candidly about the often circuitous paths that led them to their current jobs and why they took them—tales in which the students had a vital interest. And they described the kinds of writing they did, passing out samples of their work and indicating the features of their particular work culture that affected the writing. In question-and-answer time, speakers were able to address directly students' questions about their work.

Relevant Readings and Writings

We required students to read about different applications of writing, such as strategies for designing a brochure, and to bring in samples they had written during their internship or earlier or ones they had seen or received elsewhere. These samples, along with their reflective analyses, stimulated class discussion. In this way, class members were prepared for the many kinds of writing they were asked to do in their internships. Students also worked throughout the semester on building a writing portfolio that was turned in at the end of class. Included in the portfolio were several samples of writing they had done in their internships, along with their reflections on the writing; a log of at least thirty pages of reflections on their on-the-job experiences; responses to readings and preparations for class discussions; and, finally, a formal paper reflecting on the job, the class, their writing, and any insights or plans that may have developed as a result of the course.

Evaluation of Assigned Work

Unlike traditional writing courses in which the quality of finished pieces counts toward a final grade, in this course we asked students to submit samples of finished writing they did on the job, but we did not evaluate them at all. Rather, we focused our evaluations on the quality of reflectiveness and active participation through the many venues of formal and informal writing, group work, and discussion. Was it thoughtful, thorough, and detailed? Did it take into account the rhetorical issues we had discussed in class? Did it consider the professional and vocational issues the entire class was wrestling with, that speakers were discussing, and that the co-teacher and I were foregrounding?

Much has been written on the key role reflection plays in the service-learning classroom in helping students process their experiences through formal and informal writing and through group discussion in which students collaboratively work through these issues. (See, for example, de Acosta 1995; Reed and Koliba 1995; Giles, Eyler, and Schmiede 1996; Anson 1997; Rhoads and Howard 1998; Eyler 2001; *Service Learning Faculty Handbook* n.d.; Hamner 2002, among others.) The point unfailingly emphasized is that reflection needs to be structured to encourage deeper critical awareness rather than superficial reactions. In evaluating students' final portfolios, we were once again reinforcing the things we were encouraging students to do all along: to think about rhetorical differences between academic and non-academic/public literacies; to think, in particular, about the culture of the workplace context in which they found themselves; and to draw some conclusions, however tentative, about concrete career directions that may have opened up for them as a result of the class.

Conclusions

In recent years, English departments have eagerly embraced service-learning, especially in composition courses. Its values and

aims—encouraging both intellectual and social development—
have proved particularly compatible with the sociopolitical emphasis found in so much contemporary composition theory. As
Schutz and Gere (1998) point out, service-learning "provide[s] a
venue for students to connect with the situated complexities of
issues and communities outside the classroom" (130). In literature courses too, service-learning can provide a site for students
to extend their critical textual analyses to those of real-world
rhetorical situations (Comstock 1994). As the emphasis on teaching diversity has shifted from the classroom to providing students with direct experience of this diversity in the community
(Herzberg 1994; Schutz and Gere 1998, among others), from
writing as writing across the curriculum to writing beyond the
curriculum (Parks and Goldblatt 2000), and from academic literacy as an exclusive focus to making connections to public literacy (Peck, Flower, and Higgins 1995; Flower 1998; Ervin 2000),
so too our theories of service-learning have expanded in the field.

Our application of service-learning to the career development
needs of undergraduate English majors, however, reflected current disciplinary changes within English departments as we
grapple with redefining our professional purposes and ourselves.
Our primary goals, in other words, were concrete and practical.
Some students certainly dealt with issues of diversity and learned
an "ethics of care" (Rhoads 1997). The student who worked in a
rape crisis center, for example, got a crash course in learning
varied cultural constructions for the experience of rape. The student who tutored non-native speakers came away with great com-
passion and respect for her clients. But though students wrote
and talked about these experiences, these insights were still not
the primary focus of the course. Rather, in order to get at the
concrete outcomes, we encouraged students to think hard about
what Peck, Flower, and Higgins (1995) call "community literacy."
How was preparing a press kit different from writing an academic paper? What did one need to know about cultural constructions of rape in order to write appropriately about it in a
brochure? Why did the supervisor of one workplace sit down
with a student for two hours to help her understand the altruistic
philosophy of his organization? We wanted students to understand the gap between the world of Dickens and Woolf they had

been immersed in for the better part of four years and the non-academic world of writing jobs. And we wanted them also to see the commonalities of these two worlds—that the critical thinking and writing skills at which they excelled in the academy could also transfer beyond it.

Through this process, we led the students to concrete outcomes. What did our students decide they could do with their English majors? Most of them edged closer to clarity on that question. Some managed to at least rule out some possibilities they had been entertaining—for instance, finding brochure writing too tedious a prospect compared with the creative writing they loved. Others discovered new and definite directions, such as our student who came away inspired to go into technical writing. Our sportswriter found it really did offer the perfect combination of his interests. Most students also simply learned something about writing beyond the academy from both their own experiences and those of their classmates. One student left virtually on his own to develop both a catalog and Web site learned much about integrating the visual with the verbal and about establishing a company image through his language and design choices. Another student learned much about the vagaries of collaborative writing on the job when she wrote a personal profile of an employee for a newsletter. Assuming that her discursive piece was final copy, she was shocked to see it treated as boilerplate and transformed into unrecognizable bulleted material. Students learned about differences in writing in organized and in disorganized workplaces and about differences in writing for congenial and for hostile bosses.

Though the course was largely successful in its first run, if I were to teach it again or to offer advice to anyone interested in starting such a course, I would plan on allowing plenty of time before the course both to set up internships and to talk with students individually. Further, it would be wise to investigate the conditions and kinds of writing tasks at the internship sites. In our case, some students had the opportunity to write several pieces crucial to the organization and were invited to feel part of its overall mission. Others, however, wrote very little and were not treated with professional courtesy. Since the writing that students did on the job occurred outside the classroom, it was also difficult to set up a support system or mechanism for feedback on their writing. A listserv in which students actively participate might provide some needed support, as would providing service-learning sites where two or more students could work. And, finally, I would certainly continue to invite a variety of speakers to talk about their writing careers and to keep the class size small enough to offer plenty of one-on-one attention to students, since these were two of the most instructive components of the course.

Service-learning writing courses focused on career development have an important practical role to play for students interested in writing careers. Our course helped English majors sort out the range of choices available to them and gain some writing experience beyond the academy. They came to a broader understanding of community/public literacy and how it differs from the academic literacy in which they had been immersed. Such a course could also be constructively adapted to the needs of many other fields across the curriculum, particularly in the humanities, in which undergraduates, like English majors, must often make a huge leap from academic writing to writing for the inevitable world of work.

Appendix

Excerpts from Syllabus

Overview

The world of writing at work can be vastly different from the world of academic writing when you first encounter it. Many students in the humanities feel as if they've landed in a parallel universe as they try to decipher the new literacy codes of the workplace. This course is designed primarily to help you bridge that gap by providing an opportunity for you to apply what you are learning in class to what you are doing during a ten-week internship. Beyond that, it will also give you firsthand experience in performing community service for a nonprofit organization. These organizations provide people in the Twin Cites with meaningful services, helping with violence in families, diseases, housing needs—the list goes on. If you have social causes that you care deeply about, this class will provide you with a way to use your writing talents to make a difference. So look at this course as a 2-for-1 opportunity: you will learn about literacy practices in the workplace while giving something back to the community. In addition to your internship outside class, we will study public relations writing within the class. You will learn about how to write newsletters, annual reports, brochures, and other kinds of writing, and, most of all, how to analyze rhetorical situations in the workplace. You will assemble a portfolio of your work due at the end of the semester using pieces you write on the job, reflective writing, and course log entries. And you can expect to collaborate in small groups on readings, writings, and presentations throughout the course.

Materials
Text: Public Relations Writing, 4th Edition, by Thomas H. Bivins, Contemporary Publishing Group, 1999.

Internships
In consultation with the Service-Learning Center, we have selected a number of interesting sites around town at which you might intern. Or you may wish to select your own site. Either way, you will need to talk with us and settle on a place by at least the first week of class. On the internships, you'll help the organization by writing for them—newsletters, brochures, reports, manuals, and other kinds of writing. Don't feel daunted by this prospect. We'll be studying these forms in class, and you'll have instructors, supervisors, and other students in the class to provide guidance along the way. These internships are similar to regular jobs except that you are not paid and are instead doing them on a volunteer basis. Keep in mind that you need to be as responsible and professional on these internships as you would on a regular job. Plan on spending a full ten hours a week on both the internship and class time. You'll also need to provide your own transportation to and from work.

Course Description
Weeks 1–4: Meet in class twice a week. We'll introduce and review basic concepts of advanced expository writing: how to analyze a rhetorical situation; invention, revision, research, and editing techniques; how to do group work successfully; and understanding the world of community service. During this part of the course, you'll need to line up your intern site, begin your course log, participate in class activities. In week 4, you'll begin your internship.

Weeks 5–12: Meet once a week for class; you continue your internship. For our weekly meetings, we'll focus on various public relations forms of writing. You'll read, discuss, and write about them and bring in writing samples to share. For some class sessions, we'll have outside speakers. During this part of the class, you will need to keep your course log, contribute to listserv and class discussions, and work on preparing materials for your course portfolio.

Weeks 13–16: Meet twice a week for class; during week 13, you'll finish your internship. In weeks 13 and 14, you'll workshop drafts of writing for your final portfolio. In weeks 15–16, you will give a brief oral presentation on your experience at work (what you learned about the social concerns, rhetorical situation, and writing at your site and the kinds of writing you did). You'll also finish preparing your portfolio for the last day of class.

Course Requirements

This isn't the kind of writing course in which only final texts of papers count toward your grade. Instead, it is highly participatory. Plan to

- Attend classes prepared with assigned activities completed—readings, writings, reflections.

- Participate actively in the arranged internship.

- Contribute to all collaborative activities—discussions in class and on the listserv, providing commentary on one another's work in small groups.

- Keep a course log (at least 3 pages a week) for reflections on readings, writings, and the internship experience. Some reflections will be assigned and others will be created by you.

- Turn in a final portfolio* including writing, process and participation work, the course log, and reflective memos.

* **Your portfolio must be complete in order for you to pass the course.**

Final Portfolio Contents

Writings for the Portfolio: (50%) Consists of your reflective paper on writing, the job, and the rhetorical situation (4–5 pages); the course log; and 2–3 pieces of writing you did on the job. (The number of pieces will vary depending on the kind and length of writing you did on the job. Check with the instructors before you assemble your portfolio.) You need to include the paper trail of drafts and process work, group commentary, and reflective memos.

Course Log: (25%) Plan on writing at least 3 pages a week or about 30 pages total for weeks 4–13 while you are on the job. This should be put in your final portfolio.

Participation: (25%) Consists of participating in class discussions, workshops, and listserv discussions—showing up for class prepared, contributing oral and written comments on the work of others, getting writing in to workshop partners on time, various group and individual presentations, and the results of your group/partner evaluation of your contributions to their success. The evaluations of others should be placed in the portfolio.

Works Cited

Anson, Chris M. 1997. "On Reflection: The Role of Logs and Journals in Service-Learning Courses." Pp. 167–80 in *Writing the Community: Concepts and Models for Service-Learning in Composition*, ed. Linda Adler-Kassner et al. Washington, D.C.: American Association for Higher Education.

Brown, Bettina Lankard. 1998. "Service Learning: More Than Community Service." *ERIC Digest No. 198.* Columbus, OH: ERIC. Online EBSCOhost, 21 May. Accessed 17 December 2001.

Comstock, Cathy. 1994. "Literature and Service Learning: Not Strange Bedfellows." Pp. 83–90 in *Building Community: Service-Learning in the Academic Disciplines*, ed. Richard J. Kraft and Marc Swadener. Denver: Colorado Campus Compact.

de Acosta, Martha. 1995. "Journal Writing in Service-Learning: Lessons from a Mentoring Project." *Michigan Journal of Community Service Learning* 2: 141–49.

Deans, Thomas. 2000. *Writing Partnerships: Service-Learning in Composition.* Urbana, IL: National Council of Teachers of English.

Ervin, Elizabeth. 2000. *Public Literacy.* New York: Longman.

Eyler, Janet S. 2001. "Electronic Journaling: Using the Web-Based Group Journal for Service-Learning Reflection." *Michigan Journal of Community Service-Learning* 8: 27–35.

Flower, Linda. 1998. *Problem-Solving Strategies for Writing in College and Community.* Fort Worth, TX: Harcourt Brace.

Giles, Dwight E., Janet Eyler, and Angela Schmiede. 1996. *A Practitioner's Guide to Reflection in Service Learning: Student Voices and Reflections.* Nashville, TN: Vanderbilt University Press.

Hamner, Doris. 2002. *Building Bridges: The Allyn & Bacon Student Guide to Service-Learning.* Boston: Allyn & Bacon.

Herzberg, Bruce. 1994. "Community Service and Critical Teaching." *College Composition and Communication* 45: 307–19.

Jacoby, Barbara. 1996. *Service-Learning in Higher Education: Concepts and Practices*. San Francisco: Jossey-Bass.

Parks, Steve, and Eli Goldblatt. 2000. "Writing beyond the Curriculum: Fostering New Collaborations in Literacy." *College English* 62: 584–605.

Peck, Wayne Campbell, Linda Flower, and Lorraine Higgins. 1995. "Community Literacy." *College Composition and Communication* 46: 199–222.

Reed, Julie, and Christopher Koliba. 1995. *Facilitating Reflection: A Manual for Leaders and Educators*. Georgetown University Volunteer and Public Service Center. Accessed 17 December 2001. <http://www.uvm.edu/~dewey/reflection_manual/>.

Rhoads, Robert A. 1997. *Community Service and Higher Learning: Explorations of the Caring Self*. Albany: State University of New York Press.

Rhoads, Robert A., and Jeffrey P. F. Howard. 1998. *Academic Service Learning: A Pedagogy of Action and Reflection*. In *New Directions for Teaching and Learning* Vol. 73. San Francisco: Jossey-Bass.

Schutz, Aaron, and Anne Ruggles Gere. 1998. "Service Learning and English Studies: Rethinking 'Public Service.'" *College English* 60: 129–49.

Service Learning Faculty Handbook. n.d. Virginia Technical University. Accessed 17 December 2001. <http://www.majbill.vt.edu/sl/fachand.html>.

Silcox, Harry. 1995. "The Need to Consider Service Learning in Developing Future Vocational Education Programs." In *Enriching the Curriculum through Service Learning,* ed. Carol W. Kinsley and Kate McPherson. Association for Supervision and Curriculum Development. Accessed 17 December 2000. <http://www.ascd.org/framebook.html>.

Chapter Six

Managing Diverse Disciplines in a Junior-Level WID Course

Mark Schaub

Grand Valley State University

Teaching Context

Grand Valley State University (GVSU) is a regional comprehensive university and one of fifteen state-supported four-year universities in Michigan. GVSU's main campus is located in Allendale, Michigan, and in 1999–2000 had an enrollment of 17,200 students. Situated near the urban center of Grand Rapids, GVSU serves a large and diverse community, and the student body (60 percent female) can best be described as nontraditional; undergraduate students tend to be older than the national average (at GVSU the average age is about 22.5). Fewer than 19 percent of the students live in on-campus housing units; these on-campus students are overwhelmingly traditional students, eighteen to twenty years old, from communities across Michigan.

Writing 305: Writing in the Disciplines exists in relation to the following writing requirements in the GVSU curriculum:

First-Year Writing Requirement. This is generally fulfilled by taking Writing 150: Strategies for Writing, the standard first-year composition course. In order to fulfill the first-year writing requirement with Writing 150, students must get a C grade or better. Evaluation is by collaborative portfolio grading of selected student work; each group comprises five faculty members.

Supplemental Writing Skills (SWS) courses. Several courses in each major area are identified as SWS courses, and students must complete two SWS courses (with a C grade or better) before graduation: one within their major area and one outside the major. A minimum of 3,000 words of written work is assigned in each SWS course. These courses are taught by faculty across the disciplines.

Junior-Level Writing Requirement. To be completed within the first three years (or first ninety hours) of undergraduate work, this requirement may be fulfilled in one of two ways: (1) achieve a satisfactory score on the junior-level assessment essay (devised and evaluated by a committee of faculty within the student's major area), or (2) pass Writing 305 with a grade of C or better.

Three-quarters of GVSU students complete the junior-level writing requirement by doing well enough on the assessment essay (they are allowed two attempts at this essay) that the Writing 305 course is waived. In recent semesters, roughly 25 percent of GVSU students have fulfilled the junior-level writing requirement by completing Writing 305, the majority of these having done poorly on the assessment essay. For numerous reasons, the rest of the students who enroll in Writing 305 have not even tried to take the assessment essay that could exempt them from the course. After speaking with several of these students in the past year, I have concluded that they end up in Writing 305 either because of a failure to plan ahead for the scheduled exam dates or because of low levels of confidence in their writing—they wanted to take another writing course because they felt they needed it.

Writing 305 students bring to the course a broad range of disciplines, reflecting the offerings of the university: everything from nursing to criminal justice to engineering. To respond to this situation and still preserve the discipline-specific nature of the course mission, the Writing department designates special sections for students in particular schools or divisions. One section each semester, for example, is designated for students majoring in the health professions; another is designated for students in the Seidman School of Business. Still, half of the sections go without such designations and are labeled "general" sections of Writing 305.

Approach

The approach I describe here is geared for the general sections of Writing 305, in which the twenty-eight enrolled students can easily represent twenty different majors. Students can expect to be exchanging drafts of their papers with students outside their discipline, even though their own writing will be particular to their own discipline. I usually have students remain with one writing group of three or four students for the duration of the semester, and as the students become more familiar with the writing and disciplines of their writing group colleagues, each in turn assumes the role of the expert or representative for their own discipline.

The Writing 305 course meets twice a week (seventy-five minutes each) during a regular semester. One of the class meetings is in a computer lab and the other is held in a traditional classroom. Most of the computer lab time is spent researching, drafting, revising, or providing peer feedback within the writing groups. The classroom time is primarily devoted to presentation and discussion of writing assignments, discussion of common reading assignments, workshopping of paper drafts, and other tasks. Common readings are from either a textbook (e.g., Christine Hult's *Researching and Writing across the Curriculum* [2002]) or photocopied articles. Each semester I distribute academic articles that appear to be accessible to a general university audience, and then the classroom discussion centers on how the authors of these articles present new knowledge to their readers and what the editorial boards of the various journals seem to be certifying as appropriate new knowledge for a particular field. I often supply lists of questions in support of these discussions, questions to which students respond in writing.

Beyond these kinds of secondary reading and writing activities, my approach to this course includes three primary writing assignments, each one addressing academic writing in the students' disciplines, professional or workplace writing related to their disciplines, or a combination of both. The three assignments are as follows:

Analysis of Workplace Writing (in a career related to my discipline). This project involves students in an investigation of the role of writing in a career associated with their academic discipline. To complete the assignment, the students must actually talk with a professional about the writing he or she does on an hour-by-hour, day-to-day, or week-to-week basis. The students must also document specific audiences to whom the professional writes, the genres in which the documents are written, and the purposes for which the documents are written.

Analysis of Academic Writing in My Discipline. For this project, students analyze the content, format, and style of published writing in their chosen discipline. One important requirement is that they locate and read hard copies of academic journals, rather than gather articles from electronic databases. This requirement reflects my growing recognition that very few of the juniors and seniors I've had in Writing 305 have ever held an issue of an academic journal in their hands. One obvious reason for this is the nature of contemporary academic research: with the ubiquity of efficient and immense online databases, students can download abstracts and complete articles with relative ease. The genre of academic journal articles continues to be influential in shaping knowledge in the disciplines, but reading individual articles in isolation does not provide an understanding of the breadth and depth of the genre; articles read individually and/or online are outside the context of their original publication. Students who rely on databases alone are not privy to the editorial shape of journals and articles, the role of book reviews and commentary, and scholarly debate. They don't see the charts and tables and figures (these key visuals are often impossible to download through library-linked databases), and they don't see the advertising that may appear alongside the text of the articles.

New Directions in My Field. For this research paper project, students look for the spaces—the openings for future knowledge making in their chosen disciplines. The research is, of course, quite contemporary, since in order to locate the new directions in a field students must assess the very latest published (and soon-to-be-published) research. Students should also be able to interact with professionals and academics in their field in order to solicit the perspectives of those who will be affected by new directions in the discipline.

Reflection

For the most part, students have succeeded with these assignments, and in their feedback either during the course or in course/instructor evaluations after the semester they generally confirm my belief that the assigments are useful. The Analysis of Academic Writing assignment often prompts student complaints as they initially begin work on the project, but in hindsight the majority of students have found it interesting and helpful. One student, however, added on the evaluation sheet that he or she "did not have enough exposure to these [academic journals] outside the class." Optimistically, I take that as further evidence of the necessity for such an assignment.

For the Analysis of Academic Writing paper, one element that seems to separate the A papers from the B papers is that the A papers reflect a clear understanding of the audiences for particular journals and how the editors maintain the journals with these readers in mind. (See Appendix A for an example.) For the Analysis of Workplace Writing essay, I am particularly interested in seeing how the students are able to perceive the genres at work in a particular context. A successful response includes the range of genres addressed as well as specific examples of writing in each. (See Appendix B.) As for the New Directions assignment, I've only begun using this assignment and look forward to more carefully monitoring its success in future semesters.

Rationale

My approach to the Writing in the Disciplines course connects two compatible notions: (1) the course should prepare students for the academic writing they will continue to encounter within their discipline, and (2) the course should help students with the workplace writing they will encounter as professionals in their discipline after they leave the university. I try to follow the advice found in numerous critical works, which call for a bridging of these two purposes for college-level writing courses. Reither (1993), Spilka (1993), and the authors published in the collections edited by Garay and Bernhardt (1998) and Cope and Kalantzis (2000) all argue that college writing classrooms need to reflect more of the genres, contexts, and situations of workplace writing. The Analysis of Workplace Writing essay is clearly designed to get the students to look ahead to the writing they will encounter in the future. The assignment embodies the bridge between academic and workplace writing.

My approach also reflects an attempt to remain faithful to the catalog description for Writing 305, which emphasizes the academic nature of the course. Two of the three assignments described reflect this goal for the course. Still, these assignments are designed to broaden the repertoire of the students' academic writing beyond the skills and genres emphasized in the other writing courses in our curriculum.

Students already have some experience as academic writers, and not just because they've already taken one first-year composition course. Nelson (1995) summarizes the understanding of contemporary students as "somewhat experienced" academic writers, arguing that there is "a powerful legacy of school experiences that students bring with them every time they step into the classroom and undertake a writing assignment" (411). At the same time, students often are quite reluctant to view themselves as "inventing the university," much less adding something worthwhile to the daunting collection of published knowledge already at play in their fields. They are humbled if their essays or papers are seen, as Bazerman (1994) puts it, "as an answer to the question, 'Against the background of accumulated knowledge of the discipline, how can I present an original claim about a phenomenon to the appropriate audience convincingly so that thinking and behavior will be modified accordingly?'" (162). Unfortunately, only a fraction of my new Writing 305 students will be able to confidently answer that question. The New Directions assignment—difficult as it is—appears to provide a boost in students' confidence.

The role of the New Directions in My Field paper in my course is to acknowledge that students do have some expectations about academic writing but that they will generally lack confidence in their ability to add anything new to the conversation. By framing the paper in terms of observing the process of knowledge being shaped, I better position students to evaluate or critique that process—and that's just what they do in the Analysis of Academic Writing assignment.

Each of the three assignments described here addresses the issue of genre. As Segal et al. (1998) point out, we help students understand "how discursive systems work in order to improve the ways in which people learn from those systems" (75). The tools for doing this are using, imitating, and evaluating the range of available genres. Walvoord and McCarthy (1990) concur that the key to understanding a discipline is to understand its genres. The Analysis of Workplace Writing assignment requires that students not only look at genres in the workplace but also actually talk about genres with professionals in their field, an activity most students are never asked to engage in elsewhere in their university curriculum. The Analysis of Academic Writing assignment mandates a close reading of the various genres prevalent in the dominant and knowledge-shaping publications in the disciplines. Finally, the New Directions in My Field paper takes the understanding of academic genres even further but makes it relevant to the students' own visions of their disciplines.

Appendix A

Here is an excerpt from a successful analysis of medical journals by Kate Kryger, a biomedical science student:

Editorial Control and Review

The content of medical journals is primarily dictated by the journal's intended audience. A medical journal directed towards experts within a specific field often publishes recent studies and research projects performed by other medical experts within their field. Furthermore, journals geared towards medical and scientific specialties tend to include advanced studies or information about cutting-edge technology. These works are often indicative of the future of medicine. To illustrate, *The American Journal of Cardiology* published a study titled, "Increased Platelet Aggregability in Response to Shear Stress in Acute Myocardial Infarction and Its Inhibition by Combined Therapy with Aspirin and Cilostazol after Coronary Intervention." This study examines a *prospective* treatment route using a combination of two drugs.

In contrast, medical literature such as *Journal of the American Medical Association* may publish articles and studies encompassing a variety of topics. A journal that is directed toward a broad audience tends to be less distinctive in topic specification. (However, less distinctive in topic specification does not negate the expertise of the author. Thus, there is no compromise in quality of more generalized journals.) These journals tend to take articles and studies that pertain to current "real-life" situations (instead of new ideas and technology that may apply in the future). Articles are often inclusive of case studies or manifestations of common diseases/medical problems, monthly features, and articles that may be considered more "sociological" in nature. Furthermore, these journals are more likely to publish book reviews and editorials, thereby satisfying the general needs of a physician or student.

Typically, the majority of authors/researchers published by medical journals have received terminal degrees of M.D. or Ph.D.-M.D. However, manuscript submission is nondiscriminatory, provided the submission is medically significant and scientifically valid. Thus, researchers and students lacking terminal degrees are also considered for publication. Regardless of scholastic achievement, each author must follow the same article submission guidelines. Although these guidelines tend to be uniform between all medical journals, some variability in minor aspects, such as article length, does exist. An example of such variability is found when comparing *The American Journal of Emergency Medicine* and *The American Journal of Cardiology,* whereby "brief reports" are limited to 2,000 words and 2,500 words, respectively.

Appendix B

Here are some segments from a successful analysis of workplace writing. The author, a communications major, reports on the writing done by a high school principal.

What Kinds of Documents Does She Write?

In her job as principal Mrs. Clooney writes in the various genres, as well as writing in areas specifically related to her job, such as teacher evaluations.

Memos

There are sixty people on St. Monica's staff. Mrs. Clooney communicates with most of these people through memos, which she writes almost daily. . . .

Letters

Supplementary letters are sent to parents if something special comes up that cannot wait for the monthly newsletter. Parents also receive thank-you letters at times as well as letters describing their tuition statements and other school accounts.

Reports

Mrs. Clooney writes three different kinds of reports. The first is written on the level of the Catholic school itself, to the educational committee or school board. The second type is written on the diocesan level. These reports can be anything from statistical reports to narratives. Finally, an annual report for accreditation is sent to the state.

A special kind of report is written once every seven years. During this time, the school undergoes a complete review for accreditation. Over the course of several days, fifteen to twenty people evaluate the school to see how it is operating according to 12 standards. Their reports are kept in a large binder.

Staff Evaluations

As part of her job as principal, Mrs. Clooney must review her staff's performance. These evaluations include observation notes Mrs. Clooney writes while sitting in on a teacher's classroom, as well as written critiques. All the documents involved in an evaluation are put in the personnel file.

"Things you don't even give a second thought about"

This type of writing, as described by Mrs. Clooney above, includes such tasks as writing articles for the local newspaper about her school. In addition, this genre encompasses daily rituals. Mrs. Clooney keeps written logs of all the phone calls she makes or takes. She also takes notes at every meeting she attends, whether it be a meeting with a parent, student, staff member, etc. She keeps these notes in binders that she brings with her to the meetings. She also writes preparation notes for every meeting, including, but not limited to, weekly office staff meetings, weekly faculty meetings, and twice monthly/monthly maintenance, play-ground, and kitchen staff meetings.

Mrs. Clooney also makes extensive use of e-mail, which she says is "as important as some business letters . . . because it's direct and to the person."

Works Cited

Bazerman, Charles. 1994. "What Written Knowledge Does: Three Ex-amples of Academic Discourse." Pp. 159–88 in *Landmark Essays on Writing Across the Curriculum*, ed. Charles Bazerman and David R. Russell. Davis, CA: Hermagoras Press.

Cope, Bill, and Mary Kalantzis. 2000. *Multiliteracies: Literacy Learn-ing and the Design of Social Futures*. London: Routledge.

Garay, Mary Sue, and Stephen Bernhardt. 1998. *Expanding Literacies: English Teaching and the New Workplace*. Albany: State Univer-sity of New York Press.

Nelson, Jennie. 1995. "Reading Classrooms as Text: Exploring Student Writers' Interpretive Practices." *College Composition and Com-munication* 46: 411–30.

Reither, James. 1993. "Bridging the Gap: Scenic Motives for Collabora-tive Writing in Workplace and School." Pp. 195–206 in *Writing in the Workplace: New Research Perspectives*, ed. Rachel Spilka. Carbondale: Southern Illinois University Press.

Segal, Judy, Anthony Pare, Doug Brent, and Douglas Vipond. 1998. "The Researcher as Missionary: Problems with Rhetoric and Re-form in the Disciplines." *College Composition and Communica-tion* 50: 71–90.

Spilka, Rachel. 1993. "Influencing Workplace Practice: A Challenge for Professional Writing Specialists in Academia." Pp. 207–19 in *Writ-ing in the Workplace: New Research Perspectives*, ed. Rachel Spilka. Carbondale: Southern Illinois University Press.

Walvoord, Barbara E., and Lucille P. McCarthy. 1990. *Thinking and Writing in College: A Naturalistic Study of Students in Four Disci-plines*. Urbana, IL: National Council of Teachers of English.

CHAPTER SEVEN

Letting Students Take Charge: A Nonfiction Writing Workshop

STEPHEN WILHOIT

University of Dayton

When I arrived at the University of Dayton over a decade ago, I was asked to teach a graduate course in nonfiction prose. Though this course was listed in the catalog, no one had taught it for some time. When I looked at the last syllabus used, I could see why: it had been a traditional teacher-centered writing course with lectures on various nonfiction genres, critiques of sample readings provided by the teacher, and five original essay assignments based on topics the teacher chose. As someone trained in creative writing, I knew I couldn't teach a course this way. I was much more interested in turning responsibility for the class over to my students. I wanted them to choose the genres we would study, help one another develop and revise their essays as a community of writers, and decide how their work would be evaluated. A writing course designed along these lines would build on my strengths as a classroom instructor and teach the students much more about writing than would a more traditional class.

As I began to plan the course, though, I faced a real problem—finding a suitable textbook. None of the rhetorics or readers on the market fit my needs. First, I wasn't sure which nonfiction genres my students would elect to study. Second, I couldn't find a textbook with the kind of readings I wanted—samples of contemporary professional nonfiction prose from a wide variety of academic and nonacademic publications. Third, because I wanted my students to learn to write nonfiction prose inductively, I needed a textbook with minimal directions. Rather than being told how to write how-to essays, travelogues, or interviews, for example, I wanted my students to study these genres themselves, to identify together the defining features of each genre, and to decide themselves how best to produce similar publishable work. Almost in desperation, I decided to try something new: instead of ordering a textbook for the class, I decided to have my students compile their own reader-rhetorics. Fortunately, this assignment has proven to be one of the most productive and popular elements of the course, playing a central role in almost every aspect of the workshop.

First, the context: my university, the course, and my students. The University of Dayton is a private (Catholic), residential, comprehensive institution with an undergraduate enrollment of around five thousand students. The English department offers both the B.A. and the M.A. with two graduate tracks, one in literature and one in writing. English 629, Non-fiction Writing, is primarily filled by graduate students in the writing track, though advanced undergraduate students have twice taken the course with permission. About half of the students in the writing track go on for their doctorate; the others enter the workforce with their M.A.s. Most of these students find jobs in technical writing, editing, advertising, marketing, and teaching.

The class meets for three hours once a week for sixteen weeks. The first five class meetings are devoted to compiling the "textbook"; for the rest of the semester, the class functions as a writing workshop. I participate in the class as a writer as well, having my work critiqued along with the students'. During those first five weeks, the students select the eight nonfiction genres we will study in the course and build their reader-rhetorics by collecting and analyzing professionally published samples of each genre. The students then compose five original texts, choosing to work with any five of the eight genres they have studied. I respond to all of the students' manuscripts, and at least two of them are workshopped by the entire class. The students face no deadlines for their manuscripts; they can complete the work at their own pace. They may not, however, turn in more than one manuscript a week, which helps me avoid toiling over mountains of work at the end of the term.

At the first class meeting, we decide which eight genres we'll study, and for the next four weeks we discuss two genres a class meeting. If, for example, the students decide they want to examine interviews and how-to essays first, over the following week they have to collect at least three professionally published interviews and how-to essays and place them in a binder to be turned in at the end of the course. I suggest they gather their sample texts from a variety of publications: mass-market magazines, newspapers, newsletters, trade journals, and so forth. Once they gather their samples, students compose a rhetorical analysis of the genre. In this three- to four-page informal essay, they discuss their conclusions concerning the content, structure, and style of the sample texts they found: what kind of material is generally found in the sample readings, how the sample texts tend to be organized, how they sound on the page. I ask the students to note any significant exceptions to the generalizations they form and to pay particular attention to format (what do they notice about the use of sidebars, pictures, or graphics in these texts?) and audience (who is the target audience of each publication they consulted and how might that audience influence the content, structure, style, and format of the sample texts?). The day we discuss the genre the students bring their binder and two copies of their rhetorical analysis to class, one to keep in their binder and one to turn in to me.

As we discuss each genre in class, I use an overhead projector and transparencies to compile a "master list" of the rhetorical features for each genre. When I ask the students to share their conclusions about the typical content, organization, and style of each genre, I list their comments on the overhead under appropriate headings. Everyone contributes to the discussion, passing around sample texts from their binders to illustrate points when necessary. I also ask the students where they collected their sample texts so that we also have a master list of publications that publish this sort of material. During the following week, I type up and duplicate this master list of rhetorical features and distribute it to the students at the next class meeting so that every student has a copy for his or her binder. (See the appendix for a sample master list.) By the end of the fifth week, the students' binders are complete, each containing (1) the sample texts the student collected, (2) his or her own analysis of each genre, and (3) the master list of rhetorical features and publications compiled during the class discussion. This binder becomes the students' "textbook" for the class: a reader (the sample texts) and a rhetoric (the analytical essays and lists).

Building these reader-rhetorics helps the students in several ways. First, most of the students are studying these genres seriously for the first time. Locating, reading, and analyzing the sample texts familiarizes them with each type of writing. Second, analyzing the sample texts rhetorically improves the students' critical reading and writing skills. They come to see what their sample texts have in common and how they differ according to the target audience of the publications. Third, their analysis of the readings, plus the master list compiled by the class, helps them write texts of their own. As we discuss each genre in class, we identify some of its common attributes and features, including typical opening and closing strategies, use of examples and evidence, use of graphics and illustrations, paragraph and sentence length, diction, and tone. Based on this work, the students have a good idea how to draft their own manuscripts.

Finally, the students can refer to their reader-rhetorics when they critique one anothers' manuscripts. Around week seven of the course, the workshop sessions begin. Each week we review the work of three writers in class, and every writer has at least two of his or her manuscripts critiqued in class. The class meeting before they are scheduled to have their manuscripts workshopped, the writers distribute a copy of their work to everyone in class, indicating a target publication they have in mind. The rest of us then have a week to review these manuscripts, mark up the texts, and prepare our comments. Since the students are free to experiment with any genre they like in any order they like, each week we have a variety of manuscripts to review: a review, a travelogue, and an editorial, for example, or a how-to essay and a profile. As the students review each manuscript, they can compare it against the sample texts they collected and the lists of rhetorical features in their binders. How is it similar to or different from the sample texts? How well does it exhibit the key rhetorical features of the genre that the class identified? What suggestions for improvement can be drawn by comparing this manuscript to the sample texts in the reader-rhetoric?

When we critique a writer's manuscript in class, I act as manager, leading the discussion, pulling in all the students, drawing connections and distinctions between the students' comments. During this session, the writer is not allowed to speak; he or she has to listen quietly to the comments and take notes. Toward the end of the session, I summarize the students' comments, offer my own observations and suggestions, and then turn the class over to the writer, who has the last word. (When one of my manuscripts is scheduled for class discussion, I ask one of the students to lead the session.) Participating in a writing workshop can be difficult for students, especially if they are new to the procedure. As writers, the students need to develop patience, good listening skills, and the ability to accept constructive criticism; as peer critics, they need to develop a vocabulary for talking about writing like writers, good critical reading skills, and the ability to offer respectful, constructive commentary on draft manuscripts.

Having the students put together their own textbook for this course succeeds, I think, because it combines two tested approaches to teaching composition: classical imitation and modern rhetorical analysis. Imitation comes first. If students plan to submit their work for publication—a stated goal of the course—they need to know what type of work tends to get published today. What constitutes "publishable quality" work for each genre? How is it structured? What is its style? If the students can form generalizations concerning the content, organization, and style of the various genres we study, then they have standards to imitate when they write their own pieces. Imitation offers students a starting point for their work, a template or paradigm to follow, which most students need since they have not studied these genres before.

Yet, as the students collect and analyze their sample texts, they always discover important variations in each genre—the content, organization, and style of each genre vary in interesting ways by publication and intended audience. Here is where more modern theories of rhetorical analysis aid the course. Instead of mechanically imitating models as they compose their own texts, the students must adapt content, organization, and style to suit their targeted publications and readerships. An interview intended for publication in *Rolling Stone,* for example, will look and sound different from an interview published in *TIME* or in *Modern Fiction Studies.* As modern rhetoricians such as James Kinneavy (1971) and Wayne Booth (1963) point out, the content, format, and language of any piece of writing is closely linked to the needs of the reader. Successful writers adapt their prose to the needs and interests of their audience. As they compile their reader and compose their rhetorical analyses of each genre, the students must examine how writers make these adaptations, how they tailor their work for a particular publication and a particular readership. These lessons help the students compose effective manuscripts themselves and offer insightful, constructive comments on their peers' work.

Every semester that I teach this course the students mention the reader-rhetoric as one of the most important aspects of the class. Here are some of the comments students wrote on their course evaluations the last time I taught the class:

> The idea to make our own textbooks was clever and highly appropriate for a graduate-level course. I learned more from doing that than from any textbook I've ever read.

> Thanks for inspiring me to write and making me explore new genres I have never written about. The "textbook," assignments, and portfolio make this class—it is truly a writing workshop. The feedback from the other writers in this class was very helpful and constructive.

> I learned a lot from this class. . . . This course gave me an opportunity to learn about a type of writing I had never done before. I like the way that the class was organized. It gave us the opportunity to give each other feedback and to learn about our own writing. This is one of the most valuable classes that I have taken as a grad student.

The project puts learning into the students' hands but also encourages collaboration: the students have to gather the sample texts on their own and draw their own conclusions about each genre's content, organization, and style prior to class discussion; however, in class they share their insights and collectively establish standards for composing and evaluating each genre. The exercise even helps me determine the students' course grades. Every student composes five draft manuscripts for the course. They revise four of these manuscripts for their final class portfolio, which receives a grade. When evaluating this work, I rely on the master list of features we developed for each genre, applying the criteria we agreed on in class. In the end, the standards we develop as a community of writers largely determines the students' grades.

Appendix

Sample Rhetorical Feature Master List: Editorials

Sources

Dayton Daily News	*New York Times*	*Columbus Dispatch*
Media Info.	*Newsweek*	*Detroit News*
English Journal	*Computer World*	*Wall Street Journal*
NEA Today	*InfoWorld*	

Content

Arguments

Testimonials

Pathos

Human interest appeals

True stories

Calls for action or reform

Statistics as evidence or examples

Opinions

Pro-con debate

History of issue

Comparisons

Analogies

Interview material

Summaries

Quotations

Organization

Summary→commentary

Summary/comment→summary/comment

Problem-solution format

Move from past to present

Opposition→refutation

Picture of author

Biographical sketch

Sidebars/inserts with highlighted quotes

Openings

Subheads to announce topic/stance

Change in typeface

Announce topic

Appeal to ethics

Historical overview

Description

Shocking story

Call to action

Pictures

Generalization

Endings

Call to action

Restate main point

Promote one solution

Scary statistic

Quote from expert or layperson

Offer last point to ponder

Summary

Caption

Thanks

Aim

Persuade

    through information/facts (logos)

    through rhetoric (pathos or ethos)

Warn

Inform

Move to action

Fortify own position

Style/Audience

Assume audience interested in topic/issue

Assume audience can relate to topic (or help them to)

Tend to be short

Sentences may be longer than in news stories

Allusions to current events/historical events

Writer poses as "everyman," relates his/her experiences to topic or readers

Writer speaks for self or for community

First person possible: *I, we,* or *our*

Serious tone

Lecturing tone possible, offering moral lessons

Little humor, but tone can be light at times

Some with wit, biting comments

Tends to be subjective and one-sided

Tone is authoritative; few hedges

Middle diction common

Use of rhetorical questions

Match diction and syntax to purpose and audience

Often sound like a speech

Audience can be very localized

Some jargon possible

Works Cited

Booth, Wayne. 1963. "The Rhetorical Stance." *College Composition and Communication* 14: 139–45.

Kinneavy, James L. 1971. *A Theory of Discourse: The Aims of Discourse.* New York: Norton.

II

WRITING ASSIGNMENTS

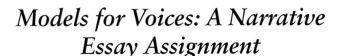

CHAPTER EIGHT

Models for Voices: A Narrative Essay Assignment

TONYA M. STREMLAU
Gallaudet University

Narrative essay assignments are fairly standard fare in first-year composition, so there is nothing radical about my using a narrative essay as the first writing assignment in first-semester English courses that combine reading and writing for students who enter our university with strong English skills. (We label these courses "accelerated" and "honors.") There is something unusual about the context. Gallaudet University is the world's only liberal arts university dedicated to the education of deaf and hard-of-hearing students. Classroom instruction is conducted in sign language, and the rare hearing students (who are visiting, nondegree students) in undergraduate classrooms are expected to sign as well.

Like my students, I am deaf. During my own education (always in hearing schools), I was never assigned a deaf author to read; the only one I even knew about was Helen Keller (who was, of course, blind as well). I had no models for how to write about this experience that was so much a part of my life until I set myself to search for deaf writers when I was in graduate school. Since many of my students have been mainstreamed in hearing schools, it is unlikely that they have been exposed to deaf writers. I want to provide such models for my students.

Therefore, before I hand out the narrative essay assignment, students begin to read and discuss a memoir/autobiography by a deaf writer. I usually use *What's That Pig Outdoors? A Memoir of Deafness* by Henry Kisor (1990), a deaf journalist, because it does a good job of addressing the language-learning issues I want to discuss with the students and because it offers perspectives that are controversial on our campus. (Specifically, testimonial for the success of oral—rather than signed—instruction and communication for the deaf.) Kisor is an extreme example of what is known in the Deaf community as "THINK-HEARING"—a deaf person who tries to be like a hearing person (and who considers being able to do so a sign of success) instead of embracing the Deaf[1] world. This parallels the label "oreo" for a black person. Students who strongly identify as Deaf are frequently so upset with Kisor that they do not notice that he states several times that he is not against sign language; he even says that if he had a deaf child who was not benefiting from oral instruction, he would have the child—and the entire family—learn to sign. Other students identify with Kisor more closely. All, however, can identify with the problems of living in a world in which most people can hear.

After beginning this discussion, I pass out their first essay assignment. Following is part of what I handed out in a recent semester:

> For your narrative essay, write a mini-memoir. Tell a story of an occasion when your hearing status was a central issue. How has where you fall along the continuum of deaf to hearing affected who you have become (and are becoming)? The story you pick should tell of a significant event in your life. It might not seem significant to anyone else, or even to you at the time it happened. In your essay, show how the event proved important.

The assignment also asks that students carefully consider who their audience will be. Kisor pointedly addresses his book to a hearing audience. In the first chapter, he explains, "most important, this volume is intended to help the hearing public understand something of what life is like for those who cannot hear" (1990, 10). Many students also choose to address hearing people for similar reasons—and because they hope hearing people can come to understand that there are many different ways of being deaf.

All of these reasons for giving this assignment I share with my students. I tell them that I can't imagine a greater success as an English teacher than for one of them to become a well-known

Deaf writer who will help the rest of the world see and understand what our world is like. I tell them how important deaf and Deaf writers are to me. What I don't tell them is that I choose to use a deaf writer to inspire them when they write their own papers because I want them to be very aware that "deaf writer" is not an oxymoron. I need to exorcise a ghost that haunts both our English department and deaf students in English classes— even honors classes—everywhere: the ghost of Deaf English.

"Deaf English" refers to the error-prone syntax of many deaf writers. It is a common malady, but the reason does not lie in deafness itself. Its roots lie in the lack of exposure many deaf people have to English in any form, in the fact that English is a second language for many of them,[2] and in the many problems of deaf education systems in the United States. Deaf English resembles ESL writing—limited vocabulary, limited understanding of English idioms, nonstandard phrasing and word order, problems with subject-verb agreement and verb tense, and so on. One book focusing on these English problems of deaf students is Jacqueline Anderson's *Deaf Students Mis-Writing, Teacher Mis-Reading: English Education and the Deaf College Student* (1993). Although she is focusing on deaf students, Anderson argues that her methods "are equally applicable to hearing students, and can be utilized in any mainstream, ESL, or English for Special Purposes classroom" (18). In other words, deaf students need what hearing students need: the chance to learn English in meaningful context.

In this case, that meaningful context is one in which deafness is not a barrier but a boon to developing as a writer. As Peter Elbow (1995) says, "Writing is a struggle and a risk. Why go to the bother unless what we say feels important?" (81). Elbow argues that it is important to provide students with a class in which they can see themselves as writers and in which they can feel they have something important to write about; reading the deaf autobiography or memoir sets up this situation by showing that a deaf person can be a successful published writer and can do so by writing about being deaf. Even the good students worry about being judged negatively as deaf writers, that any flaw in their writing will be blamed on their deafness; this assignment provides a context in which it is expected that deaf writing and good writing can be one and the same.

The worry my students feel was part of my experience as a student, too; knowing that people expected deaf students to have poor English skills, I worked even harder to prove that I was a good writer. I tried so hard to write like a hearing person that I even avoided writing about deaf-related topics; deafness was something to brush under the academic rug if I could. My students themselves comment on experiencing the effects of the common (mis)perception that deaf students have problems with English. One of my honors students, Tom, wrote the following in his final self-evaluation for the course, explaining how he had developed a low-confidence level in his English skills by the time he entered my class:

> In my third year of high school I was identified as "gifted and talented" in English by the Gifted and Talented program. I was quite shocked because for years everyone would not believe in the possibility a Deaf student could actually have good reading and writing skills, let alone possess potential for the Gifted and Talented program.

He goes on to say that a family crisis caused him to fall behind on schoolwork; when a teacher commented on the neglected work, he began to doubt his ability with English.

I have hope that the very act of writing about being deaf, in tandem with reading good deaf writing (Kisor's book and the writing of their peers), will banish the ghost of Deaf English (much as it did for me) and create a positive writing experience to start off the course. Does it work? Tom wrote, "my narrative paper . . . proved to be an easy paper for me to write." Tom had chosen to write about an experience he had when he was four years old when it first hit him that he could not communicate with the rest of the world the way he communicated with his family; this was his story, so he was the authority with something important to say. He went on to explain that getting positive feedback on the paper helped him regain the confidence in his ability to write that he had lost in high school. My experience with this assignment is that it helps create a positive atmosphere in the classroom in which students understand and trust one another (and me).

What I think I see happening is what Peter Elbow talks about in *Writing with Power* (1981) when he discusses his students finding their "voice" in a course he taught in autobiography. By writing about their own experiences, students "begin to like writing more, to write about things that are more important to them, and thus to feel a greater connection between their writing and themselves. I think this process leads not just to learning, but to growth or development" (284).

What kinds of stories do students share? I end by summarizing those of two students, Tom and Arin. Both wrote papers about developing their self-awareness of being deaf. Arin's paper was about how difficult it was for her to accept herself as deaf. She began, "The day I couldn't hear the birds anymore was the day I knew it was permanent. There would be no magic doctor, surgery, nor medicine to fix this. I was deaf. It took 5 years and 10 surgeries to come to this realization." She goes on to describe the many ways she tried to avoid seeming "handicapped" and difficulties that resulted when people were actually fooled by the results of her hard work to appear "normal." At the end of the paper, she describes her growing acceptance of herself for who she is and her excitement at being in a deaf environment at Gallaudet.

Tom's paper is very different from Arin's. One day when Tom was four, his father took him out to eat. The weather was bad, and Tom did not want to go out in it, so his father let him stay inside the restaurant while he went to get the car. A small group of teenagers came in and gave the boy an experience he would never forget. Tom describes:

> Pointing right at my face, the girl started moving her mouth and laughing. A boy suddenly stooped down and smiled right in my face. Another boy stooped down behind him and started moving his mouth and started to laugh. Who were these people, and what were they doing? A funny feeling started to grow in my stomach, up my chest and into my throat. These people were starting to scare me.

Tom, despite his fear, managed to see one of the teenagers saying the word *Daddy*, and he responded by signing *Daddy*, which only made the teenagers make more fun of him, mocking his sign. Tom concludes the paper by explaining that this was the first time he knew he could not understand other people the way he could understand his parents and that other people could not understand him the way his parents could.

These are the kinds of papers I had hoped for when I gave the assignment; the papers show how the writers' hearing status affected the development of their self-identities. Of all the papers I assign in this course, this is the one I look forward to reading the most. Students find (or rediscover) their writing voices, and the confidence that comes with that seems to carry over into papers later in the semester. Because the students hear one another's stories, an added benefit is that the process of writing this paper helps create a positive classroom community. Gallaudet classrooms have unpredictable mixes of different facets of deaf experience. Some students are born deaf; others become deaf later. Some students are completely deaf, some can hear well enough to talk on the phone with a hearing aid, and many are somewhere in between. Many students are the only deaf person in their families, while others have deaf family members. Some were raised with no sign language at all, some grew up using American Sign Language, and still others were taught a version of sign based on English. Students form cliques based on these and similar differences, and this can spill over into tension in the classroom. The increased understanding of one another that comes from exchanging their stories helps diffuse this tension.

It is difficult to know if the benefits of this assignment stay with students past the end of the semester. I passed Arin in the hall recently, however, and she was excited to tell me that she was signing up for another course I teach, The Deaf in Literature. She could have chosen a number of other classes to satisfy our general education literature requirement, but she picked the one in which she will have further opportunity to explore the intersection between the writing world and the deaf world.

As a footnote, the university is beginning a pilot study of admitting some hearing students as regular, degree-seeking undergraduates (known in campus terminology as HUGs—hearing undergraduates). If they show up in my classroom, I will give them this assignment; they might need to think harder about how being able to hear has affected them, since as a majority trait hearing is usually transparent. I am interested to see how such an addition to the classroom might increase everyone's understanding.

Notes

1. *Deaf* with a capital *D* is used to refer to those who are members of Deaf culture, while lowercase *deaf* is used to refer to the physical condition. Deaf culture's prime distinguishing characteristic is the use of sign language (in the United States, American Sign Language) and participation in the deaf community. No hearing person is considered Deaf, although many hearing people are involved in the deaf community. A notable example is hearing children of deaf parents, known as CODAs (children of deaf adults). As native users of ASL and lifelong participants in the deaf community, they frequently strongly identify with Deaf culture, but they are not Deaf. On the other hand, people whom the medical community would classify as hard-of-hearing—for example, someone who has enough hearing loss to need a hearing aid but who with it can hear well enough to function as a hearing person—can be accepted as Deaf if they choose to use sign and be involved in the Deaf community.

2. American Sign Language is the primary language of Deaf culture in the United States.

Works Cited

Anderson, Jacqueline Joy. 1993. *Deaf Students Mis-Writing, Teacher Mis-Reading: English Education and the Deaf College Student.* Burtonsville, MD: Linstok Press.

Elbow, Peter. 1995. "Being a Writer vs. Being an Academic: A Conflict in Goals." *College Composition and Communication* 46: 72–83.

Elbow, Peter. 1981. *Writing with Power: Techniques for Mastering the Writing Process.* New York: Oxford University Press.

Kisor, Henry. 1990. *What's That Pig Outdoors? A Memoir of Deafness.* New York: Penguin.

CHAPTER NINE

Writing with/in Identities: A Synthesis Assignment

HEATHER E. BRUCE
University of Montana

Context

The first-year writing and rhetoric seminar I teach has been of-fered at two state research institutions in the intermountain West (student populations 20,000+ and 12,000+ respectively) and at a private college in the Pacific Northwest (student population 2,500). The course fulfills the first-year writing requirement. Co-listed at the college as a women studies course, enrollment is capped at seventeen. Although open to all, predominantly white, middle-class females register. At the universities, enrollment is capped at twenty-three, and a diverse range of students register.

Approach

Composition theories discuss how identity markers such as race, class, gender, and sexuality are inscribed on the bodies of stu-dents enrolled in writing classes and the ways in which these identities influence students' composing practices. But theoreti-cal discussions generally do not address teaching strategies that take into account students' personal histories and identities and the ways they influence being, learning, and writing at the uni-versity. To address this gap, I organize my course around three focal points: college students' identities, ways of knowing and writing across disciplines, and composition research about stu-dent writing at the university. I use composition scholarship such as David Bartholomae's "Inventing the University,"[1] Peter Elbow's "Writing for Teachers," and Linda Flower's "Reading to Write" to teach conventions of academic discourse and to help students understand university expectations for student writing. The curriculum introduces students to the university's systems and techniques of scholarly inquiry but does not stop there. It also addresses the power of academic discourse and acknowledges its assimilative intentions; it helps students not only use academic discourse, but also learn to exploit, negotiate, and resist the university's expectations for student writers.

The curriculum advocates alternative conceptualization of the first-year course as one that explicitly examines composition's historically irresolvable tensions, highlighting inherent contradictions between (1) the interests of students who wish to develop as college writers and gain the cultural capital offered by higher education; and (2) the interests of the university, which as gatekeeper must answer to political and economic constituents by dismissing weaker students, who more frequently are students of color, students from working-class backgrounds, first-generation college students, and non-native speakers of English (Rose 1987), or all of these. The course curriculum positions student identity at the center of the curriculum so that student writers can determine how composition best serves their educative interests.

Synthesis Assignment and Examples

The synthesis assignment is an example of ways in which my students explore how gender, race, class, and other identity markers influence ways of knowing and writing at the university. Synthesis is a common technique college writers can expect to use. Professors assign synthesis papers so that students can demonstrate their understanding of multiple perspectives on a given issue as well as its context. Synthesis requires that writers make connections between activities, ideas, texts, and theories—to name a few of the possible range of options. A synthesis depends on a thoughtful, compelling thesis and selectively combines information from several sources into a coherent discussion. To complete a synthesis, students first need to summarize main points other writers have made and then analyze required components before they can synthesize, or make connections, between other components.

The topic for this assignment is Ways of Knowing. The purpose is twofold: (1) to practice the process of bringing together ideas generated from scholarly reading to make a point, and (2) to compare academic ways of knowing with ways of knowing from personal experience. This synthesis asks students to explore influences of identity on both knowing and writing. Students first consider how they have come to know what they know about something with which they have a great deal of experience. They then identify, analyze, and explain how two or more academic writers are "talking" with each other and to them about disciplinary ways of knowing. Finally, students examine how their views about knowing from experience come to terms with academic conversations.

Students read several scholarly discussions about ways of knowing—or epistemologies—in various academic disciplines (Fitzgerald et al. 1998, 89–243) and write informal responses to the readings. When responding, students consider the rhetorical situation (Who is the writer's intended audience? What is the writer's purpose? What evidence does the writer use?); intertextual conversations (How do this writer's points respond to, connect with, and build on the ideas of other writers we have read? Who is participating in this conversation? How are they participating in this conversation?); and joining the conversation (What do I think about this? What might I add to this discussion?).

Students warm up for the first draft through in-class writing and demonstrations, which combine art, music, performance, and narrative. During warm-up, students brainstorm things they like to do in their free time. They then share with one another and add ideas during feedback sessions. Then writers focus on an activity in which they have spent so much time that they might consider themselves something of an expert. Students freewrite "all that they know" about their selected topic. Each day students engage in similarly structured exercises, which ask them to further consider ways of knowing. Students write about ways they came to know about the topic; ways their thinking about the topic has changed over time; ways certain techniques, skills, and attitudes have influenced what they know about the topic and how they know it; and ways in which they might teach others to engage in and think about the topic. Students read out loud in small groups, and each group chooses one person's work to share with the rest of the class.

During this prewriting phase, students also engage in several activities designed to illustrate ways of knowing. They create multimedia fanfares. They assemble collages from photographs and images in magazines. Some produce videos. They select music and choreograph images of knowing from experience. They perform. They compose rap and other rhythmical lyrics. They conduct field trips for the class. They demonstrate what they know and how they have learned it. The purpose of these activities is to embrace knowledge gained from experience and to highlight connections between personal identity, knowing, and writing.

During this phase, we build connections between all activities. We examine themes and patterns in the epistemological content we are reading; discuss various ways in which identity influences ways of knowing, being, learning, and writing; and talk about how personal experience influences subjectivity—our sense and production of ourselves—and intertwines with individual and group-mediated ways of knowing. We enjoy exhilarating performances. During these discussions and extravaganzas, we examine our notions about concepts such as "expertise," "knowledge," "learning," and "epistemology."

Eventually, students draw from all these activities to explore ways of academic knowing through the lens of their personal experience and expertise. They write five- to seven-page papers that synthesize evidence from experience with evidence from performance with evidence from at least three sources we have read. Potential themes for this synthesis include, but are not limited to, the following:

- How can we be sure of what we know? (Certainty of knowing and frameworks of knowledge construction)

- Who gets to say what and why? (Issues of authority)

- How do we determine fact from fiction? or, How do we know folly when we see it? (Criteria by which we judge our beliefs to be true)

+ How do identity and personal history affect ways of knowing? (Roles of gender, race, religion, class, ethnicity in ways of knowing)

+ Whose views are considered of most worth? Why those people? To what effect? (Role of cognitive authority in ways of knowing)

+ How do our religious, spiritual, philosophical, or ethical beliefs affect what we take to be true? (Role of metaphysical commitments in ways of knowing)

+ How does status construct social and professional hierarchies and influence whose knowledge is considered of most worth? (Role of social arrangements in ways of knowing)

+ What roles do native language, word choice, or jargon play in knowing? (Roles played by language in ways of knowing)

+ What counts as evidence?

+ How do writers demonstrate their credibility? (Constructing a "scientific" or "academic" or "scholarly" ethos)

+ What rhetorical strategies does the writer use to persuade the reader? What appeals? What language? Whose voices? (Rhetorics of knowledge)

Students have drawn on their experiences to write on such wide-ranging topics as mountain bike racing, laws restricting use of personal watercraft (jet skis and waverunners) in the San Juan Islands, Puget Sound, discrimination against Jews, and the disproportionately high rate of diagnoses of attention deficit/hyperactivity disorder (ADHD) in Native American children. Students also draw on theories advanced by a range of scholars including philosopher Kathryn Pyne Addelson (metaphysical commitments and social arrangements); historians Joyce Appleby, Lynn Hunt, and Margaret Jacob (social arrangements, metaphysical commitments, and professional status); literary theorists Stanley Fish and Jane Tompkins (interpretive discourse communities and perspectivism); gender theorists in science and history, Evelyn Fox Keller and Londa Schiebinger, respectively (effects of gender, race, and class on "scientific" or scholarly ways of knowing); and philosophers of science E. D. Klemke, Robert Hollinger, and A. David Kline, Bryan Magee, and Karl Popper (lines of demarcation between science and nonscience, scientific method). Student writers use their own experiences as evidence to make claims about the role of expert knowledge at the university. They find themselves able to analyze, contribute, and speak back to "expert" conversations about disciplinary ways of knowing. With evidence garnered from experience, students provide additional support for and critique of epistemological discourse and "scientific" notions of academic expertise.

Justin, for example, writes about "cognitive authority" and "professional hierarchies" in the "science" of mountain biking. He describes hierarchies of influence and, invoking Addelson, identifies those who have the most "cognitive authority" to evaluate the quality of particular bike products and riding techniques:

> Levels of subordination in the hierarchy are not based solely on questions of skill or professionalism. This is simply because the people determining the criteria seldom hold the honored professional positions which lie at the very top of the hierarchy. Knowing the reliability of a new [bike] part or component is key, but sources for obtaining that information are often biased and inconsistent. Racers who endorse certain products are often paid to do so, while mechanics often use parts well past any modest consumer's price range.

Justin analyzes how social hierarchies influence ways of constructing knowledge in the mountain biking community, comparing them to "scientific" ways of constructing knowledge in the academy. In a reflective phase following submission of his final draft, Justin discusses what he has learned about personal and academic ways of knowing. He critiques ways in which the university reduces learning to a matter of completing courses and acquiring grade point averages: "I feel that in order to be happy with my progress at this institution, I need to be confident that what I am learning is for the purpose of something greater than a grade or 'good mark.'"

Student writers generally introduce the theme of their synthesis with a personal anecdote that illustrates points they will be making in their papers. Their rich narratives are enhanced by the performance phase of the project. Justin, for example, gave a breathtaking mountain biking demonstration, and it helped him write a gripping narrative anecdote, which introduced the thesis of his paper. To support their theses, student writers organize the body of their papers around points scholarly writers make. Students synthesize textual points made by scholars with their own understandings of coming to know. Their focus is on connections between these points themselves and *not* on the points made by scholars. Others' work bolsters students' points about ways of knowing but is not the focal point of concern. In this way, first-year writers enter the conversation of others—who presumably have more authority and privilege to speak on these issues than do students—by connecting personally with the themes they address. Thus, student writers find something unique to add to ongoing conversations about disciplinary epistemologies. On the basis of their own personal experiences, students have the opportunity to speak back to "authorities."

A Caveat and My Theoretical Rationale

This synthesis assignment is an experimental pastiche of genres intended to help students gain facility with, manipulate, and play with genre conventions typically required in academic writing. Their experiences allow students to acknowledge ways in which the meaningfulness of education is always woven through learners' personal histories, and the techniques developed through this process help dissolve rigid boundaries between student ways of knowing and "expert" ways of knowing. Expressive composing processes are juxtaposed intertextually to serve the interests of first-year students in an institution that historically has belittled and condemned their abilities. These composing processes serve students extratextually as well. We discovered just how well when Justin demonstrated "ways of knowing" mountain biking by careening down a steep set of university steps and splashing through the college fountain in perfect rhythmic time to an amplified song by Jane's Addiction with enough speed and agility to outwit the waiting campus security force. He deftly illustrated what composition theorists have termed "those slippages" in which writing (and riding) bodies are caught between "bodies that write as they are written" (Fleckenstein 1999, 297).

Justin's performance was both exhilarating and instructive. But a gendered caveat remains. Although diverse groups of students generally enroll in my class, one semester sixteen women and one man registered. Teaching a predominantly white, middle-class, heterosexual female group alerted me to ways in which gender-conscious teaching can make a mess in classrooms. In this female-majority class, the gendered nature of knowing, learning, and writing percolated uneasily to the surface. During prewriting, many women chatted and wrote blithely about things they knew a great deal about—dieting, sleeping, applying makeup, crocheting, and shopping. Jackie worried out loud, "Even though I consider myself an expert at shopping for bargains, especially at *J.Crew* and *The Gap,* it's knowledge that isn't valued in college. It's *silly*. Why would I write about it?" Others agreed. I wanted students in general to draw on expert knowledge derived from experience, but I had not considered how academic ways of knowing in particular alienate female students' experiential expertise.

Although academic texts often undermine tales of feminized expertise, women students are continually expected to perform "femininely" in their social worlds, including classrooms. To succeed as college students, they often must resist, silence, and/or abandon female-identified experiences. Women find themselves needing to choose between experientially learned knowledge and a seemingly separate knowledge of the mind. I was in a quandary, uncertain how to help students synthesize expertise about "shopping" with rhetor Kenneth Burke's discussion of "terministic screens," for example. I proceeded with the synthesis as described, however, because I did not want to devalue women's claimed experiences of expertise.

I encouraged students to play with their topics of dieting, sleeping, makeup, and shopping. I said I would help them write plausible academic syntheses about the expertise they claimed if only they would claim it. They might consider, I suggested, how drawing on "feminized" claims of expertise and appropriating them in service of academic writing could help us discover writing strategies that might contest masculinized expectations for academic writing and disrupt the status quo. They might create a space for transforming gender politics in classrooms.

Some of the students became enamored with the possibilities. Jackie's thesis drew from her knowledge of shopping trends to claim that scientific ways of knowing are constructed through prestigious social arrangements in interpretive communities. She performed a very funny parody of high fashion runway exhibitions. By appropriating academic conventions and deploying them in service of cultural critique, Jackie critiqued the cultural phenomenon known as "power shopping" and assessed power hierarchies that conspire to profit from the systemic disenfranchisement of (female) shoppers. Her work put her readers out of synch with normal expectations for college fare. Jackie exposed how feminized epistemologies might disrupt misogyny embedded in disciplinary ways of knowing and masculinized domination of academic discourse. In that, her paper was not unique. Kamala used her expert knowledge of friendship to claim that both cognitive *and* emotional authority affect scientific ways of knowing; she analyzed how affective domains are excluded from scientific ways of knowing and drew connections to Evelyn Fox Keller's biography of geneticist Barbara McClintock. Jesse wrote about diet fads, eating disorders, and how they "discipline" female ways of knowing.

Teaching this class, I realized that I had been pedagogically blind to what it might mean to write academically as a white woman, a working-class student, or person of color. Female students' experience with this synthesis assignment stubbornly reminds me that it is one thing to write feminist analyses and another thing to enact critical feminist pedagogy and (female) ways of learning with women students in writing classes. This oversight demands redress. As Kristie Fleckenstein (1999) explains,

> In sacrificing bodies to some illusion of either transcendent truth or culturally constituted textuality, we cut ourselves adrift from any organic anchoring in the material reality of flesh. We—and the knowledge we create—lose our *proprioception*, "our secret sense, our sixth sense" by which neurophysiologist Charles S. Sherrington says a body knows itself to be real (qtd. in Sacks, *Man* 43). (281)

It was pedagogically impossible and totally unacceptable not to take critical stock of the gendered nature of the bodies sitting in my class—a factor, I argue, that warrants consideration in every writing class.

Acknowledgments

The author wishes to thank the editors for their thoughtful and generous reviews of earlier drafts of this essay. She also must thank Kathryn Fitzgerald for ongoing inspiration and Connie Hale, Bruce Adams, and Mary Ellen Hughes for close and careful readings.

Note

1. All the readings discussed in this chapter that are listed by author and title but no year of publication are assembled in Kathryn Fitzgerald, Heather Bruce, Sharon Stasney, and Anna Vogt, editors, *Conversations in Context: Identity, Knowledge and College Writing* (Ft. Worth, TX: Harcourt Brace, 1998).

Works Cited

Addelson, Kathryn Pyne. 1998. "The Man of Professional Wisdom." In Fitzgerald et al.: 117–30.

Appleby, Joyce, Lynn Hunt, and Margaret Jacob. 1998. "Discovering the Clay Feet of Science." In Fitzgerald et al.: 180–98.

Bartholomae, David. 1998. "Inventing the University." Reprinted in Fitzgerald et al.: 249–67.

Burke, Kenneth. 1998. "Terministic Screens." Reprinted in Fitzgerald et al.: 233–44.

Elbow, Peter. 1998. "Writing for Teachers." Reprinted in Fitzgerald et al.: 273–89.

Fish, Stanley. 1998. "How to Recognize a Poem When You See One." Reprinted in Fitzgerald et al.: 219–32.

Fitzgerald, Kathryn, Heather Bruce, Sharon Stasney, and Anna Vogt, eds. 1998. *Conversations in Context: Identity, Knowledge and College Writing*. Ft. Worth, TX: Harcourt Brace.

Fleckenstein, Kristie S. 1999. "Writing Bodies: Somatic Mind in Composition Studies." *College English* 61: 281–306.

Flower, Linda. 1998. "Reading to Write: Exploring a Cognitive and Social Process." Reprinted in Fitzgerald et al.: 267–73.

Keller, Evelyn Fox. 1998. "A Feeling for the Organism." Reprinted in Fitzgerald et al.: 135–45.

Klemke, E. D., Robert Hollinger, and A. David Kline. 1998. "Introductory Comments on 'Science and Nonscience: Introduction.'" In Fitzgerald et al.: 92–100.

Magee, Bryan. 1998. "Scientific Method—the Traditional View and Popper's View" and "The Criterion of Demarcation between What Is and What Is Not Science." In Fitzgerald et al.: 103–16.

Popper, Karl. 1998. "First and Second Thesis." Reprinted in Fitzgerald et al.: 101–2.

Rose, Michael. 1989. *Lives on the Boundary: The Struggles and Achievements of America's Underprepared*. New York: Free Press.

Schiebinger, Londa. 1993. "Who Should Do Science?" Reprinted in Fitzgerald et al.: 146–63.

Tompkins, Jane. 1998. "Indians: Textualism, Morality, and the Problem of History." Reprinted in Fitzgerald et al.: 199–218.

CHAPTER TEN

Conflict, Context, Conversation: Rethinking Argument in the Classroom

MARGARET M. STRAIN
University of Dayton

Ethos, logos, pathos. Warrant. Rebuttal. Ad hominem. Induction. Claim. *Kairos.* For those of us who have spent any number of years in writing classrooms and for those preparing to enter them, one of the most challenging areas of writing instruction is the arena commonly referred to as argumentation. Composition students at community colleges, research institutions, and private universities alike are expected to develop a level of expertise that allows them to analyze the persuasive elements of another's text/speech and to formulate a critical stance of their own.

And there is no short supply of readers and argument textbooks on the market to assist teachers. Typically, these texts rely on the fundamentals of classical rhetoric or Toulminian argument as the theoretical underpinning for understanding and composing persuasive discourse, and they are often organized into units of thematically linked readings. At many institutions, my own included, students who successfully pass both sections of first-year composition, or their honors English equivalent, may well have fulfilled their writing requirement for graduation. Thus, students must be able to bring discourse skills to bear on the writing and research they do throughout their collegiate experience.

While I find both classical and Toulminian strategies valuable theoretical grounding for students' introduction to persuasion, I am less satisfied with the adversarial, argument-as-conquest model that overshadows many discussions of persuasion and rhetors' relationships with audiences. Student writers risk reducing the complexities of persuasion to a binary dynamic, the aim of which is to "win" by defending one's position or attacking another's. The possibility that interlocutors might *share* assumptions, that the means of conflict resolution might entail cooperative negotiation, or that the end result might mean an enlightened understanding of another's view is lost. A second concern is the decontextualized, ahistorical manner in which conflict can be portrayed—devoid of its social, political, economic, and local exigencies. Greek rhetoricians, understanding the importance of the "opportune time . . . or right measure in doing something," valued the role of *kairos* in moving audiences (Kinneavy 1986, 80).

A number of contemporary scholars—feminist rhetoricians, in particular—have addressed the limitations of argument as hierarchical, linear, and patriarchal (Ayim 1991; Dietrich n.d.; Fulkerson 1996; Gilbert 1994; Jarratt 1991; Lamb 1991). One attempt to challenge pro/con approaches to argument is Patricia Bizzell and Bruce Herzberg's *Negotiating Difference* (1996). This text situates conflict, providing students with the primary documents that chronicle controversies in our nation's history (e.g., first contacts between Puritans and Native Americans, the women's sphere in nineteenth-century U.S. society, the Japanese American internment). Each unit's introductory materials and readings highlight an awareness that lines of debate are seldom clearly drawn, nor do they unfold among constituencies of equal power.

Contexualizing Conflict: A Prewriting and an Assignment

The assignment and prewriting activity I developed encourage a multiperspectival, contextual view of conflict and an alternative to argument's traditional linear structure. (See Appendix A for the prewriting activity and Appendix B for the writing assignment.) What is more, they can be adapted to reflect the varying skill levels of student writers. The prompts emerged from an English 102 course I taught at an urban, largely commuter institution the spring that Los Angeles was engulfed in riots following the acquittal of four police involved in the Rodney King assault. The day our local newspaper covered the story, students' reactions were lively, diverse, and fervent. For the following class meeting, I clipped newspaper articles that covered the events from a number of positions: responses to the verdict from local African American and white citizens; reactions from the jurors; reports that hailed the looters' actions as a form of social justice; responses from local clergy; the anger and frustration of Korean merchants whose businesses were vandalized; and reports from the police and troops called in to quell the uproar.

Dividing the class into groups—one for each viewpoint—I asked each group to respond to a set of prompts: What reaction(s) did this party have to the verdict? What kind of evidence do they provide for their position(s)? Can you identify examples of ethical/pathetic/logical appeal in their position? With what other group(s) might you find agreement/disagreement? As a class, we considered how factors such as the shared assumptions of a given speaker, the type of appeals employed, and the degree of participation or proximity each speaker had to the pivotal events affected her or his assessment of how (in)justice was served.

The assignment I designed for the final unit on argumentation asked students to create a conversation between three speakers brought together to ponder an issue or question of their choice. Students might use fictional characters, historical individuals, or figures drawn from the course readings. Although formal research was not a requirement for the assignment, if the speakers were debating a topic that demanded specialized knowledge, writers had to do some background reading to reflect a position a given character might reasonably assume. I also provided some basic guidelines:

1. Provide some initial description of the speakers and background context to orient readers and introduce the issue under discussion. This tactic will also provide a way to develop connections between the issue under discussion and the characters' lives.

2. The discussion should have a form, not merely ramble. We will be doing in-class work to help you think about the kinds of things your characters might say. In the revision process, look for emerging themes in the characters' speeches that can be developed. Remember, the conversation should have a point; the speakers are attempting to persuade one another.

3. It is not necessary that the speakers resolve the issues they raise—just that they flesh them out enough so the reader can follow the strands of conversation and the position of each.

4. Make sure that the characters' participation in the discussion is balanced and interactive. That is, avoid a dynamic in which a speaker simply serves as a "yes man" for another's comments.

5. Read the draft aloud to yourself before duplicating it for your readers. An important aspect of this assignment is creating authentic voices for your speakers. Reading aloud will allow you to "hear" them and convey ideas meaningfully.

As a prewriting exercise, I asked students to write a short (250-word) character sketch of each participant in the conversation. Writers considered several questions: How do factors such as the individual's race, class, gender, or cultural background affect her or his position? How would you describe this person's personality? What is important to him or her? Student responses were then shared in peer writing groups, and they had an opportunity to ask the class for suggestions. In adaptations of this assignment, I have required a research component (five sources) and an annotated bibliography describing how each source was used to develop the discussions.

Pedagogical Rationale

I now teach at a private, residential Catholic university and have found versions of these assignments appropriate for advanced writing and writing-across-the-curriculum courses, with students often engaging issues important to their majors or career paths. Here are a few examples of the work students produced: (1) one advanced composition student, following a church trip to Haiti during his spring break, wrote a powerful discussion between former Presidents George Bush and Jean-Bertrand Aristide regarding U.S. subsidy of foreign governments; (2) a pre-law major placed two Supreme Court justices with opposing interpretations of the First Amendment in a stalled courthouse elevator, with a repairman calling down periodically to add his ideas; (3) following a unit on Mary Shelley's *Frankenstein,* two English 102 students collaboratively constructed a series of letters that focused on nine-teenth-century women's rights, including letters by Mary Shelley, Mary Wollstonecraft Godwin (Shelley's mother and author of *A Vindication of the Rights of Woman*), Swiss magistrates (fictional), and an unjustly executed character from *Frankenstein,* Justine Moritz; and (4) focusing on perceptions of beauty and identity, guests on a mock Oprah Winfrey telecast—Georgiana (a charac-ter from Hawthorne's "The Birthmark"), Cher, a bodybuilder, and a fifteen-year-old patient—debated the merits of cosmetic surgery.

No single writing assignment addresses all students need to know to deftly maneuver argumentative discourse, but I have found several benefits to this assignment. Students are often drawn to write about issues they care about. A conversation between several speakers helps them avoid dichotomous thinking. The design of the assignment requires that writers situate their dis-cussion in place and time, so they employ *kairos* and are able to recognize fallacious reasoning in the "voices" of the speakers they create. In so doing, they come to terms with issues of audi-ence—a difficult concept for many writers—and become aware that rhetors might easily share concerns without being "con-verted" to another's view.

Finally, since the situated nature of learning and teaching lies at the heart of this collection, I'd like to close with a few observa-tions on the implications of a multiperspectival approach to teach-ing argument. Over the years, the student audience for this assignment has differed across skill level and institutional makeup. While the political, economic, gendered, and racial features of the classrooms and schools differed, the need for a multifaceted approach to teaching persuasive discourse remained strong pre-cisely *because of* a given school's or course's specific identity as an academic community. That is, first-year writers at a private school were no more prepared, and no less willing, than their urban counterparts to consider alternate sides of an issue. The writers actually experienced some of the same challenges in at-tempting to construct views other than those shaped by their re-spective locations. The same observation could be made about students with different writing abilities or those who compose from particular disciplinary vantages. Each one must learn to appreciate the importance of context, see shared connections, recognize that all tensions cannot be reconciled, and live with difference. This lesson applies to writing students and teachers alike: By working together toward a multivoiced, contextualized view of argument, we can acquire the persuasive strategies to become effective rhetors in the twenty-first century.

Appendix A

Prewriting: Creating a Persona

N.B. As part of my introduction to argument, I often rely on a small group in-class workshop similar to the one described in the Contextualizing Conflict section. Once I've distributed the major writing project, I assign the following journal/homework exercise.

Up to this point, you have examined an array of possible issues which might serve as the basis for your dramatic dialogue. What we need to do now is pay attention to the fact that behind any issue is a *person* who holds those beliefs—an individual whose economic, racial, gendered, geographical, and political experiences have shaped the ideas she/he holds. In this writing prompt, you will be concentrating on constructing personas for your discussion. That is, you need to discover for yourself who these people *are* as a subtext for writing, uncovering why it is they might hold the views they do before you actually engage them in an informed dialogue.

Part I

In the space provided, create a character sketch for each of the personas in your dialogue. Introduce each character. Who is she/he? What kind of background does each come from? What standards does she/he value? In what way(s) is the individual's family, economic, or political beliefs relevant to the discussion she/he will be involved in? What experiences has she/he had that might explain why she/he thinks as she/he does?

Persona One:

Persona Two:

Part II

Based on the information you have generated above, do two rushwrites for each individual and bring all your materials to our next class.

Appendix B

Writing Assignment

N.B. This assignment was used in conjunction with William Vesterman's Juxtapositions: Connection and Contrasts (JCC) (1996) *and Dona J. Hickey's* Developing a Written Voice (DWV) (1993).

Your final assignment asks you to investigate the range of middle voice and builds on the theme of *juxtaposition* which has characterized many of the readings we have discussed for this course. The essay also expands upon your experimentation with writing genres and incorporates an element of research, requiring you to create a special kind of works cited page called an annotated bibliography.

You will need **five** library sources; you may count any readings from *JCC* or *DWV* as sources. "Library sources" are defined as those materials in the university, public, or other participating libraries as well as Internet sources (a maximum of two). You may share a source or two with another writer; however, I expect the annotation you compose to reflect *your* use of the document.

Before committing to one of the writing options, produce about five pages of "prewriting" (e.g., clusters, lists, freewriting, notes, talking to your peer group), playing with a couple of ideas first. This tactic will allow you to see which of your ideas will generate the richest material for the assignment. And remember—your peer readers and I will be available to help you think/write/talk through the rough spots.

Audience: Instructor and peer group

Writing issues: Using evidence to substantiate a position or an interpretation you hold; experimenting with alternate forms of argument, research, and document design; learning genre conventions; adopting a middle voice(s).

Length: 5–6 pages

Due Date for Rough Draft 1: Copies for peer group and instructor. Compose a reflective memo for your readers.

Due Date for Peer Review 1:
Due Date for Rough Draft 2:
Due Date for Peer Review 2:

William Vesterman's text *Juxtapositions* presents clusters of thematically linked essays. They cross cultural contexts, historical circumstances,
gender, race, and personal and public styles of composing. In a way,
these essays are in dialogue with one another about any number of issues.

This assignment invites you to develop your own "juxtaposition" by
creating a dialogue between three figures (or people of your own choosing) brought together to discuss/ponder a particular issue. Your dialogue will not explicitly lift quoted material from the research materials
you gather so much as the conversations will reflect each individual's
position on a question and a voice he/she might reasonably assume.
How might, for example, the young Orwell's struggle with racism and
imperialism ("Shooting an Elephant") intersect with Malcolm X's sen-
timents in "The Ballot or the Bullet"? How would Georgiana ("The
Birthmark") react to her contemporary counterparts who endorse plas-
tic surgery? How might Walt Disney counter Vlahogiannis's criticisms
of Mickey Mouse? What might Frederick Douglass have in common
with Mr. K*A*P*L*A*N concerning the power of language?

For this assignment, you need to provide some initial background or
context for the conversation. It is not necessary that you resolve the
issues you raise—just that you flesh them out enough so the reader can
follow the strands of conversation and the position of each speaker. To
help you get started, here are some basic guidelines: (Refer to itemized
list above).

Works Cited

Ayim, Maryann. 1991. "Dominance and Affiliation: Paradigms in Conflict." *Informal Logic* 13: 79–88.

Bizzell, Patricia, and Bruce Herzberg, eds. 1996. *Negotiating Difference: Cultural Case Studies for Composition*. Boston: Bedford/St.
Martin's.

Dietrich, Julia. n.d. "Feminism and Argument: 'One Cannot Hope to
Tell the Truth.'" Unpublished essay.

Fulkerson, Richard. 1996. "Transcending Our Conception of Argument in Light of Feminist Critiques." *Argumentation and Advocacy* 32: 199–217.

Gilbert, Michael. 1994. "Feminism, Argumentation, and Coalescence." *Informal Logic* 16: 95–114.

Hickey, Dona J. 1993. *Developing a Written Voice*. Mountain View, CA: Mayfield.

Jarratt, Susan. 1991. "Feminism and Composition: The Case for Conflict." Pp. 105–23 in *Contending with Words: Composition and Rhetoric in a Postmodern Age*, ed. Patricia Harkin and John Schilb. New York: Modern Language Association.

Kinneavy, James. 1986. "*Kairos*: A Neglected Concept in Classical Rhetoric." Pp. 79–105 in *Rhetoric and Praxis: The Contribution of Classical Rhetoric to Practical Reasoning*, ed. Jean Dietz Moss. Washington, D.C.: Catholic University of America Press.

Lamb, Catherine. 1991. "Beyond Argument in Feminist Composition." *College Composition and Communication* 42: 11–24.

Vesterman, William, ed. 1996. *Juxtapositions: Connections and Contrasts*. Mountain View, CA: Mayfield.

CHAPTER ELEVEN

Liberal Arts in a Cultural Studies Composition Course

MARY M. MULDER
Jefferson Community College SW

My composition teaching takes place on the suburban campus of the community college in Louisville, Kentucky. The challenge I face is one of introducing students to the critique of our capitalist culture, on which they have based their aspirations for success. I also, however, want to affirm their faith in the American Dream and inspire them to create a vision of the United States that can sustain and enrich their lives as well as accommodate diversity and inclusivity. I recommend the approach I take because it is a means not only of acknowledging the weaknesses of our American system but also of providing a vision and a series of goals that can affirm the hopes and dreams of these students. I attempt to accomplish this through teaching with a "reconceived" liberal arts tradition that complements and complicates the critical pedagogy/cultural studies approach to teaching composition.

Our blue-collar suburban campus includes three thousand of the eight thousand Jefferson [County] Community College students who make up our student body. It includes only a tiny fraction of the minority and international students who attend our college; most of them take classes on the downtown main campus. What this means is that rather than dealing with the diversity of students and cultures many community college instructors face, my colleagues and I face a similarity of views, usually those supporting "the American way." This unanimity of views presents its own challenge for composition teaching. Our students are almost universally first- generation college students, typically working students in their twenties or thirties, but often displaced middle-aged workers. They are trying to find their way in an economy that no longer offers the kinds of jobs in manufacturing that enabled their parents to move into the middle class by relocating to the city from small Kentucky towns or the military life of nearby Fort Knox. Furthermore, while many of these students are heavily invested in their part-time jobs, working long hours to be able to attend college, they need to be encouraged to make a similarly serious investment in their college course work. My approach, using both cultural critique and the liberal arts, helps them see that their investment in higher education must include such things as critical thinking as well as more specific job skills.

The text used by most faculty for the first-semester writing course in our college is Cassebaum and Haskell's *American Culture and the Media* (1997). The text begs for a cultural studies approach to its material since its essays argue that the media have a heavy influence on commodity-hungry Americans. Missing from the text is any challenge to the argument the text mounts against the inadequacies of our consumer culture and our bankrupt capitalism. The problem we face is that students can simply dismiss the critique the text attempts to introduce to them. They may then become more vehement in their support of "the American way" and its assumption of the success of the work ethic. Alternatively, students may become disillusioned and despair about their prospects.

To complicate the text's critique and the critique that post-structuralist and postmodernist theories make on American life, I draw on the body of theory known as liberal humanism. This material was known in earlier eras of composition teaching as the liberal arts tradition. But the tradition as I envision it is "reconstructed" using insights from critical pedagogy and cultural studies (see Mulder 2000). As I define it, the liberal arts tradition includes recognition of the importance of Western humanism, with its emphasis on the dignity of all people and the maximizing of the individual's freedom, a focus on responsible citizenship, and acknowledgment of the importance of the American Dream to American life.

The Assignment

How these ideas and goals become incorporated into my assignments and how they reflect current thinking about language, knowledge, and learning becomes clear in my handling of the students' third paper assignment. In the initial assignment of this first-semester composition course, students discuss a general social issue, such as the health or damaging effects of the new configuration of "family," from a personal perspective. For their second assignment, they must incorporate a quote from their text into their discussion of an issue raised in one of the essays from their text. The third assignment calls for an argument paper in which students are to assert a position on a controversial issue of personal interest to them (see the appendix) and back it with research as well as their own opinions and/or experience. In preparation for this assignment, we continue our discussion of readings from the text, focusing on ways our American system can respond to its challenges. We discuss the ideals of U.S. democracy, and, in the face of postmodernist thought, we discuss the possible legitimacy of foundationalist ideas. As part of this process, we review the Declaration of Independence and analyze the activist role that arises out of involved citizenship and social responsibility. Critical pedagogy also encourages political activism, but I situate the discussion in the context of the humanist tradition of the "good life." Rather than focusing on the Great Books as icons, the earlier typical humanist approach to the liberal arts tradition, I emphasize the importance of individual self-critique as well as self-realization to "the good life." We note ways in which our U.S. democracy can inspire as well as dismay us and ways in which individuals can create fulfilled and satisfying lives no matter what their origins and later circumstances. They can aim to fulfill their own dreams, personal if not financial, and gain satisfaction from contributing to the improvement and enrichment of our American system.

Specifically, although I assert confidence in the American Dream, we discuss the dream as one of personal fulfillment rather than financial success only. I emphasize the importance of standard forms of language as a means of communicating ideas, believing that its value of clear communication makes up for its supposed elitism. Finally, I concern myself with the moral development of my students as a legitimate pedagogical concern, another basic tenet of liberal humanism. We speculate about where the "right" or the "good" lies in various U.S. social policies and cultural practices—for instance, noting the way family life is ignored for glamour in U.S. advertising and movies. As I emphasize liberal humanist ideals, I draw on the work of numerous humanist scholars, such as Booth (1998), Boyer (1987), Farnham and Yarmolinsky (1996), Gless and Smith (1992), Kernan (1997), Nussbaum (1997), Oakley (1992), and Orrill (1995). In composition, Kurt Spellmeyer's *Common Ground* (1993) has been an especially helpful example of drawing on multiple theories to enrich teaching, and Mike Rose's *Possible Lives* (1995) has been a useful model for cultivating positive attitudes about our diverse situations.

For their response to the argument assignment, I encourage students to write about an issue that affects their own lives, hoping to stimulate their motivation. I encourage students to do the kind of research that answers their questions and to write at a level of formality and in a genre appropriate for the issue they choose to discuss. According to liberal humanist theory, the goal of higher education should be as much to enable students to enrich their lives as to give them a career. As part of their preparation, I insist that the discussion of readings and issues students identify as important to them cover the range of positions society demonstrates. Thus, students have the chance to discuss their issue from all angles. To enhance their opportunity for growth and their confidence in presenting their ideas to a wider forum, over the semester I move the class discussions to one large circle in which students face the entire class and not just their peer review group. Vygotsky's scaffolding (1986) provides the theory behind this practice.

In peer response sessions, students must address specific questions their classmates pose to them about their position on the issue they have chosen. Furthermore, before students do their peer responding, they must take home classmates' papers and write responses. Their comments are more thoughtful and far-reaching when they can respond at their leisure rather than in the pressured atmosphere of the review session itself. Discussion in both venues moves beyond the immediate implications of issues to connections with priorities for life. Students learn academic discourse (Bartholomae 1985; Rose, "Language," 1985) but also political, social, and personal discourse and some of the issues related to establishing social and personal priorities.

A recent student response to this assignment demonstrates the cultural critique these teaching procedures foster, as well as the personal growth that is one of the most important goals of liberal humanism.[1] Coming from eastern Kentucky coal country only a couple of years before attending the college, Amy (a pseudonym) was of mixed mind about strip mining. Mining had been a boon to her family Amy's entire life; they had had to leave eastern Kentucky when strip mining was discontinued and no longer offered her father a good job. At the same time, though, she appreciated unspoiled natural environments.

Amy's discussion of strip mining moved from lyrical passages describing the beauty of the mountains as she experienced them in her childhood to an analysis of the implications of recent legislative moves to restrict strip mining at the top of Kentucky's tallest peak. Amy writes,

> I can remember many great times on Black and Colmar Mountains [the latter of which had been strip-mined in earlier years] with my Uncle James and family. Spending the day on top was such a great experience. Climbing the trees, fishing in the ponds, wading in the creeks, and trying to catch a rabbit or butterfly to keep for the day.

Yet she also becomes aware of the larger issue of environmental damage caused by the mining and experiences a shift in her thinking. She quotes the Louisville *Courier Journal,* which suggests that "under the agreement [being negotiated], mining and timber cutting above 3,800 feet would be prohibited on the 4,145-foot [Black] mountain." Mining is a necessity, even if it in part feeds our voracious American appetites, because people make a living in mining. Yet nature's beauty needs to be preserved. Neither the coal companies nor the environmentalists would find Amy an easy ally as she evaluates the issue for herself.

Although much of the validity of this paper lies in its combination of reminiscence, research, and critique, more important is

Amy's realization that she is personally deeply committed to the saving of the mountains and therefore opposes excessive strip mining even as she accedes to the necessity of some surface mining. In addition, she realizes that her childhood experiences have academic legitimacy as vehicles to move her audience emotionally to share her commitment. Speaking of her self-discovery in her cover letter, she says, "It may mean nothing at first, but after you finish reading my piece you will discover that it has a lot to do with your life as well." Further evidence of her recognition of her growth as a writer comes from her last-day assessment of her progress in the course: "I admit at first I was not too sure of my writing and how it would be interpreted by others in the class. Once I found that I was comfortable with others and with you, I began to come out of my shell."

Not all students, of course, respond as favorably to the assignment. Several have taken positions that simplify the complex factors involved in evaluating particular issues. Insisting that parents must monitor children as they watch television exemplifies this kind of argument, as does the argument that affirmative action is wrong because it prevents individuals from succeeding on their own. Students have more success when they take a middle-of-the-road approach that reflects a mild shift in thinking. A student who had been laid off from the Fruit of the Loom garment plant demonstrated this in her paper on the North American Free Trade Agreement (NAFTA). While she opposed NAFTA, she was able to recognize that the company could pay workers in Mexico less and that those workers needed jobs just as she did. I consider her response indicative of a greater sensitivity to human life and dignity than she had on entering the class.

My students often come to college bearing the assumptions, insecurities, and prejudices of their families and economic class. Using the liberal arts tradition in my composition classes, especially its liberal humanism, enables me to complement the critique of U.S. society with a reaffirmation of our democratic goals, with our more altruistic personal goals, and with the interest in the moral development of students that has been a part of the tradition of U.S. higher education (Connors 1997; Crowley 1998). Composition, as a core course in the higher education curriculum, has a stake in producing good citizens as well as critical citizens. The liberal arts tradition gives me a means of tackling both goals. The American Dream is alive and well in community college students. I want to help them learn to use it as sociologist Robert Wuthnow (1996) suggests U.S. society in general uses it—as both an inspiration and a curb on American desires.

Appendix

English 101 Third Paper Assignment: Taking a Stand on an Issue

Write a 4-page researched argument paper on an issue that is in dispute in our society, one that matters to you or affects you. Your claim, the stand you are taking on the issue, should be something that you care about, have a personal interest in, or something you have had experience with. For example, you might want to argue that noise pollution laws are not strict enough because you and your roommate are being bothered by a noisy business that has recently located close to your apartment building. You might consider issues of the media and culture, of gender, or of poverty and wealth as we have discussed them in class.

Research handled in the MLA format is required for the paper. The paper must cite 3 sources outside of our book (only one of which can come from the Internet) and thus must include a works cited list. This is not to be a long research paper but rather a brief argument paper for which you do research. Magazine, newspaper, and journal articles found through library databases, along with your experience, are to be your sources.

Determine whether you will follow the five-part argument or the problem-solution structure of organization for your argument. Establish your audience considering your issue and those interested in it. You are writing to persuade them to agree with you or to be open to considering your claim of fact, value, or policy. Your own position should be clear and you should establish your ethos as credible through your knowledge, your reasonableness, and your willingness to consider other views as possible. Use a reasonable, logical, persuasive tone establishing facts and offering your opinion.

Note

1. This response is used with permission of the student.

Works Cited

Bartholomae, David. 1985. "Inventing the University." Pp. 134–65 in *When a Writer Can't Write: Studies in Writer's Block and Other Composing-Process Problems,* ed. Mike Rose. New York: Guilford Press.

Booth, Wayne C. 1998. "The Ethics of Teaching Literature." *College English* 61: 41–55.

Boyer, Ernest L. 1987. *College: The Undergraduate Experience in America.* Report of the Carnegie Foundation for the Advancement of Teaching. New York: Harper & Row.

Cassebaum, Anne, and Rosemary Haskell, eds. 1997. *American Culture and the Media: Reading, Writing, Thinking.* Boston: Houghton Mifflin.

Connors, Robert J. 1997. *Composition-Rhetoric: Backgrounds, Theory, and Pedagogy.* Pittsburgh: University of Pittsburgh Press.

Crowley, Sharon. 1998. *Composition in the University: Historical and Polemical Essays.* Pittsburgh: University of Pittsburgh Press.

Farnham, Nicholas H., and Adam Yarmolinsky, eds. 1996. *Rethinking Liberal Education.* New York: Oxford University Press.

Gless, Darryl J., and Barbara Herrnstein Smith, eds. 1992. *The Politics of Liberal Education.* Durham, NC: Duke University Press.

Kernan, Alvin B., ed. 1997. *What's Happened to the Humanities?* Princeton, NJ: Princeton University Press.

Mulder, Mary Margaret. 2000. "Toward a Theory of Ethical Values in Freshman Composition: The Contribution of the Liberal Arts Tradition." Ph.D. Diss., University of Louisville.

Nussbaum, Martha Craven. 1997. *Cultivating Humanity: A Classical Defense of Reform in Liberal Education.* Cambridge, MA: Harvard University Press.

Oakley, Francis. 1992. *Community of Learning: The American College and the Liberal Arts Tradition.* New York: Oxford University Press.

Orrill, Robert, ed. 1995. *The Condition of American Liberal Education: Pragmatism and a Changing Tradition.* New York: College Entrance Examination Board.

Rose, Mike. 1985. "The Language of Exclusion: Writing Instruction at the University." *College English* 47: 341–59.

———. 1995. *Possible Lives: The Promise of Public Education in America*. Boston: Houghton Mifflin.

Spellmeyer, Kurt. 1993. *Common Ground: Dialogue, Understanding, and the Teaching of Composition*. Englewood Cliffs, NJ: Prentice-Hall.

Vygotsky [Vygotskii], Lev. 1986. *Thought and Language*. Trans. Alex Kozulin. Cambridge, MA: MIT Press.

Wuthnow, Robert. 1996. *Poor Richard's Principle: Recovering the American Dream through the Moral Dimension of Work, Business, and Money*. Princeton, NJ: Princeton University Press.

CHAPTER TWELVE

Writing to Save the World

MARGRETHE AHLSCHWEDE
University of Tennessee at Martin

The University of Tennessee at Martin, a public four-year university, is the smallest, most rural, and most residential campus in the University of Tennessee system. Although there are some graduate programs, the focus at UT Martin is on undergraduate education. Many of the 5,500 students are the first in their family to attend college, and the reading-writing literacy they bring with them is mixed. It is not uncommon to hear a student say, "Oh, I never read a book in high school." Many students come to campus writing minimally and writing what they believe is "correctly," too often with little excitement. Few express joy, amazement, or wonder about "the research paper" written in high school. For most, writing from research has been a chore.

English 112 is the second course in a two-semester sequence taken by most first-year students. For many years, the course description and texts emphasized genre study, with a particular emphasis on literary analysis. A department committee recommended anthologies and faculty selected. The first semester "taught" fiction and essay; the second semester "taught" poetry and plays. But two years ago the department, after a year's work by the curriculum committee, adopted a new course description that included the option of theme-based classes in which students read trade books rather than anthologies.

The description also listed the following purposes for English 112. The course

◆ . . . seeks to expand students' understanding of and opportunities for practice in persuasive and analytical writing, including research writing and documentation.

- Continues to engage students in thesis-directed writing while encouraging students to see writing as a process . . . through which students discover ideas and develop those ideas into coherent . . . essays.

- Continues to involve students in a variety of writing situations, including those they are likely to encounter in other classes, while emphasizing the value of writing beyond the university experience.

- Deepens students' engagement with ideas introduced through several types of texts . . . and uses these texts as a basis for extended analysis, reflection, and writing.

- Enables students to refine their control of style, organization, logic, rhetoric, and grammar.

- Engages students in library research.

The first semester the new course description was implemented my two sections of English 112, From Private Lives to Public Dialogue, were among a handful of theme-based courses. (The number of theme-based sections continues to be less than one-fourth the total number of sections offered.) The new course description set a minimum of sixteen to twenty-five pages of finished writing. Students would write more than that, of course, through drafts in which they could warm up, try out ideas, and receive responses in a school version of Natalie Goldberg's writing practice. I believe, as Brooke, Mirtz, and Evans (1994) do, that writers need time to write, ownership of their writing, and response to their writing throughout a semester, as well as opportunities to hear what other writers are doing. The many opportunities for writing-based interaction would help students grow as writers in a community of writers. While two weeks of my sections of English 112 focused on poetry (to take advantage of a visiting poet who read as part of the campus academic speaker program), most of the writing assignments and the reading worked incrementally toward the Save the World writing task near the end of the course.

Because students often remain timid writers even into the second semester, we began by reading and discussing *Wild Mind: Living the Writer's Life* by Natalie Goldberg (1990). Those students who had been with me first semester had already read

Goldberg's *Writing Down the Bones* (1986). But for the rest, Goldberg's notion of writing as practice was new. We continued with *Into the Wild* by Jon Krakauer (1996); *Reviving Ophelia: Saving the Selves of Adolescent Girls* by Mary Pipher (1994); and *Near Breathing: A Memoir of a Difficult Birth* by Kathryn Rhett (1997). I wanted to immerse my students in real books and the music of language. I wanted them to be startled into learning something new and relevant to their lives. I wanted to implement a principle of the writing classroom to which Zemelman and Daniels (1988) and others subscribe—much, varied, and ongoing reading. I wanted students to read writing from research that worked in opposition to students' perception of nonfiction writing as dull and boring and that combined the writer's experience and observation with other facts. Finally, I wanted my students to approach writing from research because they cared, not simply because they had to. I wanted them to revel in choices, to see that they could write well and with enjoyment, and that their writing could make a difference, either on campus, back home, or somewhere else.

We began working toward the Save the World project in early February when class met in the library for the reference librarian's orientation to the online public access catalog (OPAC) and electronic searches. The point was to become acquainted with library sources, to read in them, and to absorb them, rather than, in the case of electronic sources, merely figuring out how to cut and paste from them. In my experience, the problem students have with writing is not that they can't write. They can. The problem in their writing is a lack of *knowing*. Too often students locate too many sources that are too complex or too remote too close to deadline with no time left to let information settle and gel. To work against these habits, I created a "search and learn" writing task that asked students to do several things. First, using what they had learned about electronic databases, students were to look up an interview, one or more reviews of one of the books on our list or another book by one of our authors, an essay by one of our authors, or a news article about one of our authors. The rationale for this activity was that students were already familiar with, or had an investment in, a topic or an author and therefore would have an easier time engaging with the task. In a three-page essay, they were to write about what they had read—what they learned, why what they had read mattered—but also about their process of discovery, being as detailed about this process as the authors of these texts were about their own experiences. Students were asked to mimic, in an abbreviated form, the narratives of the course texts. They were to tell their story—in this case, the process of discovery—and describe what they learned from the discovery.

The next time we met, moving ever closer to the Save the World project, I borrowed a strategy from one of my graduate school professors and asked students to list what irritated them: big things, small things. Any irritation was appropriate: lousy parking, lousy cafeteria food, slow drivers, fast drivers, campus safety, people who snap gum, people who take the wheelchair-accessible elevator with no apparent need to do so, and so on. As I wrote my list on the board, students wrote in their notebooks.

When we talked about the lists, there were lots of chuckles and "oh, yeahs." Then each of us chose one problem from our list and wrote a letter to the person who could solve the problem. We then exchanged writings, and the next task was to "become" the person to whom the letter was addressed and respond to it. After writing, we reexchanged these quickwrites and read some aloud. One of the funniest—it kept showing up the rest of the semester—was Duffy's humorous account of "the blue-haired lady" who prevented him from roaring down the road to get to the parking lot, and to class, on time. Since I had received Duffy's letter in the class exchange, I responded as "the blue-haired lady." I had a great time defending my rights to the road and my years of seniority as an authority to be deferred to.

In between all the fun, the exercise got us thinking about issues that needed illumination or problems that needed solutions. For the next class meeting, students brought in draft writing—their first thoughts about an issue or a problem, why it was a problem, why the issue was important, and some solutions, if possible. At the start of class, students, like students in Nancie Atwell's (1998) middle school classes, shared their topics in a quick status-of-the-class update. Then they met in writing response groups to hear one another's drafts and talk about what would be needed to clarify the problem and further illuminate a topic. They could field additional questions that needed answers and talk about additional sources of information to strengthen the writing. For the following week's writing response groups, students brought in the next version of their essay. Before the essay was due, everyone met with me in an individual writing conference.

The final version of their essays required a minimum of four and a half pages of writing plus a works cited list. As with all finished essays, each was followed by a brief author's note explaining who helped the student with the essay and how. Each essay also was accompanied by a separate one- to two-page process memo recounting the story of the writing of the essay from empty page to finished composition. The process memo is a spin-off of Eve Shelnutt's (1989) source essay and helps students understand the sources of topics for writing and how, when, and under what circumstances they write best. The author's notes verify the social and communal nature of writing and constitute a classroom version of the acknowledgments that are increasingly included in professional journals. Both the process memo and author's notes move students toward academic integrity.

As usual in my classes on the day a final essay is due, each of us read a classmate's essay and made written comments. Then each of us in the circle read aloud one to two pages of our own writing so that our community of writers could hear what we had been up to.

What did the students write about? They wrote about campus issues: parking, food service, malfunctioning showerheads in the residence halls, disparate funding for athletic teams, and the campus work-study program. They also took on larger issues. One student's essay about teen drunk driving was prompted by her experience with the alcohol-related deaths of seven friends her senior year of high school. One student's writing on anorexia was prompted by a friend's obsession with weight, while another student's paper drew on compelling first-person interviews on the same topic. What in early drafts had seemed like frivolous writing about mold on dorm walls turned into an essay that explained how and why mold affects those plagued by allergies.

After the read-aloud, I asked, "How could what you have written become an essay that saves the world? How could what you have researched and discovered be turned into something that works for change?" I suggested revisions such as statements to campus groups and letters—letters to the editor of the campus newspaper and to administrators and staff who could change what was wrong with parking or food service or other campus annoyances. And because I know from teachers in our West Tennessee Writing Project the thrill for students of writing to an author—and receiving an answer—I suggested a last alternative: a letter to one of our authors. This writing might not save the world, but it would provide practice with a particular part of the third side of the rhetorical triangle—audience.

Finished writings had to identify real problems and letters had to be sent to real people with real addresses or presented to real campus or other groups with real presidents who called real meetings with real meeting times and places. No "To whom it may concern." All letters had to conform to the business letter style.

What happened? I had expected most students to write position papers, essays that could be printed in guest columns for the student newspaper, and material that could be used for speeches to student groups. But except for three or four pieces, all were letters. I had also expected that most of the Save the World pieces would be revisions of the students' research writing. Some were; some weren't.

To save the world, one student wrote to the head of UT Martin's physical plant, with a copy to the chancellor, pointing out problems with campus lighting. Another wrote the president of the Student Government Association with ideas for SGA-sponsored weekend activities, copies to the vice chancellor for student affairs. The student who had written about the sizzling hot showerhead in her dorm and had discovered an article about a faucet attachment that could control shower temperature wrote a letter—enclosing a copy of the article about the attachment—to the director of housing. Several students wrote to the head of campus security about the need for more parking. A couple of students wrote to the vice chancellor for student affairs citing their problems with roommates and recommended approaches that could have eliminated some of the problems. One student wrote a short letter about the politeness of college men to college women and sent it to *Ebony Appeal,* a new campus newspaper, which printed it. Another student composed a statement that she read at a meeting of the Student Government Association where she admonished students to study rather than party. Four students wrote letters to authors.

How did the students feel about this assignment? A student who had suggested a more complete menu board for the cafeteria reported that a menu board was put up after her conversation with the head of food service. Another was aghast at what seemed to her to be the frivolousness of her classmates' concerns. She had written to the head of the National Farm Bureau to protest the Farm Bureau's objection to reinstatement of wolves in natural areas. "I thought this was supposed to be writing to save the world," she announced to the class, clearly disdainful of much of what she heard around the room. Though some students made an obvious effort to keep a straight face, if they took additional offense at the rebuke, they didn't say anything.

Through a combination of all three writing tasks—search and learn, writing to illuminate a topic or solve a problem, and writing to save the world—the students did the work described in the English 112 course description. Students read in new texts, documented from them, drafted and revised, and in various ways combined the personal with the public. Research methods included interviews, observations, thick description, informal opinion polls, and library searching. All constructed a works consulted list, a requirement for much college writing. All students wrote on topics that mattered to them. All sent their writing out into the world. And I enjoyed reading all of it.

Students come to English 112 dreading "the research paper." Their previous context for "research writing" is writing about which they care little and about which they believe their teachers care even less. "Research" to students has meant red ink and a grade. Through the reading—the books were spaced throughout the semester, and we spent a day of class time discussing each— I hoped students would see that research writing could read as interestingly as a good novel. I wanted them to believe that others could read their writing with as much interest. I had wondered about the progression of the writing assignments and the success of the culminating Save the World piece. But the voice of

Deborah Meier (1995) sounded in my head: academic excellence is not the goal of school. The goal is to produce citizens. Steadily reading and writing our way toward the end assignment—writing to save the world—valued students as thinkers and makers of meaning. It provided an opportunity for students to draw on what they knew, to argue a position in which they believed strongly, and to send their words off into the world where they might actually make a difference.

Works Cited

Atwell, Nancie. 1998. *In the Middle: New Understandings about Writing, Reading, and Learning*. 2nd ed. Portsmouth, NH: Boynton/ Cook.

Brooke, Robert, Ruth Mirtz, and Rick Evans.1994. *Small Groups in Writing Workshops: Invitations to a Writer's Life*. Urbana, IL: National Council of Teachers of English.

Goldberg, Natalie. 1986. *Writing Down the Bones: Freeing the Writer Within*. Boston: Shambhala.

———. 1990. *Wild Mind: Living the Writer's Life*. New York: Bantam.

Krakauer, Jon.1996. *Into the Wild*. New York: Villard Books.

Meier, Deborah. 1995. *The Power of Their Ideas: Lessons for America from a Small School in Harlem*. Boston: Beacon Press.

Murray, Donald. 1987. *Write To Learn*. 2nd ed. New York: Holt, Rinehart, and Winston.

Pipher, Mary. 1994. *Reviving Ophelia: Saving the Selves of Adolescent Girls*. New York: Putnam.

Rhett, Kathryn. 1997. *Near Breathing: A Memoir of a Difficult Birth*. Pittsburgh: Duquesne University Press.

Shelnutt, Eve. 1989. *The Writing Room: Keys to the Craft of Fiction and Poetry*. Atlanta: Longstreet Press.

Zemelman, Steven, and Harvey Daniels. 1988. *A Community of Writers: Teaching Writing in the Junior and Senior High School*. Portsmouth, NH: Heinemann.

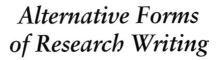

CHAPTER THIRTEEN

Alternative Forms
of Research Writing

EVE GERKEN
Concordia Lutheran High School

Teaching Context

Concordia Lutheran High School, located in Fort Wayne, Indiana, has an enrollment of 750 students and employs fifty-five teachers. The mission of Concordia is to minister to each student as a chosen and redeemed child of God. This Christian mission reflects the background of many students who attend Concordia, a majority of whom graduated from Lutheran elementary schools and attend Lutheran churches. Twenty-two congregations own and operate Concordia. Minority students constitute 11 percent of the student population. Many students at Concordia take college preparatory courses since 90 percent of Concordia graduates continue in postsecondary education. Concordia offers both Advanced Placement and honors courses. Recognized for its academic programs locally and nationally, Concordia has also been noted for its strong athletic, music, and video production programs. In addition, its JROTC, drama, and journalism programs have earned national recognition.

Students at Concordia take English courses all four years. First- and sophomore-year courses are genre based. The sophomore curriculum also includes a semester of speech. The junior-year curriculum focuses on U.S. authors, and the senior-year curriculum includes British and world authors. Juniors may elect to take creative writing, and seniors may choose to take humanities. The senior curriculum includes one semester of expository writing. College preparatory and honors courses in English are available at all grade levels.

Approach and Rationale

Our senior composition curriculum involves each student writing a research paper, typically at the end of the semester. Through the years, the research paper assignment has been passed on to each new senior teacher. Having graduated from Concordia, I returned to my alma mater four years later to teach courses I once took as a student. I inherited files of handouts from previous teachers, including handouts I remember receiving as a student. Research handouts spelled out instructions for note cards, source cards, sentence outlines, parenthetical citations, and thesis statements. When I first started teaching the research paper, students did what they had always done: found and read eight to ten sources, took notes from these sources, and integrated summary, paraphrase, and quotations into eight to ten pages of carefully constructed paragraphs. Students wrote straightforward, detached prose, careful not to reveal personal bias, basing observations and conclusions solely on research they could document. I presented accuracy and form as paramount to good research writing. Although many students met the deadlines I set, their research writing seemed stale. My students did not share my excitement for research. And the writing I asked them to do failed to have the intensity I wished to foster intellectually and personally.

When I started teaching, I held romantic notions about how I would inspire my students. Quickly I learned that effective teaching also means being both organized and structured. I needed clearer expectations of myself and of my students. Although I wanted to develop my own pedagogy, during my first years of teaching I often relied on those teaching materials and assignments previously developed by former teachers of the courses I inherited. Those materials provided some of the direction I needed as a new teacher. Not perceiving them then as a crutch, I used those resources to help alleviate my constant fear that I was not doing what the school expected of me. What I grew to understand, however, were the needs, not of the school per se, but of the students I taught. And I understood my students' needs better when I considered the larger context of the profession, not just my department and school. My initiation into the profession started with attendance at National Council of Teachers of English (NCTE) and Indiana Teachers of Writing (ITW) conferences and developed further in graduate composition courses. From these conferences and courses, I learned to consider many ways to teach writing and many ways to foster students' thinking, writing, and research skills.

After trial and error, as well as deliberate reflection, I became more comfortable in my role as writing instructor. I began to realize how the teaching materials I inherited failed to address and foster the growth I wanted in student writing. This observation was important in rethinking what I asked my students to do. The procedures seemed sound: selecting a topic, finding sources, developing a thesis statement and outline, taking notes on note cards, and writing and revising drafts. Yet these expectations proved especially problematic when, in my fourth year of teaching, I completed the assignments a few steps ahead of my students. I quickly became frustrated by the constraints. Imposing structure on the research process seemed necessary, yet the very process I was pushing students through did not work for me as a writer. I needed to rethink this process.

The neatly packaged approach with specific deadlines failed for me as a writer. Rather than wrestling with substantive issues and perspectives in my research, I became more concerned about fulfilling the conventions of the specific tasks (e.g., number of note cards, length of outline). Writing the research paper along with my students helped me understand the limitations of the assignment and my expectations. More important, the experience made me think through audience, focus, and documentation. I learned through the process how the final product seemed to overshadow the smaller steps along the way. I learned that students had too many deadlines to meet and that the deadlines assumed all writers write in the same way: basically, the deadlines I asked students to meet failed to recognize the messy and sometimes chaotic musings of a researcher and a writer. I learned that some skills such as documentation and writing transitions needed less evaluation and more practice. And I learned that my expectations of the final product needed to be more elastic to reflect students' interests and abilities.

After five years of assigning and correcting the "traditional" eight- to ten-page research paper, I needed to assign something different, something more engaging. The skills and knowledge I would review would mirror those in previous years: summary, paraphrase, MLA documentation, and integrating quotations. But I wanted to make the research process less rigid, less a cookie-cutter approach to research writing. I wanted the writing of the research paper to be more engaging than the traditional research paper had previously encouraged.

My revised approach was a mix of standard research-writing activities and activities meant to encourage personal connections, reflection, and innovation. All students began their research projects by generating annotated bibliographies, listing and evaluating at least ten sources. Students then used at least four sources to develop four- to five-page traditional research papers, which included thesis statement, MLA parenthetical citation, and a works cited list. Drafts of these papers were presented to peer groups and the instructor along with cover memos addressing students' concerns about their drafts. The written and oral response to cover memos and drafts prompted revision and for some students prompted new directions for their research and writing.

For the second part of their research project, students had the option of developing their initial four- to five-page paper into a longer eight- to ten-page paper or treating the second part of their paper in a new way. Guidelines and expectations for the second part were less formal and prescriptive than those for the first section. Students could choose one of four options:

- ◆ a continuation or longer revision of the first paper
- ◆ a four- to five-page new "chapter" on a related topic, also showing MLA documentation
- ◆ a four- to five-page creative response to the topic
- ◆ a four- to five-page reflective response to the topic

Martha, one of my seniors, chose the reflective option as a way to understand her sister's decision to give up her baby for adoption. After a five-page researched and documented section about teenage pregnancy in the United States, Martha wrote a reflective narrative recounting her sister's experience and Martha's involvement in the process. Martha's reflective narrative captured the emotional difficulty and intensely personal struggle a pregnant teenager and her family face: "[My sister] held Nick in her arms and whispered softly, 'please . . . don't hate me.' Then, she kissed his head ever so softly as to not wake him, and handed him to the adoptive mother, who was crying herself. . . . She scribbled down her name on the papers as if it were being chiseled into a rock, . . . and watched as the adoptive parents admired their new son." Martha revealed her own feelings of first surprise, then anger, and later admiration for her sister's decisions: "My heart was really at ease when my family and I left the last time. . . . [I]t brought closure to my sister's soul—to know that he is doing well, and that the decision she made was a good one. . . . I commend her for being so courageous." Whereas Martha's first section showed her ability to integrate information from a variety of sources about teenage pregnancy, her second section helped her think through the personal difficulty surrounding teenage pregnancy and giving up a baby for adoption. Although the first section of the project needed to be clearly and closely researched and documented, the second part did not require students to proceed with documented writing as long as the new section used the research in the first section as a foundation. Similar classroom procedures continued with the second part, namely informal conferences, peer response groups, and cover memos. Students were encouraged to reflect on what they had learned from their research and writing and consider what perspectives on their topics they wished to share; they were not limited to sharing these growing awarenesses in traditional research form. For some students, the creative and reflective responses allowed them to shelve formalistic documentation concerns and instead focus more closely on what they had come to know and understand about their topics. These alternative forms of relating research allowed students to take risks in expression and do important personal reflection and critical thinking, examining their attitudes toward their subjects and what formed those attitudes.

My earlier expectations for the traditional research paper had encouraged the very dullness in student writing I wanted to avoid, but adjusting deadlines in the research process was not enough to encourage more engaging writing. I also needed to rethink what type of writing I wanted to encourage in the final paper. In "Teaching Griselda to Write" (1979), Joan Bolker describes the student who is a "good girl," the student who meets readerly expectations of form without showing personal stake in the writing. Bolker describes this writing as competent but dull: "Ambivalence is out, changes of mind are out, the important nagging questions are out, because they are not neat, and they might offend—and because they involve paying some attention to one's own state of mind while one is writing" (907). I paused to consider whether my assignments, such as the research paper, encouraged students to demonstrate competency or to write compelling, interesting prose. Bolker encourages teachers to "let [the 'good girls'] know that most readers are more pleased by the sloppy sound of the human voice in a piece of writing than they are by neatness and goodness" (908). I needed to consider this risk taking in my instructions to students. If I wanted students to take risks in their writing, I needed to be prepared to respond to their writing in ways that took into account not just competency but also inventiveness and personal expression. Allowing students the choice of genre in the second part of their research project allowed me to encourage various forms of writing and risk taking even within the parameters of a research project.

Rethinking the final paper meant I took risks as an instructor. I felt constrained by having to assign a researched and documented paper while wanting students to write intensely, even personally. Because I wanted my assessment to better reflect changes in the assignment and the revision process to move students to write stronger papers, I solicited advice from Peter Elbow about how, without becoming overburdened by teacher response to drafts, to move from assessment of structure, content, and mechanics of student writing to encouraging expressive papers. His response solidified both the necessity and the importance of my rethinking the research paper I was asking my students to write:

I don't think you have to assume their writing will get terrible if you get it longer and more personally involved. How about using the revising process to help students move early exploratory germs in two slightly different directions: a kind of more formal tight paper and a more personal essay kind of paper—but using the same thinking. It's great for them to feel the differences in tone/register/genre/audience.

Rather than define the final paper in regimented terms, I could offer students alternatives for presenting their research. As Elbow suggested, I could use the revision process to help students develop, even change, the direction of their writing.

Assigning my students more writing and more revision at first seemed a daunting task as I envisioned several hours of paper correcting. But I recognized the importance of feedback, as Nancy Sommers explains it in "Responding to Student Writing" (1999): "Without comments from readers, students assume that their writing has communicated their meaning and perceive no need for revising the substance of their text" (339). What I needed to learn were new methods of response: broader ways of providing feedback and a less rigid notion of what teacher and peer response meant. Therefore, I adopted writer's memos, suggested by Jeffrey Sommers (1989), in an attempt to keep the revision process student driven. Revision shifted from being initiated by teacher suggestions to being shaped by and "directed from" a writer's own concerns about a particular draft. The effectiveness of using writer's memos varied in my classes. Some students understood the concept and used the process to help their writing. Other students mimicked almost verbatim the examples of writer's memos I displayed in class. Other students focused only on editing and grammatical correctness despite my attempts to shift emphasis to content and development of ideas.

I also heightened the importance of peer response groups in the revision process of the research paper. Before I could address minimal, even ineffectual revision, I first had to rethink my expectations for peer response. My fears reflected those of Tom Romano expressed in his book *Clearing the Way: Working with Teenage Writers* (1987): "A good part of my unease stems from my excessively high expectations for how peer groups should work" (69). Like Romano, I feared that peer groups did not give enough direct feedback to writers about their work. What I grew to understand was the necessity of social interaction between writers as they talked about and read their work and saw their writing from different perspectives. I learned to loosen up my guidelines for peer response at times and provide stronger direction at others. I learned to shift focus to content and clarity issues and to show students different ways of responding to drafts, including the use of writer's memos. I learned that peer response could be as basic as listening to drafts being read aloud. I encouraged peer groups to do more reader-based responses, as Peter Elbow and Pat Belanoff suggest in *Sharing and Responding* (1995). Students needed practice as critical readers, listeners, and responders. Although helping them gain skill in responding took time, the effort paid off by making my writing classroom more student centered and by allowing students to receive meaningful feedback to their writing. But I also needed to remember that sometimes peer response groups do not work: "no matter how the peer response groups are formed, some work winningly, some competently, some adequately, some poorly" (Romano 69). Even when I provided an environment that supported revision and reflection, students had varying expectations, abilities, motivation, and preparation. I needed to encourage them to develop and change over time, and I needed to be patient when students did not respond as I had envisioned they would.

Several components of this research project invited students to reflect on their writing and on the subject of their writing. Through formal and informal conferences and peer group discussions, students began to form perspectives on their topics and to present their new understandings about their topics. Cover memos encouraged reflection as students thought about the development of their writing in draft form. Cover memos helped keep revision student directed as instructor and peer response groups reacted to drafts in light of a writer's concerns. Approaching the project in two stages allowed both my students and me to focus on developmental concerns, if needed, and encouraged their interest in their topics to grow and take new directions. Allowing for alternative types of writing in the second section of the research project also prompted student reflection. The freedom and choice embedded in the second part of this project implied that students could write and could learn to write in a variety of forms and that research could be the foundation for this writing.

The new directions students took in their research projects were exciting. Some students clearly became personally invested in their topics. After researching a topic that directly affected her life, Martha wrote compelling reflection, her personal reaction based not only on emotions and memory but also on a larger, cognitive understanding of her topic. Researching teenage pregnancy helped Martha place her teenage sister's pregnancy in a larger context as she learned to respect her sister's decision to give up her son for adoption. Students had the freedom to present their information in a manner of their own choosing. Many welcomed the opportunity to vent, to express their opinions, and to reflect, revealing a fluidity and intensity in their writing that some lacked in their initial documented sections. The alternative forms of writing encouraged in the second section of the research project allowed some students to become more expressive and more reflective about their subjects than the traditional research paper had allowed or encouraged. Mastering formalistic concerns in a lengthy paper became secondary to expressing perspectives and learned understandings about research topics. The flexible nature of the assignment encouraged students to discuss their subjects in ways not always accessible in traditional research papers. Some students liked the reflective option because it allowed them to reveal how their faith in God shaped their perspective on the issue; witnessing their faith is encouraged at CLHS. Loosening up the rigidity and predictability of the research assignment helped some students move from "safe" yet stale documented discussion to more engaging and complex ideas and prose.

Works Cited

Bolker, Joan. 1979. "Teaching Griselda to Write." *College English* 40: 906–8.

Elbow, Peter. 1999. "Re: questions about assessment." E-mail to the author, 12 November.

Elbow, Peter, and Pat Belanoff. 1995. *Sharing and Responding.* 2nd ed. New York: McGraw-Hill.

Romano, Tom. 1987. *Clearing the Way: Working with Teenage Writers.* Portsmouth, NH: Heinemann.

Sommers, Jeffrey. 1989. "The Writer's Memo: Collaboration, Response, and Development." Pp. 174–86 in *Writing and Response: Theory, Practice, and Research,* ed. Chris M. Anson. Urbana, IL: National Council of Teachers of English.

Sommers, Nancy. 1999. "Responding to Student Writing." Pp. 339–47 in *The New St. Martin's Guide to Teaching Writing,* ed. Robert J. Connors and Cheryl Glenn. Boston: Bedford/St. Martin's. First published in *College Composition and Communication* 33 (1982): 148–56.

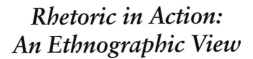

CHAPTER FOURTEEN

Rhetoric in Action:
An Ethnographic View

DAVID SEITZ
Wright State University

Teaching Context

Although Wright State University claims an address in the city of Dayton, Ohio, I find it more accurate to locate it nearby off the interstate. From this location, Wright State offers higher education to approximately seventeen thousand students from primarily rural and suburban areas in the surrounding four counties of southwestern Ohio. Until recently, these students were almost entirely from white, working-class backgrounds, and most of them worked more than part-time hours to pay for their education. But with the academic and research successes of the university over the past five to ten years, this population has shifted, and now between 30 and 40 percent of students live on or near campus. So while the majority of our students still work outside of school, we cannot so easily assume they share common patterns of experience with regard to social class and family background.

Even with these recent demographic changes, our students hold a practical worldview of their education and future work. Among our English majors, the students concentrating on secondary education in particular maintain this perspective toward their classes. Our department kept these students' worldview in mind when we created an integrated language arts major. To prepare these future English teachers for various rhetorical situations they might encounter in their teaching, we chose to make a junior/senior-level course in rhetoric part of that program. My department and I did not intend this quarter-length course to be a watered-down version of a graduate course, a class on argumentation, or a historical survey, which was already available in the communications department. Nor could I develop the course around rhetorical issues of the corporate workplace, as some undergraduate rhetoric courses have done. Given students' work-oriented motivations, I wanted the course to complement and critically inform the student teachers' experiences observing and assistant teaching in the local schools. So with audience and purpose in mind, I designed Rhetoric: Language, Power, and Persuasion, a course whose main goal is to develop critical rhetorical awareness. Through their projects and analyses of readings, students ask how different forms of oral and written language intersect with power relations and acts of persuading others in specific social contexts that will be common in their future lives, particularly in the setting of the public classroom. Over the term, the projects focus on three key areas of rhetorical study: discourse, metaphor, and persuasion.

The Ethnographic Project: Studying Rhetoric in Action

Despite the practical nature of our students, many have a hard time imagining a rhetorical study of the everyday world. If they have considered rhetoric at all, they have associated its practice with big-time politics and mass media communications, as most Americans do. Although I tend to discourage this limited view throughout the course, their final project explicitly challenges this reduction of rhetoricians' philosophical stance and purposes. The Rhetoric in Action assignment moves the students from a global view of rhetoric to a study of local situations and people's agency within them. Through ethnographic methods of participant observation and interviewing, students examine which strategies, appeals, and assumptions might be persuasive for a particular social group from the perspectives of various insiders. As one student later put it, "It allowed me to research whether or not these lofty theories of rhetoric really applied to a real-life situation."

As students choose field sites and begin their observations, our readings in the course shift from more theoretical works and textual analyses to ethnographic studies. Along with excerpts on ethnographic methodology from Chiseri-Strater and Sunstein (1997), we discuss the relationship of identification, persuasion, and local knowledge in three communities. The students read ethnographies of a multicultural eighth-grade classroom (Fine 1993), a white, working-class neighborhood's responses to a speech by Mayor Richard J. Dailey (Philipsen 1992), a Chicago Mexican American community's criteria for powerful oral performance (Farr 1993), and finally a few model student papers from my previous classes. Students eventually write an eight- to ten-page paper based on four to five weeks of ethnographic research.

To focus their ethnographic observations toward rhetorical research, students must consider the connections between social interaction, acts of persuasion, identification, and use of discourses in their field site. To understand which statements persuade different group members, for instance, students need to consider what values and social roles members identify with, as well as what assumptions underlie their actions and discourse choices. To accomplish this rhetorical analysis, students must interpret their observations as tensions between solidarity and status within the group. (See the appendix for the specific rhetorical and ethnographic questions from the assignment.) In this way, their research projects help them perceive more fully the relations of rhetoric and power within the everyday, the areas of their life in which they can have more agency and control. For the English education majors in particular, this research can give them new ways to examine complicated interactions they encounter in their teaching observations and practicums.

This ethnographic perspective toward rhetoric, for instance, offered Charity another way to make sense of the strong, confusing teen personalities she encountered in her student teaching observations at a nearby inner-city school (Harris 1999). In the course of her observations in this ninth-grade class, several groups of girls, both white and black, confronted Charity, a white, middle-class student originally from the rural West, with talk and behaviors she would not expect if she were their teacher. Some of the girls tended to confide intimate secrets Charity did not think she was entitled to hear, while a few others publicly tested her in-between role of student teacher with a barrage of sexual street talk. To complicate matters, Charity's supervising teacher often left her in charge of a discussion or activity, even though her education program expected her to observe only in this first phase of her field experience.

Based on this difficult situation, Charity came to ask: What are these particular girls trying to convince others about themselves through their very public performances? Although Charity encountered problems focusing and organizing her study, as all ethnographers do, she eventually framed her work around common issues of female adolescent identity. She writes, "Adolescent girls wear many masks, but their performances are acts of persuasion; they make themselves the center of attention in hopes that their audience will recognize them as individuals." Charity then showed how this common need for teen girls ranges across gender, class, and race (although she did not explicitly point this out) by describing the tense situations of three very different girls "who worked hard to separate themselves from their peers." Betty performed the role of naive innocent at her own (comical) expense to differentiate herself from the bad sexual reputation of other girls on the volleyball team. When classmates claimed she was having oral sex with her older boyfriend, Betty whispered loudly to her friend, "Is that talking about sex on the phone?" Beth, however, responded to the rumors of her as "white trash" "by living up to the rumors." Beth explained to her friend Sam, "They think I'm white trash, so I'll show 'em white trash . . . ; at least I'll be something." Carrie, an African American, fashioned a strong black-girl persona who would not put up with Charity's "rich bitch white attitude." Charity was at first overwhelmed by Carrie's behavior, but she came to understand that "Carrie wants to be seen as something more than 'black' and nothing less."

When Charity evaluated the personal value of her project and the course, she reflected on her greater rhetorical awareness, now noticing how "rhetoric plays a role in . . . conversations or situations. You can almost identify where a person is coming from or going with their thoughts." Charity's research and writing demonstrate what the rhetoric students can and do accomplish with this project. In this excerpt from her paper, Charity draws on dialogue recorded in her field notes to illustrate her sociocultural analysis of Beth's complex ambivalence toward her rhetorical performances of "white trash":

> During proficiency tests, Beth and I spent a little bit of time alone together. At first Beth wouldn't even look up at me when I spoke to her, but I kept trying.
>
> > Me: Beth, I can't believe how badly your Mom treats you? It must be hard.
> >
> > Beth: It fuckin' sucks, but it's not that bad.
> >
> > Me: It sure sounded bad the other morning.
> >
> > Beth: You heard that? I didn't know I was talkin' that loud. What'd you hear?
> >
> > Me: I heard about everything.
> >
> > Beth: Don't believe everything you hear.
> >
> > Me: Okay.

> After Beth and I spent sometime together, I realized that she was doing a lot of performing for her peers. What was confusing was that I couldn't figure out why she wanted all the attention. Then I overheard a conversation she had with her friend Sam in the hallway last week.
>
> > Sam: Beth, I don't know why you let those guys get to you. Just tell them to fuckin' shut up.
> >
> > Beth: That's easy for you to say because they notice you; they don't notice me. They think I'm poor white trash, so I'll show 'em white trash.
> >
> > Sam: That ain't cool. Why do you want to be something you're not? You're trippin' or something.
> >
> > Beth: At least I be somethin'.

Beth will do anything to be noticed. She is acting out a self-fulfilling prophecy. Obviously for some time, she has heard the words "white trash" in relation to her name. She acts aggressively because she severely dislikes being called such names, but she admits that people do recognize her as someone; they're "noticing" her. Beth is trying to live up to the rumors that are spread about her. She gains everyone's attention by breaking school policies through her language and clothing in order to be identified by her behaviors. Beth will settle for "white trash," as long as she is seen as having her own identity.

As this excerpt from Charity's paper suggests, the ethnographic project fosters writing in a hybrid genre that interweaves rhetorical and sociological analysis with descriptive stories and dialogue.

Theoretical Rationale

I intend this project to shift the students' focus from rhetoric's traditional concern with speaking to the ethnographic importance of cultural listening. The dominant practice of teaching rhetoric and communication in first-year composition classes tends to privilege the speaker over the audience. In the Aristotelian model (1991), the rhetor seeks to shape his ethos to the values, beliefs, and motivations of his intended audience.[1]

Through the way the rhetor constructs the logos of his speech or text, he intends to persuade his auditors by eliciting their pleasure of recognition. This is the common structure of the enthymeme, in which the rhetor leaves the auditor to fill in the missing premise of informal logic with his or her own understanding. In this model of rhetoric, the rhetor only listens to his auditors in order to conform to their pathos, not necessarily to further his own critical understanding of others' perspectives.

Rhetoric scholars such as Ross Winterowd (1994) have pointed out that Kenneth Burke's theories of identification challenge the assumptions of this dominant model, encouraging a shift of terms from persuasion to understanding. Of course, feminist rhetoricians (such as Ratcliffe 1999) also emphasize this view, and their tenets hold much in common with ethnographic methodology. As a rhetoric of listening, ethnographic methodology fosters this emphasis on critical understanding, rather than an emphasis on the rhetor's persuasion through ideological recognition. From this rhetorical perspective, when ethnographers set out to understand situated insider perspectives, they are consenting to be persuaded by the people they talk to, participate with, and observe. They need to rethink their worlds and perceptions of their reality based on a dialectic with the approximated perspective of others.[2]

This assignment also encourages students to research the complexities of an entire rhetorical situation, rather than just rhetorically analyzing a print or other text as they have done earlier in the course. When students pay close attention to the rhetorical actions of a social group and the power relations within it as they occur, they see for themselves the inadequacy of the traditional rhetorical triangle of rhetor, text, and auditor. The traditional model cannot describe and interpret well the reciprocal and circulatory nature of language use in a social group, much less group members' multiple interpretations of others' rhetorical actions within the group. Thus, the students come to see how the direct application of rhetorical theories rarely allows for the complex variations of a group's locally defined perspectives. Ethnographic research, on the other hand, treats culture as a process of emergent meanings and knowledges, rather than as a series of positions and texts.

Derek's project illustrates this complex process of rhetorical inquiry (Boggs 1999). Derek chose to study the persuasive strategies of a seventeen-member committee, of which he was a member, in his Assembly of God congregation. The committee needed to select a new pastor for the assembly of five hundred to six hundred congregants before the previous pastor of thirty-five years retired. Knowing the members of the committee well, Derek initially described them as "17 diverse personalities" and assumed that his paper would emerge from various controversies in the meetings. But when he responded to his field notes and discussed them in class, he saw little controversy, believing he would now have a tough time writing the actual paper. Although frustrated, Derek found himself becoming "more aware of the opinions, possible motives, and methods of my fellow committee members as we attempted to persuade each other how to proceed with our difficult process. . . . This assisted me in expressing my opinions and in voting about potential candidates." Eventually, Derek examined several moments that could have erupted into disagreement and possibly argument. He analyzed why committee members, himself included, implicitly consented to stifle legitimate questions and complaints in their arduous selection process.

When Derek took an ethnographic insider's perspective, he was able to articulate a valuable paradox. Committee members couldn't work to persuade one another because their religious faith told them they had to somehow "find and follow the will of God" to "find the pastor that God had prepared for our church." Derek described this paradox as walking a "difficult tightrope," because the group members believe that knowing God's will is "an internal spiritual process," a scriptural, personal relationship with God through prayer for an absolute inner peace that "passeth all understanding." As an intellectual student, Derek clearly understood that this cultural analysis of the committee's faith questioned the boundaries of academic reasoning, and he "enjoyed the challenge of trying to explain this spiritual process in an academic paper." I, and other students in Derek's class, also enjoyed this challenge to more conventionally academic conceptions of rhetorical study that ethnographic methodology allows for. Ethnographic methodology applied to rhetoric helps keep me more attentive to the students' emerging theories of what they observe, listen to, and experience. Inevitably, the process of the students' ethnographic research opens new spaces for me to continually rethink my positions and perspectives on rhetoric.

Appendix

For the sake of brevity, I present here only the essential questions that guide the students' field notes, interviews, reflection notes, and cultural/rhetorical analysis. For comprehensive teaching models in the writing process of ethnographic research, I recommend Chiseri-Strater and Sunstein (1997), Zebroski (1994), and Zebroski and Mack (1992).

Questions for Rhetorical Inquiry

Social Interaction: How would you describe the kinds of social interaction going on? What is the relationship between speakers and audiences (or rhetors and auditors)? Does it change?

Acts of Persuasion: Who seems to be persuaded by whom? At what moments? When do people seem unpersuaded? What are they granting consent to?

Identification: What values and social roles do different people seem to identify with? What assumptions and values underlie the statements, actions, and motives that group members find internally persuasive?

Use of Discourses: What kinds of discourse (general ones and ones specific to the group) are used by individuals in the group? For what purposes and ends? How persuasive to others is the use of this discourse?

Questions for Ethnographic Inquiry

Talk: What is said, who says it, and in what contexts? What communications are openly stated and what are unspoken? What patterns of language use can you see?

Behaviors: How do people act and react to each other? Do members act out any "rituals" of expected behavior? What values might be associated with these behaviors? What might they be saying to each other about their dress, manner, and so on?

Power Relations: How might people be showing solidarity and/or status through their talk and behaviors? How might talk and behaviors relate to different social roles within the group and culture? Do they relate to gender or social class or other social positions?

Location: How do people relate to the setting(s) they are in? What does it suggest about the values and attitudes of the culture and the individuals in it? How does setting influence behaviors and talk?

Notes

1. I purposely use the masculine pronoun here to indicate the dominant male mythos in the rhetorical tradition.

2. I owe much of this rhetorical view of ethnographic method to conversations with my colleague Julie Lindquist.

Works Cited

Aristotle. 1991. *On Rhetoric: A Theory of Civic Discourse.* Trans. George A. Kennedy. New York: Oxford University Press.

Boggs, Derek. 1999. "To Choose a Pastor: The Rhetoric of God's Will." Unpublished paper, English 480. Wright State University.

Chiseri-Strater, Elizabeth, and Bonnie S. Sunstein. 1997. *FieldWorking: Reading and Writing Research*. Upper Saddle River, NJ: Prentice-Hall.

Farr, Marcia. 1993. "Essayist Literacy and Other Verbal Performances." *Written Communication* 10: 4–38.

Fine, Melinda. 1993. "'You Can't Just Say That the Only Ones Who Can Speak Are Those Who Agree with Your Position': Political Discourse in the Classroom." *Harvard Educational Review* 63: 412–33.

Harris, Charity. 1999. "Rhetorical Ethnography of Adolescent Girl Identity." Unpublished paper, English 480, Fall Semester. Wright State University.

Philipsen, Gerry. 1992. *Speaking Culturally: Explorations in Social Communication*. Albany: State University of New York Press.

Ratcliffe, Krista. 1999. "Rhetorical Listening: A Trope for Interpretive Invention and a 'Code of Cross-Cultural Conduct.'" *College Composition and Communication* 51: 195–224.

Winterowd, W. Ross, with Jack Blum. 1994. *A Teacher's Introduction to Composition in the Rhetorical Tradition*. Urbana, IL: National Council of Teachers of English.

Zebroski, James. 1994. *Thinking through Theory: Vygotskian Perspectives on the Teaching of Writing*. Portsmouth, NH: Boynton Cook.

Zebroski, James, and Nancy Mack. 1992. "Ethnographic Writing for Critical Consciousness." Pp. 196–205 in *Social Issues in the English Classroom*, ed. C. Mark Hurlbert and Samuel Totten. Urbana, IL: National Council of Teachers of English.

CHAPTER FIFTEEN

Creating an Online Newspaper

DAN MELZER
Florida State University

Teaching Context

I teach first-year composition at Florida State University, which is located in the northwest Florida panhandle in the state's capital city, Tallahassee. FSU is a public, coeducational university with a student population of approximately 33,000. Women constitute 55 percent and minorities 22 percent of the enrollment. FSU prides itself on its commitment to technology, and it was voted the eighteenth most wired campus in the United States in a 2000 *Yahoo! Internet LIFE Magazine* survey. Because of the number of computer labs on campus and the free Internet connections in each dorm, access is not a major issue for FSU students.

In anticipation of an online version of our introductory composition course, English 1101, our composition program conducted a survey of forty first-year writing courses, with 1,200 students responding. The results of the survey show that our student population is computer savvy: 75 percent began using computers in elementary school, and more than half use the Internet to conduct research or send e-mail. FSU encourages teachers to integrate technology into their classrooms, and our students are responsive to assignments that require them to use electronic bulletin boards, e-mail, or the World Wide Web. I've been assigning hypertext projects since 1998, and I've found that students are excited about learning to create Web sites.

The Assignment

My assignment is a collaborative hypertext project based on the format of a student newspaper. I use this assignment to organize my entire semester of writing, but in the past I've also used it as a three-week project to end the semester. Students write articles for various sections of this online college newspaper (sports, entertainment, opinions, travel, etc.) individually and in groups, and with the help of three or four computer-literate students who serve as editors, the articles are published on the Internet in the form of a class hypertext. Examples of hypertext essays from past class Web sites include a guide to Florida beaches, reviews of local restaurants, opinion essays on the parking problem at FSU, and a research hypertext on Pete Rose and the Baseball Hall of Fame.

The first time I tried this assignment, I knew very little about Web publishing. But you don't have to be a computer expert to create a class Web site. I found that many of my students had already published their own Web sites, and I relied on these computer-literate students to both create the site and act as technical support for the other students. In fact, my role in the actual creation of the Web site was minimal. Students simply e-mailed their essays to editors, who added links and images and published the final version.

I begin this project by having students do a rhetorical analysis of the *FSView*, Florida State's college newspaper, focusing on issues such as audience, genre, and style. Students also look at the online version of the *FSView* and other local newspapers and magazines, and we compare the online versions to the print versions. We analyze the use of images and links and the ways hypertext differs from printed text. Last semester, for example, we discussed the way an image of the Seminole mascot holding a flaming spear seemed to undermine an article in the online version of the *FSView* that argued in favor of Native American mascots. One student pointed out that even though the article claimed to respect the point of view of Native Americans, the list of links that appeared at the end of the article all led to other pro–Native American mascot articles.

After they've analyzed online newspapers and discussed the ways hypertext differs from print text, students propose categories for the organization of the Web site they will create. Categories students have chosen in the past include fiction and poetry, opinions, health and fitness, entertainment, sports, and travel. After the class has decided on the basic design of the hypertext, I choose two or three of my most computer-literate students to be editors.

The editors are in charge of publishing each student's articles to the Internet and linking the different sections of the hypertext. I ask students to e-mail their articles to the editors for publication to the Internet, although I also give students the option of creating their own Web sites with the assistance of the editors. Usually, the editors use free Web publishing tools such as AOL Personal Publishing, Tripod, or Geocities, but some editors choose to use Netscape Composer and publish the hypertext using FSU server space. The editors are collaborators, and they add images and links to the articles. Because they are editing the articles, publishing them, and adding links and images, editors are assigned less writing.

If I use this project to organize my class for the entire semester, I have students write in similar genres and divide the assigned essays by sections of the hypertext. During the first three weeks, for example, we'll write fiction, poetry, and personal essays and then publish them in the creative writing section of the hypertext. During the next three weeks, we'll write editorials and publish them in the opinion section of the hypertext, and then we'll write reviews of movies, restaurants, and campus activities and publish them in the entertainment section of the Web site. For the final three weeks of class, I let students choose the genre of the articles and the section of the Web site they want to write for. As we practice different genres of essays, we analyze examples from the student newspaper.

I organize my class in a workshop format, but because of the need to analyze hypertext in terms of links and images, we hold both print and online workshops. If I'm not teaching in a computer classroom, we conduct online workshops at the English department or library computer lab. During the online workshops, I ask students to analyze the use of links and images and the visual organization of the text on the screen, as well as look at focus, development, audience, and style.

At the end of the semester, when the hypertext is complete, I have editors search for places to publish it on the Web. In the past, editors have connected our site to local travel and entertainment guides, FSU Web rings, and larger search engines. Some students have gotten e-mail responses from people surfing the Internet who found our site, and I've also had students in the spring semester send e-mail responses to the articles students wrote in the fall semester. I use previous class hypertexts as reading material for each new semester.

Theoretical Rationale

My hypertext assignment is informed by social constructivist theorists such as Kenneth Bruffee (1984) and Mikhail Bakhtin (1981) and digital literacy theorists such as George Landow (1997) and Johndan Johnson-Eilola (1998). Even though the assignment creates a public and social rhetorical situation, it also allows space for expressivist writing.

Kenneth Bruffee (1984) believes that knowledge is an "unending conversation" and that writing is a social artifact. Because this hypertext assignment links students in conversation, it mirrors social constructivist theories. Students write collaborative articles and write responses to one another's articles, creating a public conversation. Because I use the hypertext from each semester as a model for the next semester, the conversation and collaboration is unending. When the hypertext is linked to search engines and Web rings, the conversation becomes public. Hypertext theorists such as Landow (1997) and Johnson-Eilola (1998) have compared this kind of hypertext linking to Bakhtin's (1981) dialogic discourse, in which multiple voices are linked in social conversation. This kind of dialogic discourse certainly isn't impossible in a print environment, but I've found that the linking power of hypertext makes it easier to connect essays, connect students, and connect to the larger discourse of the Internet. Because this assignment encourages students to use links and images and forces students to think about the ways hypertext differs from print text, it gives them a sense of digital literacy.

Even though this assignment is social constructivist in nature, it is also informed by expressivist pedagogy. Theorists such as James Britton (1975), James Moffett (1968), and Toby Fulwiler and Art Young (1982) argue that genres such as the personal essay, poetry and fiction, and diaries and journals should not be abandoned in first-year composition if we want students to gain experience writing across the universe of discourse. I often begin the course by having students write fiction, poetry, and personal narrative for the creative writing section of the hypertext; this gives them a chance to explore their own experiences and work in expressivist forms before shifting to genres such as opinion pieces and interviews, which are more public forms of discourse.

Students also get an authentic sense of audience and rhetorical situation with this hypertext project. Because the format is a school newspaper online, and because they know their peers will be reading their articles, students have a real audience other than the teacher. They also know that the hypertext will be made public and used in my classes the next semester, so there is a sense of audience beyond the classroom. This focus on an audience beyond the teacher helps create a more realistic rhetorical situation as well. When students write movie reviews or editorials to a student audience, they have a sense of purpose, audience, and genre that was difficult for me to achieve before I began using this assignment to organize my class. Rather than assigning writing modes, I encourage my students to choose their purpose and audience and then use the mode or genre that would be most effective for the specific rhetorical situation. Because of this emphasis on the rhetorical situation and an audience in an online dialogue with the writer, this assignment reflects the most recent theories of language and pedagogy in composition studies.

Despite the advantages I've discussed, there are some problems that seem to be unique to hypertext writing. Although I've argued in favor of the linking quality of hypertext, sometimes links are problematic. When students link essays to their homepages or to other Web sites, the material that appears on those linked sites is beyond my control. I'm always concerned that students will link to sites that contain material inappropriate for a school project. One student, for example, linked an essay about his hometown to his personal Web page, which displayed images of *Sports Illustrated* swimsuit models. Although I'm pleased when students tell me they've given the address of the class hypertext to friends and family, or when students receive e-mail from someone who has found our site in a search engine, the public nature of hypertext writing can be negative if the site is linked to inappropriate material. The public nature of hypertext writing can also be problematic for basic writers. Students who struggle with grammar need encouragement, not pressure. These students often see the public nature of hypertext writing as a negative, since their grammar problems are exposed for all to see on the Internet.

Despite these disadvantages, I've found that my students put more effort into hypertext than print text assignments, especially if they know that future students will be reading—and even responding—to their writing. If you're considering doing a hypertext project in your class but you still have questions or concerns, please feel free to e-mail me at dlm6871@garnet.acns.fsu.edu. I'd be happy to talk with you about teaching hypertext writing.

Works Cited

Bakhtin, Mikhail M. 1981. *The Dialogic Imagination: Four Essays*, ed. Michael Holquist, trans. Caryl Emerson and Michael Holquist. Austin: University of Texas Press.

Britton, James. 1975. *The Development of Writing Abilities (11–18)*. London: Macmillan.

Bruffee, Kenneth A. 1984. "Collaborative Learning and the 'Conversation of Mankind.'" *College English* 46: 635–53.

Fulwiler, Toby, and Art Young, eds. 1982. *Language Connections: Writing and Reading Across the Curriculum*. Urbana, IL: National Council of Teachers of English.

Johnson-Eilola, Johndan. 1998. "Negative Spaces: From Production to Connection in Composition." Pp. 17–33 in *Literacy Theory in the Age of the Internet*, ed. Todd W. Taylor and Irene Ward. New York: Columbia University Press.

Landow, George P. 1997. *Hypertext 2.0: The Convergence of Contemporary Critical Theory and Technology.* Baltimore: Johns Hopkins University Press.

Moffett, James.1968. *Teaching the Universe of Discourse.* Boston: Houghton Mifflin.

Yahoo! Internet LIFE Magazine. 2000. "America's Most Wired Colleges 2000." Online. Accessed 22 September 2001. <http://www. zdnet.com/yil/content/college/college2000/college2000.html>.

III

SUPPORTING PRACTICES

Being Honest about Writing and Individual Freedom—Or, Children, There Ain't No Rules

P. L. THOMAS
Woodruff High School

In education, we often have a tendency to restrict, reduce, or simplify in order to make the overwhelming task of teaching more manageable. Introducing young people to the chaotic world of formal language use—reading and writing—often makes such restrictions and reductions seem unavoidable. Yet, if an education is to empower students, the teaching of writing must ultimately become an act of individual liberation. As teachers of writing, we are left with inviting our students into the open-ended world of the writing process and the written product—in effect, admitting to our classes, "Children, there ain't no rules."

Young writers need to practice a writing process that is open-ended and chaotic. Likewise, they need to discover that the act of writing is a constant stream of choices guided by the writer's growing awareness of the conventions of writing and a sensitivity to the appropriateness of their rejecting or maintaining those conventions.

Teaching Context

I have taught for sixteen years in the public high school where I graduated over twenty years ago. I teach primarily American literature courses and Advanced Placement Literature and Composition, with my students ranging from grades 10 to 12. During my teaching career, I have also taught journalism and even American history.

A rural school in the upstate foothills of South Carolina, Woodruff High encompasses grades 9–12. We currently teach about 700 students; graduating classes waver between 100 and 135 students. The town and the school itself are both quite tradition-bound. The school received a great deal of state and even national attention for its football program from the 1950s on into the 1980s.

The students and families of the town are primarily of upper-lower to lower-middle socioeconomic status. The parents are rarely college graduates; students tend to stay in town after graduating. The school population is largely white, with the percentage of African American students dwindling over the past couple of decades. A small but growing population of people with Mexican roots is moving into town. The school and community are quite conservative—philosophically, politically, and religiously. Students experience a wide range of adult influences, from little or no parental supervision to the most inflexible, fundamentalist coercion.

In my classroom, writing is both the focus of what the students learn to do and the primary avenue for learning content. We are there to learn to write and to write to learn. Students are expected to write four major essays each quarter and are required to rewrite those essays at least once each. Further, they are always allowed to rewrite essay submissions as often as they wish throughout the quarter. In effect, students will write from thirty-two to nearly one hundred essays each year in my class, along with dozens of more informal efforts.

To me—and eventually my students—the rewriting of essays is the key to both the learning of language use (expanding a student's awareness of grammar and conventions) and the deepening of a student's understanding of content. First submissions always fall short; both the students and I know that, expect that, and can work with a determination and freedom that allow learning to blossom.

The activities discussed in the following sections are beginning-of-the-year activities that support my first-quarter focus on nonfiction and that help to establish the attitude toward writing we will follow throughout the year: writing as chaotic and as a series of choices by the writer.

Being Honest about Writing and Individual Freedom

As sophomores, students reach my English class primarily concerned with what they can*not* do in their writing (No fragments!) and the format of their writing (introduction with thesis, body, and conclusion; don't write past the right margin!); they have also been well instructed in a linear writing process—prewriting, drafting, revision, finalizing. By their tenth year in school, students often view the content of their work as of minimal importance—if important at all. My primary goal with these young people is to liberate them from all such preconceptions.

The truth about writing is that anything a writer *chooses* to incorporate is either appropriate (or effective) or inappropriate (or ineffective). What students often perceive as "rules" are actually conventions that serve as guidelines and that change gradually over time. This honest approach is messy and much more difficult to teach than rigid rules, essay form, and a linear writing process. But the rigidity of traditional approaches produces neither writers nor freethinking young people. The traditional approach often creates a hidden curriculum that teaches superficiality and a paint-by-numbers approach to writing. An honest approach allows young people to become artists before blank canvases.

Writing as Professionals Do

Briefly, I outline here a set of activities that help show both what students can do and what concepts can be fostered in students when the primary goal is student understanding and awareness of writing. The first step is allowing students to rediscover the world of professional and published writing as it compares to what they have come to believe to be rules that govern their writing in school.

In a group activity, students are placed into five or so groups, each group receiving a different genre of writing to explore—poetry, nonfiction (e.g., newspapers, magazines), novels, and so forth. They are instructed to explore and explain the conventions for sentence formation, paragraphing, and writing form they discover in their samples. The teacher can even prompt them to consider traditional ideas about fragments, introductions, and thesis statements, for example, by brainstorming their preconceptions before completing the group work.

A classroom activity that may work well to prepare students for this group activity is to have them all read a newspaper editorial that has an ironic or sarcastic tone. I often use a piece by Mike Royko about flag burning. We discover that he has no thesis (since he is being sarcastic, he never directly states his main point) and that he follows no introduction-body-conclusion format. Nonetheless, he made his living as a professional writer. Students soon learn that the possibilities in the real world of writing are virtually limitless—that the narrow essay formats they have previously produced have little to do with writing as it is practiced by writers.

Further, these same groups can be provided explanations and examples from professional writers concerning professionals' writing habits. The writing process *in practice* does include brainstorming, outlining, drafting, revision, and all the steps we have taught for years. But those steps are not linear. The active writer writes in a chaotic manner, incorporating the steps of the writing process in overlapping, holistic, and idiosyncratic ways.

Practicing What We Preach

After students' awareness has been raised about the open-ended and chaotic nature of writing forms and the writing process, they must be given the challenging task of applying that understanding, which is much more difficult than producing an essay conforming to the conventions of standard English (and in which the content is virtually irrelevant). An effective next assignment is to have students write original pieces, allowing choice of both form and content. The focus of the assignment is for students to openly defy as many of the conventions—those preconceptions they have been taught directly and indirectly in school—as they can while producing an effective and appropriate piece. They should be encouraged to challenge the introduction-body-conclusion organization as well. As they write their pieces, they must also maintain a reflective log that explains their choices—what conventions they reject and why.

This set of activities strives to move students into a much more difficult world of writing than we have traditionally approached. The truth about writing is extremely hard to teach and as difficult to learn. But when students are shown the freedom of expression within the simple act of writing, they also embrace a world of individual freedom, a gift more powerful than the credit they receive for the class.

Students Struggle with Freedom

When any teacher explains a set of activities, they appear neat and clean, not a blemish in sight. Yet in the classroom, all great plans are covered in warts. My approach to liberating students within their writing and through their writing is a painful one, for both the students and me.

Initially, most students are resistant to moving from a "rules" mentality to a "guidelines" mentality. My students have grown up in homes and in a town where conservative and fundamental attitudes are the norm, and their English classes have often portrayed learning to read and write in similarly simplified language. The black-and-white world is much more manageable for everyone than the world of gray we live in. Actually, my students have trouble trusting me, and they are afraid my approach will "get them in trouble" with other teachers. Therefore, allowing them discovery and building their trust in me as a writer and an expert on writing are extremely important.

Most students respond well after a few essays, especially after they have success with their rewrites. Not only do their grades improve, but they also often feel prouder of their work because of the time and energy invested and because they develop a deeper understanding of their own ideas. By the end of the first quarter, almost all of my students have come to trust that I have been honest with them and that the approaches and attitudes I have fostered will be successful in any classroom or real-world setting.

Of course, my approach has its pitfalls. Some students never trust me, and some never attempt the required rewriting schedule. Once again the hidden curriculum has negatively affected students; many students slip through English classes without ever passing or even completing a writing assignment (just as many never read the books we assign). Under those circumstances, they have learned that writing is not a central concern of the English classroom. As the year passes, those students fall so far behind their classmates that recovery is virtually impossible. One major factor in this failure is lack of student motivation. If a student does not want to learn to write—or even to write at all—a class in which all grading depends on writing is an instant trap for failure.

Yet I have found over sixteen years that my students go on to thrive in college writing situations. They are praised by their professors, and they have much greater confidence as writers and thinkers than many of their college-level peers. The open-ended workshop approach to teaching writing is our best hope for fostering independent young writers.

Supporting the Truth about Writing

A few essential areas of research and educational philosophy support the approach I've described: education as a vehicle to individual freedom, learning for understanding as a primary goal of education, and current knowledge about language acquisition and the teaching of writing.

Many argue that education is an act of empowerment and liberation (Freire 1993; hooks 1994; Greene 1978, 1988), especially as the acquisition of language skills is associated with individual self-direction. My activities are grounded in a belief that when young people face the chaotic and relative nature of language and the world, they are better able to take control of their own lives and better able to contribute to the good of society. Ultimately, teachers of writing must decide whether the goal of our work is to inculcate grammar rules that are at best debatable and are certainly temporal, or whether the goal is to empower and free our students through language.

Further, I contend that linear thinking and behavioristically grounded instruction produce a false appearance of being educated. Gardner (1991, 1999) argues for learning for understanding. If students are allowed to experiment with the open-ended nature of the writing process and writing forms while they are mentored by supportive teachers, they are more likely to attain an awareness and an understanding of writing that is applicable in their personal and professional growth. Again, we can indoctrinate and demand memorization of rules, assessing with grammar text–type tests, but what will that accomplish? We have known since the beginning of the twentieth century that superficial learning is of little value; young people need understanding and awareness, and through writing instruction, we can offer students a pathway to that understanding and awareness.

In addition, this approach draws heavily on the more recent reevaluation of the writing process as a chaos model (Weaver 1996, 83). The process steps themselves—brainstorming, drafting, rewriting, formatting—are valid and effective tools for teaching. What Weaver and others are arguing is that those steps occur simultaneously and chaotically as a piece is being prepared. A writer brainstorms initially, of course, but format and purpose are often in mind during that initial stage. Also, as a writer produces a first or second draft, further brainstorming is occurring, and issues of format and organization arise as the work appears on the page. (I know as a practicing poet myself that all of these steps occur simultaneously and at an unconscious level as I write.) Weaver contends that "the phases of the writing process intertwine and overlap"; thus, teachers of writing must "[establish] a writer's workshop in which writers can work on pieces of writing in their own idiosyncratic way, at their own pace" (1996, 83).

Important too is a grounding in a descriptive approach to grammar and writing form (Williams 1990; see especially Chapters 1 and 10). Teachers and students must become aware that the history of grammar "rules" is a series of often arbitrary and constantly shifting guidelines that are best presented as conventions bound to a certain time period. The tremendous number of commas in Hawthorne's *The Scarlet Letter* contrasts greatly with the relative scarcity of commas in many current works; likewise, today we never find commas following dashes, though this is common in Hawthorne. To refute a dogmatic approach to grammar, Williams (1990) argues that "learning to write clearly can help us think and feel and see, and that in fact there are a few straightforward principles—not rules—that help" (Williams 1990, 14).

Ultimately, such activities must incorporate our current but ever-changing understanding of language acquisition. The work of Pinker (1994, 1999) shows that *how* young people acquire language is still greatly debated. Yet, according to Pinker, current experts in language acquisition believe that much of grammar awareness is more or less "hardwired" into the brain of humans at birth. When small children make all verbs regular ("I goed"), we cannot make them change until they reach another level of cognitive development; we can correct them with "I went" until we are blue in the face, but nothing will change until they reach that level. When writing instruction is primarily imposed, we are wasting student time and crushing their will to learn and their opportunities for empowerment. When writing instruction springs from the students themselves, the possibilities are endless. Since our understandings shift constantly, teaching methodologies must be flexible, open-ended enough to allow for instruction to shift as our knowledge of language acquisition grows.

We are left with experimenting with the student-centered, open-ended approaches to fostering writing in our students. I contend that our work is about each student, not about preserving "Don't split an infinitive" or "Don't end a sentence with a preposition." Language conventions will shift, as they should; our energy should be on writing that contributes to the freedom and empowerment of our students.

Works Cited

Freire, Paulo. 1993. *Pedagogy of the Oppressed.* Trans. Myra Bergman Ramos. New York: Continuum.

Gardner, Howard. 1991. *The Unschooled Mind: How Children Think and How Schools Should Teach.* New York: Basic Books.

——. 1999. *The Disciplined Mind: What All Students Should Understand.* New York: Simon & Schuster.

Greene, Maxine. 1978. *Landscapes of Learning.* New York: Teachers College Press.

——. 1988. *The Dialectic of Freedom.* New York: Teachers College Press.

hooks, bell. 1994. *Teaching to Transgress: Education as the Practice of Freedom.* New York: Routledge.

Pinker, Steven. 1994. *The Language Instinct: How the Mind Creates Language.* New York: HarperPerennial.

——. 1999. *Words and Rules: The Ingredients of Language.* New York: Basic Books.

Weaver, Constance. 1996. *Teaching Grammar in Context.* Portsmouth, NH: Boynton/Cook.

Williams, Joseph M. 1990. *Style: Toward Clarity and Grace.* Chicago: University of Chicago Press.

CHAPTER SEVENTEEN

Conflicting Voices in the Classroom: Developing Critical Consciousness

ANNETTE HARRIS POWELL
University of Louisville

Although I teach at a large university set in a metropolitan area, many of my students come from surrounding rural counties that are relatively insulated. The average student age is twenty-seven, and there is a variable number of both traditional and nontraditional students. In any given class, an instructor might have students ranging in age from eighteen to thirty. Many of these students have not been introduced to diverse groups of people or contexts, so when they take their first composition class, some of them are asked to grapple with sociopolitical issues such as race, gender, class, and sexuality for the first time. They are asked to venture outside their context, something that many of them, frankly, have little time to do because of their full-time jobs and complicated child care arrangements. They also have few tools with which to negotiate new information.

Recently, the University of Louisville's designation shifted from an urban mission to a strong research focus. While the university is still dedicated to the urban mission, the mandate is to gain prominence as a research institution. Much of the work that had been done in terms of remediation is being redirected to neighboring schools (junior colleges), where students are able to make a seamless transition to the university—at least in theory. How this shift toward research will affect the focus and pedagogical goals of instructors is yet to be seen. We might, however, hypothesize that the composition of the student body, in terms of class and perhaps race, will be affected to some degree. I anticipate that this shift will crystallize the homogeneity of the current student body.

How the university and thus how the classroom is constructed ultimately influences the dialogue that takes place in our classrooms. Student response to the instructor is also significant. When students come into my classroom, see me, and hear my focus or "agenda" for the class, some feel they are about to be indoctrinated, forced to "buy" into ideologies that are in direct opposition to the values they have been taught in their home communities. As a woman of color teaching at a state university with a generally homogenous student body, I often face students who have had few or no teachers of color and who at times offer strong resistance to the issues I attempt to raise. I remember wondering, naively, what my students see first when they walk into my class: my gender or my color. The answer has become obvious to me in light of some of the reactions my students have had to my pedagogy. For many students, my color *is* my ideology. When asked to respond to the essay "Another Long Drink of the Blues: The Race Card in the Simpson Case" by popular social critic Stanley Crouch, one student declared that he had nothing to learn from any race other than his own. He rejected Crouch's critique and refused to acknowledge the validity of other subject positions and, by implication, my authority to engage him and others in discussions that involved critique of U.S. culture. This particular student's response is indicative of where he is in terms of his comfort with other discourses, as well as suggestive of a general resistance to, or suspicion of, alternative perspectives that question the existing hegemonic cultural and social structure. Another complication is that my color automatically positions me as a promoter of leftist ideology in my students' eyes; moreover, they have to deal with the power relationship that follows from this dialogue: a woman of color is directing a discussion that questions the very foundation of their narrowly defined beliefs.

Many of my students are conservative, their attitudes at times representing years of intolerance. My students of color, along with my white students, also have very definite perceptions of who I am. This creates a degree of tension, as they expect me to fulfill their vision of the monolithic black person. Some of my African American students, for example, construct me as "outsider" because of my readings of class texts. These students in particular want me to be like them, but just as their own ethnic, social class, and regional backgrounds shape their readings of me and of the texts, so too do these factors influence my performance. In addition, many of my white students resent being confronted (often for the first time) by a person of color with a degree of authority. As a northeasterner, my diction apparently signals a particular kind of background—one they associate with terms such as *elitist, liberal,* and *authoritarian* (which is problematic because of my gender and race). As Mari Matsuda (1991) argues, "accent" conveys more than just "where you have lived"; it suggests "your age, the schools you attended, the language you know, your ethnicity . . . [and] your class position" (1329). When students try to infer from my accent who I am and how I will interact with them, many become alienated. Thus, how students construct me greatly influences their feelings about the class and, in turn, my classroom practice.

Interrogating Practice

In addition to responding to how my students construct me, and because I am concerned with critical literacy, access, and race, I make these issues a central part of my pedagogical focus. I do so in concert with programmatic goals, which emphasize the academic needs of students while encouraging instructors to develop and test their own theories of language and teaching, as well as in light of the university's mission, which stresses an obligation to serve the needs of a diverse urban population. The local environment in which I attempt to construct my pedagogy, then, is one that supports helping students to negotiate academic and public discourses so that they can critique and resist both and understand different rhetorical contexts. As a result, I face the question of how, without overwhelming students, to develop critical readers, thinkers, and writers coming to voice as they negotiate new and often unfamiliar discourse communities.

Given my institutional context, I have had to revise my approach and, to some extent, my philosophy of teaching. Reflecting on my teaching experience, I realized, for example, that some students were frustrated by the decidedly liberal slant of some of the selected texts.[1] I have been somewhat aggressive in introducing my students to socially and politically progressive ideology. I believe this aggression stems from my philosophy that the classroom is a space in which students should be required to step outside their immediate comfort zone to tackle issues that demand that they engage with other contexts. The composition classroom is uniquely situated for this because it is through our study of language that we explore these various contexts. As Bakhtin (1981) argues, "One's own discourse is gradually and slowly wrought out of others' words" (345) and inevitably "enters into an intense interaction, a *struggle*" with other discourses, resulting in dialogue that offers new meaning (346). While I continue to subscribe to this philosophy of language, as my teaching has evolved I have recognized my students' right to defend their values, ideology, religion, and so forth. I do encourage them to be socially and politically aware and to position themselves as critical readers and writers, but I encourage critique from a variety of perspectives—especially their own. I am careful to convey to students that they should not have to reject their home values or who they are when they enter the classroom. This is a perspective I have arrived at after spending a good deal of time interrogating my own practices, and one that has led me to revise several aspects of my course, including the activities described in the next section.

Readings/Texts

Throughout the semester, I incorporate assignments that help prepare students to confront a number of tough issues, as well as encourage them to practice communicating their perspectives. Because I value the composition classroom as a space in which students read, critique, and construct political texts, I attempt to provide an environment in which students actually talk and write about the themes they encounter in various texts. Course activities include (1) informal written responses to short fiction and critical essays that students prepare in groups and use to lead class discussions and (2) a formal film analysis. To facilitate the informal responses, I select texts that I believe will promote dialogues that help students read, think, and write critically about a variety of topics.[2] I carefully select texts that present multiple perspectives and that encourage students to question their assumptions. Excerpts from Harriet Jacobs's *Incidents in the Life of a Slave Girl*, for example, work well to illustrate *heteroglossia* (Bakhtin's term for multiple, competing discourses) and the power of an author to represent a number of perspectives and conflicting worldviews. Prompts for response include the following: (1) Identify the voices with which Harriet speaks; (2) What perspectives can be identified by these voices? (3) Are these perspectives sympathetic (to Harriet)? and (4) What story do these voices/perspectives tell? Students are most apt to share their true perspectives in their response papers, so it is here that I discover their varied stances. I have found that this can be a double-edged sword when I am the only audience for these response papers. Whereas this makes some students more accountable for what they write, others see it as an opportunity to vent. To combat this problem, I have students share their response papers in groups, critique the points raised by their peers, and respond to one another in a whole class discussion. I use the following discussion prompts: (1) Consider the varying sides to the discussion; (2) Are there perspectives that have been ignored?; and (3) Is this person's response a balanced one? Why/why not? Students are free to highlight those issues they find compelling, interesting, and important. Of course, they must also delineate the arguments being made. Generally, I've found that students more carefully consider their perspectives and arguments if they are first asked to share them with their peers.

A more formal activity that has also worked well is the rhetorical analysis of a film. This activity is situated within a theme that focuses on literacy and texts by encouraging students to critically read texts of the world and then examine their positions in relation to these texts. Film analysis also provides an opportunity for students to critique elements of popular culture. Students seldom analyze film in a way that encourages them to empathize or identify with the characters and their experiences or to grapple with the issues presented. I stress to my students that their individual readings constitute the films they view, that their interpretive critiques of the films give the films meaning—the director has merely provided a framework within which interpretation takes place.

When I introduce the film activity, my students are generally interested because they get to watch movies, texts they consider accessible. To complete the activity, students view a couple of films (which I usually select). In the past, for example, I have chosen *Dead Man Walking* and *Higher Learning*. I try to select films that engage issues of race, gender, class, alienation, and loss. Although John Singleton's treatment of race and gender is oversimplified in *Higher Learning*, I use this film because it is popular with students and it conveniently illustrates the very issues that stagnate our discussions on difference, namely our inability to recognize the elaborate examples of people and contexts. Students select a character whom they will rhetorically analyze, looking at how he or she promotes, advances, or undercuts the argument of the movie. Students have a lot of latitude in writing their observations of these characters, but because more than one person examines the same character, the class is able to share their differing perspectives. In addition to emphasizing various rhetorical principles, this assignment encourages students to consider what it means to be authentic, how film as text writes and responds to other experiences. Students also, obviously, learn how others, who may or may not be similarly situated, view characters, and they encounter other perspectives that might contradict or challenge hegemonic prescriptions.

Discussion

Initially, I put students into predesignated groups to discuss their analyses with one another before sharing them with the class. I ask them to consider the following questions when responding to the analyses: (1) Is this character believable? (2) What about the character's experiences resonate for you? and (3) To which aspects of this character are you unable to relate? Why/why not? In the class discussion, students share their thoughts on what they believe motivates their characters and provide a rationale for the conclusions they have reached. Though some students are analyzing the same character, one student might look at how a character undercuts the film's argument while another student argues that that character advances it. Because all the students bring different backgrounds, values, and ways of seeing the world to the experience of the film, they make interesting and varied observations that seldom reach consensus. Students are encouraged to explain how they arrived at their conclusions. This facilitates interesting discussions that highlight difference. For example, during one student's presentation of his analysis of Remy, the white skinhead in *Higher Learning,* he said that he thought Remy was bigoted and racist but that he himself was not like Remy and did not know anyone like him, so racism was not really an issue for him. This prompted a response from a student who was analyzing Malik, the black track star. She noted that Malik was someone who turned everything into a black or white issue. While most students agreed that this was Singleton's point, I used this dialogue to push the conversation further to explore their understanding of the director's rhetorical aim. I asked them to consider whether Singleton himself undercuts his own film by reinstantiating the black/white binary. I noted, for example, that the film does not give voice to Asians or Latinos, but rather highlights only black/white issues.

In discussions like this one, I stress the need for us to see the complexity of the issues surrounding race and gender rather than focus solely on the extreme representations in the film that enable us to distance ourselves from the possibility of being like some of the characters. I suggest that such distance allows us to leave assumptions unchallenged. I also use my positioning as a person of color to add to the critique, explicitly stating, for example, that I understand why Malik sees everything as black or white. Despite understanding that most situations are complex, there are certainly instances in my own life when I whittle things down to race: when I'm standing in line and the person in back of the counter looks beyond me and asks, "Who's next?," how else, I ask my students, would you expect me to see this? Some students note that it is important for them to hear me articulate how and why I read the issue in a particular way, but then they proceed to explain why *they* think this is a narrow view of the situation.

Such discussions tease out the issues about which many students are either ignorant or apathetic. I choose to focus on issues of difference because talking and writing about them helps students learn how to read and interpret a variety of texts, a rhetorical act that eventually leads to the questioning and potential dismantling of the authority guiding the interpretation of established texts. This rhetorical focus has become the bedrock of my pedagogy, given the ideological stance of the students I teach. When students engage with uncomfortable issues that traditionally have been part of the silenced dialogue—e.g., race, class, and gender—I prompt them with questions: What experiences have you had that might better enable others to understand your perspective? What are some alternative ways of seeing a particular issue? I stress more rigorous discussion on issues of difference because I do not believe it is enough to simply create a space for the clash of ideology in the classroom; we need to consider where these "contact zone" discussions end up. In order to realize the contact zone, I include issues across a broad spectrum and encourage students to deal with these issues as they often are—complex and without clear resolution—rather than ask them to argue one position or another. My primary focus during class discussions is to engage as many perspectives as possible. I try to neither silence nor celebrate voices of critique or opposition (Miller 1994, 407), but rather to draw students out and have them examine their reading process to determine how they got where they are now. When we confront issues such as gender and class and especially race, the conversation sometimes stops. Everyone is tentative, afraid of offending, and quite simply afraid of confronting. Many students don't want to confront difference because for some it means confronting the privilege that positions them. When students seem reticent, I respond by doing several things: I reveal my position, my own discomfort and/or experience with particular issues, and invite others to do the same.

Often, much of the discussion goes on without me having to say much. This is significant, especially since my voice, as a woman of color, often seems to influence the analyses my students put forward. As much as possible, I position myself as an observer of these discussions, though at times I interject if I need to get a discussion back on track or if critical issues need to be further developed. In some instances, however, I talk very directly about my response as a person of color to a piece, noting why I see an issue in a particular way. For instance, during a class discussion about how issues of race, gender, and class are interrelated, one student said frankly that she was tired of race, class, and gender. I responded, "So am I." The class was amused and a little concerned about how I would proceed. I went on to relate that I too am saturated by the focus on these issues, but because of who I am, how I'm positioned in society, I cannot afford to ignore them. The class discussion continued as a sharing of how students felt about being confronted by these issues in the classroom and their daily lives.

Conclusion

My aim in the composition classroom is to develop a dialogue that helps students critically explore—and create—a variety of texts that deal with an amalgam of issues. I believe the composition classroom has a social action element that invites such exploration; therefore, I focus on topics that are somewhat charged because I believe these topics will "turn our eyes" toward substantive discussion. The classroom then becomes a site for critical thinking and good writing. When I began my teaching career, I believed like Plato that there are absolute truths and that it was my responsibility to convey them to my students. I no longer ascribe to this philosophy. I do maintain that it is my responsibility to prepare students to participate in our complex democracy, not necessarily to ensure that students are situated in a particular political plane, but to make sure they understand the magnitude of this complexity. To do this, I try to make my classroom a place where counterdiscourse occurs, providing an opportunity for multiple voices to be heard so that our writing becomes more critical and more convincing. If my students leave my classroom more politically aware, more tolerant of issues of race, class, and gender, I am thrilled. If students leave my class critically analyzing and questioning, they are well on their way to disrupting the status quo. My approach will have been successful.

Notes

1. Texts are selected from *Rereading America: Cultural Content for Critical Thinking and Writing,* 3rd ed., edited by Gary Colombo, Robert Cullen, and Bonnie Lisle (Boston: Bedford/St. Martin's, 1995) and include "The New American Dreamers," Ruth Sidel; "Rewards and Opportunities: The Politics and Economics of Class in the U.S.," Gregory Mantsios; "Social Class and the Hidden Curriculum of Work," Jean Anyon; "C. P. Ellis," Studs Terkel; and "Higher Education: Colder by Degrees," Myra Sadker and David Sadker.

2. Some of the texts we've used include "The Banking Concept of Education," Paulo Freire; "Confronting Class in the Classroom," bell hooks; "The Student and the University," Allan Bloom; "Toward a New Politics of Hispanic Assimilation," Linda Chavez; Mary Shelley's *Frankenstein* (excerpted); "Just Girls," Margaret Finders; "The Student and the University," Christian Zawodniak.

Works Cited

Bakhtin, Mikhail. 1981. *The Dialogic Imagination: Four Essays,* ed. Michael Holquist, trans. Caryl Emerson and Michael Holquist. Austin: University of Texas Press.

Matsuda, Mari J. 1991. "Voices of America: Accent, Antidiscrimination Law, and a Jurisprudence for the Last Reconstruction." *Yale Law Journal* 100: 1329–1407.

Miller, Richard. 1994. "Fault Lines in the Contact Zone." *College English* 56.4: 389–408.

CHAPTER EIGHTEEN

The Focused Reading Response

MARGARET A. MCLAUGHLIN
Georgia Southern University

Teaching Context

College-level developmental readers and writers frequently stop trying to make meaning of what they read and write because of the significant consequences of being wrong, consequences such as being placed in noncredit college classes, for example. The following assignment can help academically at-risk readers and writers realize that reading and writing are meaning-making activities and that "right" answers emerge from a convergence of reader, text, and context. This assignment has worked well with developmental reading/writing students at a rural southeastern Georgia regional university with an enrollment of about fourteen thousand students and a 75 percent Caucasian to 25 percent African American student ratio. Most first-year students are recent high school graduates, and many are first-generation college students. In recent years, around 40 percent of entering students have been admitted to the university under the provision that they pass noncredit developmental classes in math, reading, and/or English before they can enroll in regular college classes. Many of these students report that they hate to read, that they have rarely, if ever, completed the reading of an entire book, and that they have written little other than five-paragraph practice essays to satisfy graduation requirements.

When I first began teaching the developmental reading/writing classes, the postmodern theory that meaning is not inherent in a text but is created by each individual reader guided my assignments. I wanted to help students understand that reading is much more than being able to regurgitate facts but is in fact a composing process through which each reader constructs his or her own meaning. Following the response format suggested by Bartholomae and Petrosky (1986, 53), I asked students to freewrite for at least an hour on what they found to be important or significant after completing a book. All too often, however, the responses were either simplistic summaries or responses so personal that any connection to the text was indiscernible. As basic readers, these students' eyes passively glided over words while their minds wandered to faraway places. They needed instruction in how to find meaning in what they read. They needed to discover that "reading . . . [is] a process through which the moments they notice or recall in a text become the significant moments in that text. . . . Their job . . . is to find a way of using those moments to talk about a text's meaning" (Bartholomae and Petrosky 1986, 20).

Ann Berthoff (1984) encourages her students to use the type of reading, thinking, and writing that Bartholomae and Petrosky describe through keeping a double-entry journal: the reader takes textual notes on one page of a journal and interprets these notes on a facing page (30). Dialectical note taking, according to Berthoff, is analogous to "the acts of mind whereby we make sense of the world" (27) and helps students realize that "[w]e can make meaning because we see in terms of what we have seen" (30). Although Berthoff is primarily interested in how the double-entry journal enables students to "compose" revisions of their writing, the process she suggests can help underprepared readers make connections between reading, writing, and their own life experiences: first they must *recognize, or perceive,* what is noteworthy in a text, then *formulate associations* on the basis of that perception, and finally *articulate their associations with their perceptions* (31).

Berthoff's double-entry journal seemed a viable method to help my students use the "acts of the mind" throughout their reading of a text. Having to collect and transport bulky journals, however, did not appeal to me. A three-step focused reading response, based on the process Berthoff suggests, eventually emerged as a compromise solution.

The Assignment

To emphasize the necessity of reading with a pencil in hand—
annotating—in order to talk and write about the assigned readings, my classes first read an excerpt from *How to Read a Book*
(Adler and Van Doren 1972). After class discussion of this assignment, the following assignment is given to the students:

Focused Reading Response

Step 1: (Recognition/Perception) Write a phrase, sentence, or
passage that you marked at the top of your page and enclose
it in quotation marks. Put the author and page number(s) in
parentheses at the end of the quote.

Step 2: (Association) Write a paragraph explaining how the
meaning of the quote relates to what is happening or being
said on the page or in this section of the text. In other words,
*summarize the context of the quote and then explain its rel-
evance in the text.*

Step 3: (Reflection/Articulation) Write a paragraph explaining what in your own experience you can associate with what
is being said in the quote.

Students are required to write one or two focused reading
responses each week, although they may do more if they so choose.
During the beginning weeks of a semester, I collect the required
responses frequently in order to monitor students' understanding of the three-step response. At first a number of students will
have difficulty following the directions for two major reasons:
they may not know what it means to summarize and/or they
write generalizations instead of specific details or examples. Here
is an example of one student's first attempt at a focused response
when we began a semester with the reading of Bobbie Ann
Mason's novel *In Country*. In the spaces between the focused
response steps, I direct students' attention to what is well done
and what needs improvement; I have inserted my comments in
italics in the following student samples:

Student Sample 1/Focused Reading Response

Step 1: ". . . , but Mamaw acts like she knows everything about Sam. It's spooky. Mamaw is always saying, 'Why, that's just like you, Sam' or 'That's your daddy in you, for the world.' She makes Sam feel as though she has been spied on for years" (Mason 4).

Step 2: This passage is significant because it tell a little bit about Mamaw personality towards Sam. It also tells how Sam feels about Mamaw and the way Mamaw act like she knows Sam all her life.
(My response): *But she has known Sam all her life. Step 2 needs to tell (summarize) enough of the plot to explain why Mamaw does not know her granddaughter very well.*

Step 3: I marked this passage because it shows how most people feel when they see family members or friends that act as if they have known you so long and you don't have a clue who they are. In my experience in this, I felt the same way a little spooky.
(My response): *Your step 3 is much too general. You must give some specific examples or at least one account of when you experienced something similar to the way Sam is feeling.*

This sample is representative of many students' first attempts to write a focused response. It is filled with generalities. The student could have written step 2 just by pulling that one sentence out of the text without any attempt to understand why the characters speak and feel as they do. Requiring a concise, accurate summary is one way I monitor the students' reading comprehension, and it also ensures that no one can just turn to any page and select, willy-nilly, a sentence. In step 3, the student attempts to make a connection to his own experience but gives no detailed example. Because this is a developmental reading and writing class, I want the students to become accustomed to using the vivid, concrete examples that will be required for their essay assignments.

On the Focused Reading Response sheet, I leave spaces between the three steps to help me quickly read and respond to the students so that I can quickly return their work for revision if needed. During the first weeks of the semester, I require students to revise their focused responses until they illustrate an understanding of the process. For those few who continue to have difficulty with either step 2 or step 3 into the third or fourth week of the semester, individual conferences may become necessary.

Although the course integrates reading and writing instruction, I do not mark students' mechanical errors in their reading responses until they have mastered the response process, and then only when I recognize the errors as part of a pattern that is also appearing in their other writings. By midterm or soon after, I expect my students to realize the necessity of editing their reading responses just as they do the final drafts of their essays. The student samples and my responses given here are just as the students wrote them and just as I responded. The next two student responses, the first from the Mason novel assignment and the second from a student who read "A Homemade Education," an essay excerpted from Alex Haley's *Malcolm X,* illustrate what I want students to accomplish:

Student Sample 2/Focused Reading Response
Step 1: "That transmission job will take forever" (Mason 15).

Step 2: This sentence is significant because it prevents the characters in the story from reaching their destination. They are having to stay at a hotel 100 miles from Washington. It is all because of the VW Beetle. It is having transmission problems. The transmission keeps slipping out of fourth gear. While the car was in motion Sam held the stick in gear. It must of been pretty hard to do because she was tired when they arrived at a Howard Johnson. They are now going to get the transmission fixed so they can continue on their trip to Washington. The fact is they do not know how long it will take or how much it is going to cost to fix the transmission. They were then told by Bill that it would take about a day and a half and cost around $350.00.

(My response): *Quite a good summary of this section of the novel.*

Step 3: I marked this sentence because I can relate to it in some way. My Dad and I were driving to GSU for the open house in April on Interstate 16. I was hearing some noise coming from the engine. I heard this noise about three different times because I would hear it and then it would go away, so I ignored it. Later, we were almost at the exit, about five miles away, when we heard the noise again and that is when we had to stop. At first my Dad had no idea what was wrong, but when we tried to take off from the emergency lane he had trouble getting started. To make a long story short, the transmission was stuck in third gear because we had a transmission fluid leak and by that we had destroyed the working parts inside the transmission. The car took a whole week to fix. It cost us around $1500.00 plus the cost of having to rent a car to get home. Sam, Emmett, and Mamaw are in about the same situation as we were and I thought that was weird.
(My response): *A vividly described personal experience connection to the text. Well done!*

Student Sample 3/Focused Reading Response
Step 1: "Many people who hear me somewhere in person, or on TV, or those who read something I've said, will think I went school far beyond 8th grade."
(My response): *You have not transcribed the quote exactly as it is written in the text. Compare what you have written with the source. Also, remember that you must give the author and text page in parentheses immediately after the quotation.*

Step 2: Malcolm X is saying to us that a formal education is not the only kind. Being self taught can be just as well as going to a formal school. He also explains to us that self motivation is a powerful tool to possess. This type of motivation is not taught and can not be read in a book. It is up to the individual to make that decision.

(My response): *You have precisely captured the main idea of this essay in these few sentences. Good reading, good thinking, good work!*

Step 3: I have seen something similar to this. My grandfather lived and worked on a farm in North Georgia. I always remember him as being very articulate and wise. He only attended school through the fourth grade and worked on the family farm the rest of the time. But you would never know it. After the last year of his formal education, he began to teach himself math and he learned to read. It was this ambition and self motivation that made him a successful farmer and person. I hope that I contain some of his motivation and drive.

(My response): *A very appropriate personal connection to the text. You may want to use your grandfather as the subject for a character sketch, or profile, of a family member for an essay we will write later this semester.*

The focused responses of these two students illustrate that they are not only making meaning from the texts, but also making connections between what they have read and their own lives, connections they may decide to use for a future writing assignment. One of the writing assignments for this class, for example, asks students to narrate an autobiographical experience from which they learned something significant, and another asks for a profile of a family member. Step 3 of the focused reading response can help jog their memories.

As the semester progresses, students keep their responses chronologically organized in a loose-leaf notebook. Periodically, they remove the responses from the notebook; write a cover letter exploring the insights they have gained from the readings, class discussions, and focused responses; and give the packet to me for evaluation. We call this response packet a dialogue journal because the students are engaging in dialogue with the text, with themselves, and with me as I respond to what they have written as though in dialogue. When I return the response packets, students replace them in their notebooks to provide a record of their reading, thinking, and writing throughout the semester, a record they use for their end-of-semester reflective letter. The thoroughness and thoughtfulness with which students complete the focused reading responses constitute a significant percentage of their semester reading grade.

Rationale

The focused reading response has multiple instructional benefits: it accustoms students to finding and documenting sources, a skill they will need for subsequent academic papers; it gives practice in summarizing skills and in articulating how the summarized section relates to the larger text; and it helps students develop the ability to perceive texts as meaningful through the connections they make with their own life experiences. Making connections between the text and personal experience requires both thoughtful rereading and critical thinking because such relationships are not always immediately evident.

As mentioned earlier, focused reading responses can also act as heuristics for essay topics. Particularly when students are writing personal experience narratives in which they are asked to address significant incidents in their own lives and explain how they were affected by these incidents, the marked passage can trigger vivid memories that might otherwise have lain dormant. In addition, the first step, copying sentences of a professional writer, is a technique that traditionally has been used in composition instruction to accustom students to stylistic variations available to them in their own writing.

The focused reading response is also effective in initiating class discussions. In large and small group discussions, students share marked passages and explain why they chose them for marking. Because they must read a quote not already given by a previous student, they cannot get by with marking only one or two passages. By the time each student shares a passage for class response, the assigned reading is fully discussed from a number of perspectives, and all class members have initiated a discussion.

When students follow a sequence of activities that includes marking a text, writing focused reading responses, discussing passages with other students, and then using their focused response as an invention springboard for writing an essay, they can become more aware of a process that produces texts and also more capable of analyzing difficulties they encounter in reading and writing.

Works Cited

Adler, Mortimer Jerome, and Charles Van Doren. 1972. *How to Read a Book*. New York: Simon & Schuster.

Bartholomae, David, and Anthony Petrosky.1986. *Facts, Artifacts, and Counterfacts: Theory and Method for a Reading and Writing Course*. Upper Montclair, NJ: Boynton/Cook.

Berthoff, Ann E. 1984. "Recognition, Representation, and Revision," Pp. 27–37 in *Rhetoric and Composition: A Sourcebook for Teachers and Writers*, ed. Richard Graves. Upper Montclair, NJ: Boynton/Cook.

CHAPTER NINETEEN

Locating Students in Academic Dialogue: The Research Journal

JANIS E. HASWELL

Texas A&M University–Corpus Christi

Texas A&M University–Corpus Christi in South Texas is a branch campus of a large university system. We are a four-year teaching institution of over seven thousand students serving a modest-sized working-class urban center. We draw heavily from the local population, which is roughly half Mexican American and half European American. Many of our students are older returning students; often they hold down one or more jobs while attending school.

Students enroll in a configuration of community-learning courses each semester of their first year. There are eight possible configurations, including links between (1) English, political science, and history, (2) English, psychology, and music, (3) English, sociology, and environmental science, and (4) English, reading, and communication. With the luxury of composition courses scheduled in computer labs, students are able to access both the Internet and the library's computerized card catalog and electronic databases from their seats. During fall semester, students enroll in English 1301, an "intro to college writing" course, followed in the spring by English 1302, our writing and research course.

As part of strategic, long-range assessment of our writing program, Debra Dew (our writing program director), Glenn Blalock, and I redesigned the curriculum of English 1302 during the fall semester of 1999 and piloted the new course in the spring of 2000. Beginning in fall of 2000, the assessed and upgraded version of the pilot program was adopted by all 1302 faculty.

Our revised goals were based on the original vision of the core program, recent evaluations from a FIPSE consultant, and our own self-studies, as well as interviews with teaching assistants, instructors, and faculty who have taught the course. Teachers who agreed to pilot the new course worked closely with the library staff to design student orientations suited to specific assignments, and during implementation they met weekly in teaching circles to explore new ideas, discuss problems, and share assignments.

The focus of the pilot course was threefold: (1) to harness extensive reading with analysis of rhetorical appeals (a skill applied to excerpts from our interdisciplinary reader, St. Martin's *Fields of Reading, Motives for Writing,* to the students' research materials, and to their own written texts); (2) to center reading and writing assignments on a single focus for the semester that allows students to delve deeply into a subject and become experts in an ongoing scholarly dialogue; and (3) to guide the students as they identify their own positions in four research assignments after weighing and navigating multiple perspectives, debatable evidence, and conflicting conclusions. Some of the themes adopted by teaching circle team members include human rights issues, political scandals, the tobacco industry, social construction of gender and ethnic identities, the Holocaust, and the Vietnam War, to name a few.

One of the innovative and pivotal components of the pilot course is an assignment we call the research journal, intended to both deepen and lengthen the research process, transforming it from an exercise in note taking to a reflective and analytic prewriting stage (see the appendix).

The Research Journal

If we require students to explore complex and important issues, navigate through multiple sources that do not agree with one another, and produce a rhetorically sophisticated polished product, we also must propose to them a methodical, accessible, timely, and dependable means to accomplish these goals. Our solution is a research journal. In effect, we are front-loading the writing sequence, asking students to weigh evidence; analyze the rhetorical appeals of their sources; identify conflicting positions and tie those differences to the purpose, perspective, and intended readership of the author(s); and understand where and how their own thesis fits into the ongoing dialogue involved in scholarship.

We are aware that we take a certain risk in calling this pedagogical method a *research journal*. The term may remind colleagues of procedures such as Ken Macrorie's I-Search (1980), with its expressivist connections to an exploration of the self, or of personal journaling, such as Cinthia Gannett's narrative diaries (1995), with its connections to a need for marginalized groups to resist the academic establishment. Our research journal certainly buys into such assumptions, but theoretically it is more complex. It presupposes that personal connections need to be maintained as students foray into the alien world of professional literature (e.g., Fulwiler 1982) but also that introspection can lead to analysis and discovery of ideas (e.g., Elbow 1991). It also assumes with theories of heuristic methods that students can push themselves into new ideas if they are required to answer questions designed to edge them intellectually from where they are to where they might be (e.g., Lauer 1970), and it certainly assumes that reading and writing are co-enhancing activities (e.g., Nelson and Calfee 1998). Connecting all of these positions is the belief that stages in the development of skill or understanding are marked with metaconsciousness and self-reflection (e.g., Mezirow 1990).

We ask students to produce a journal entry for each source they consult (in later papers, this may entail writing eight to ten entries). Each source will have an individual entry, and then each collection of entries per paper assignment will have a final, synthetic entry about the challenges of researching that specific topic. With each entry, students are asked to evaluate their source on two levels. In dealing with content, they identify the thesis and point of view of the source, note the derivations of the author's information, assess whether the use of evidence is persuasive and whether opposing viewpoints are represented fairly, and, finally, compare what this source says to the other sources they are using. In dealing with the rhetorical setting, students identify the author's credentials, whom he or she is writing to convince and why, and the means of persuasion the author is using. Some of our faculty require formal, academic language, while others allow students to freewrite their journal entries before moving to a more formal annotated bibliography. In terms of format, the only consistent standard is correct and complete citation form.

In three specific ways, our research journal heuristic finds support in theories of adult development or growth in expertise. First, the questions requiring students to infer the "motive or purpose of the author" move them in a direction that research has shown college students taking again and again (e.g., Haas 1994; Haswell 1993). First-year students have a difficult time conceiving of books as authored, or at least authored by living people with individual motives and perspectives. Grasping this notion is a critical step for students as they gain the disciplinary know-how needed to advance in upper-division courses in their majors. Second, the questions asking students to situate the writing within an ongoing argument of conflicting opinions push them toward a more mature understanding of the nature of intellectual disputes (e.g., Hays, Brandt, and Chantry 1988). And third, the questions that force writers to locate themselves within the range of these conflicting views (e.g., "How would you characterize the sources connected to this topic?") encourage students to think beyond the relativism of this or that perspective to a new position, where they assume a personal authority or commitment to their own argument (e.g., Kegan's "fourth order of consciousness" [1994]). In short, theoretically our research journal questions exercise skills that first-year college students already have as well as ones they need to develop.

During the research phase of the assignment (the total time for each assignment runs three to four weeks), students complete their entries as they move through their sources. If they have faithfully followed through with their journal, they have done most of the thinking needed to complete a first draft (or the getting-it-down-on-paper phase). As they refine their own argument for draft 2, students might discover they need to do more research, which will require adding more entries to the journal. Students hand in the completed journal with their final paper in a miniportfolio (this ensures that students don't put off the journal the way they might for an end-of-semester portfolio). Many of our teaching circle members use conferences and one-on-one feedback with students throughout the process: selecting topics, mapping out a research plan, and wrestling with difficult material. We also find that the amount of work that goes into the research journal deserves immediate reward: either a grade or points for each journal.

Here is a sample entry from Justin's journal as he researched his first paper on the Tet Offensive:

> Edmonds, Anthony O. "The Tet Offensive and Middletown: A Study in Contradiction." 28 January 1999. 29 January 2000 <http://lists.village.virginia.edu/sixties/ HTML_docs/ Texts/ Scholarly/Edmonds_Tet/html>.
>
> This source also supported the belief that the results of the Tet Offensive made both the U.S. Government and the people of the United States less supportive and more pessimistic about the Vietnam War. See Vietnam: A Country Study, Twenty Years and Twenty Days, and Shadows of Vietnam: Lyndon Johnson's War for similar views. The author continues to reemphasize this belief through his piece. He makes the statement that the main feelings that the American people had at the time were disappointment and a concern of a long, drawn-out war. This source does contradict Vandiver's Shadow of Vietnam concerning President Johnson's role in the war. The author says that the President was very optimistic and misled the public, explaining why the public was so outraged when the news of the Tet Offensive reached home.

This is one of the shorter entries from Justin's journal, but obviously he read this source after researching several others, so he was able to align various sources that seemed to agree but also identify points of conflict.

As he completed his research and thought about writing his first draft, Justin came to the office, concerned that his sources didn't all agree. "Should I just leave out Edmonds?" he asked. "Or how do you want me to reconcile this guy with the others?" A telling question from a good student who is worried about being persuasive by making all his evidence "fit" or agree. After we talked through the intent of the assignment (developing his own position, constructing an argument that weighs contradictory evidence or conclusions), I think he understood that his own thesis and insights would develop in that fold, or that fissure, between sources.

Each separate entry in the research journal is helpful in putting together the paper, but the final synthetic component proves especially valuable. Here is Justin's final entry for his topic:

> In general, the most difficult problem that I had researching this topic was trying to find some conflicting views on the Tet offensive. In the end, I still ended up with four sources with the same basic conclusion about Tet, but all had different ways of proving their argument and viewing Johnson. Most of my sources were in some way biased toward the media. They all seemed to think that the media was the culprit that lost the war for America. The topic is significant because Tet was a real turning point in the War. My knowledge and sense of the entire war has totally changed. Since we didn't learn very much about it in high school, all this was mainly new information. From what I knew, the war was a long, drawn-out mistake. I had never known about all of the effects of the media or that some people actually supported the war. The only type of source that I would like to have would be a source about the news media at the time of the Offensive, to see its side of the story. This topic is pretty well covered by many different scholars. I think the only other thing that could be said is that the people who fought in Tet should be given a lot of credit for the outstanding job they did in holding off the NVA forces. I believe that I would be able to add the basic facts to a discussion, but there is still much more to learn about this subject.

Because Justin has stepped back from his topic to gauge its importance and place it in the larger picture, he is able to identify future interests and another path to research for the next assignment.

What do the students think about the research journal? Ryan succinctly captures the consensus of the class:

These journals were really a pain in the butt. [But he adds,] They helped me realize that the kind of research you do really effects the quality of the paper. I never used an encyclopedia during the semester. That is a lot different from when I was in high school and the encyclopedia was my main source of information. Now I know more about where to find the information I am looking for, and I am better able to analyze the material.

From the faculty's point of view, the research journal helps transform the research process from a scavenger hunt for cursory information into an extensive, analytic, and reflective prewriting stage using sophisticated material that (once completed) enables the student to approach the drafting stage with a better sense of the subject and the various sides of the issue.

We were surprised by how easily all of our students were able to meet minimum-page requirements of six to eight pages per paper. Both students and faculty experienced frustration as we learned how to translate an ambitious vision into real-life classrooms. Implementation became as much an issue as the original design. Instructors have learned that the importance of the journals must be emphasized by dedicating time to the assignment: thinking through and drafting together in class an entry for two conflicting readings and then conferencing about or commenting on each student's first set of journals. We also saw a dramatic improvement in the quality of journals by requiring that they be handed in as each final paper is due, rather than in a batch in the final portfolio. As one team member put it, "'Upping' the academic standards was no easy task, yet I feel that even though this was a 'pilot' class, the victories both I and my students experienced made the struggle worthwhile."

Appendix

Research Journal Assignment

The Research Journal
This journal constitutes a large portion of your paper portfolio and a significant percent of your final grade (20%). The purpose of the journal is to (1) deepen your understanding of the topic as you proceed through your sources, (2) evaluate how reliable each source is, depending upon

its slant, and (3) enter into an ongoing conversation or debate about your historical event/issue. It will be separate from the pages or note cards on which you write down notes, ideas, direct quotes, etc.

Format of the Journal

At the top of the page beginning each entry, identify your source in correct MLA style. Then address the following questions in essay form (understanding that not all will be pertinent to each source).

Evaluating the Content

What did you learn from this source? (in general terms—this is not your note-taking venue)

What is the thesis or claim of this reading? Is there a perspective or slant that you can identify?

Does this source acknowledge opposing viewpoint(s)? Does it do so fairly?

Is this piece intended as an argument? Is it an effective one?

How does this information connect to or contradict other sources you are reading on this topic?

Are there sources cited in this reading that you would find useful? That you would distrust?

Other observations?

Evaluating the Rhetorical Setting (who is talking to whom)

Who is the author(s) and what is his/her expertise in the subject? (Note: If your source is written anonymously, what might that suggest? If it is a government document, what does that mean?)

What do you think is the motive or purpose of the author?

Who do you think is the intended readership/audience for this source? How does that affect its content and language?

How does the writer try to persuade readers (ethos? logos? pathos?). Other observations?

Concluding Entry in Your Journal (for each paper)

At the end of your journal for each specific paper assignment, address the following questions:

1. In general, how would you characterize the most difficult problem connected to researching this topic?

2. How would you characterize the sources connected to this topic (general quality, helpfulness, bias)?

3. What is the significance of the topic? Has your sense of the issue or problem become more complex as a result of your research? How?

4. Are there any types of sources or kinds of materials that you need and cannot find?

5. What else needs to be said about this topic? Do you feel prepared to add to this scholarly discussion?

Acknowledgment

The author would like to thank Glenn Blalock, Debra Dew, and Rich Haswell for their help.

Works Cited

Elbow, Peter. 1991. "Toward a Phenomenology of Freewriting." Pp. 189–213 in *Nothing Begins with N: New Investigations of Freewriting*, ed. Pat Belanoff, Peter Elbow, and Sheryl I. Fontaine. Carbondale: Southern Illinois University Press.

Fulwiler, Toby. 1982. "The Personal Connection: Journal Writing Across the Curriculum." Pp. 15–32 in *Language Connections: Writing and Reading Across the Curriculum*, ed. Toby Fulwiler and Art Young. Urbana, IL: National Council of Teachers of English.

Gannett, Cinthia. 1995. "The Stories of Our Lives Become Our Lives: Journals, Diaries, and Academic Discourse." Pp. 109–36 in *Feminine Principles and Women's Experience in American Composition and Rhetoric,* ed. Louise Wetherbee Phelps and Janet A. Emig. Pittsburgh: University of Pittsburgh Press.

Haas, Christina. 1994. "Learning to Read Biology: One Student's Rhetorical Development in College." *Written Communication* 11: 43–84.

Haswell, Richard H. 1993. "Student Self-Evaluation and Developmental Change." Pp. 83–100 in *Student Self-Evaluation: Fostering Reflective Learning,* ed. Jean MacGregor. San Francisco: Jossey-Bass.

Hays, Janice N., Kathleen M. Brandt, and Kathryn H. Chantry. 1988. "The Impact of Friendly and Hostile Audiences on the Argumentative Writing of High School and College Students." *Research in the Teaching of English* 22: 391–416.

Kegan, Robert. 1994. *In over Our Heads: The Mental Demands of Modern Life*. Cambridge, MA: Harvard University Press.

Lauer, Janice. 1970. "Heuristics and Composition." *College Composition and Communication* 21: 396–404.

Macrorie, Ken. 1980. *Searching Writing: A Contextbook*. Rochelle Park, NJ: Hayden.

Mezirow, Jack. 1990. *Fostering Critical Reflection in Adulthood: A Guide to Transformative and Emancipatory Learning.* San Francisco: Jossey-Bass.

Nelson, Nancy, and Robert C. Calfee, eds. 1998. *The Reading-Writing Connection.* 97th Yearbook of the NSSE. Chicago: National Society for the Study of Education.

CHAPTER TWENTY

Moving beyond "This is good" in Peer Response

PEGGY M. WOODS
University of Massachusetts Amherst

In any writing class that I teach—first-year writing, upper-level composition, creative writing workshops—I attempt to do what Wendy Bishop advocates in *Released into Language* (1990): I attempt to put writers into motion, to have the students in my class experience what "it feels like to be a writer, someone who generates, drafts, revises, shares, and publishes writing, someone who experiences blocks, anxiety, elation, and success" (40). I see the use of peer workshops in a writing class as a way to put student writers into motion, and, as a result, my students take their writing through several drafts and consistently share, respond, and provide feedback to one another's work in various configurations: pairs, small groups, and the class as a whole.

Similar to Karen Spear in *Sharing Writing* (1988) and Peter Elbow and Pat Belanoff in *A Community of Writers* (2000), I consider the use of peer workshops an important component in the writing process. Like Spear, I see the sharing of work in peer groups as a way to prolong invention, to encourage students to see their drafts not as finished products but rather as steps in the composing process (5). The responses and reactions they receive from their peers enable them to work through the steps of revision.

Like Elbow and Belanoff (2000), I feel that peer workshops give students a wider sense of audience, by providing them with a variety of readers and a range of responses, that is an important aspect of their growth and development as writers (508). I also see that peer workshops enable students to participate in the decision-making process that underlies all steps of the writing process. When students receive a variety of responses and reactions on a piece of writing, they need to make decisions about how to interpret, use, and reconcile all the feedback they receive.

Despite the benefits and the importance of using peer workshops in the classroom, however, they can be a struggle—a struggle to make productive and worthwhile for writers and responders alike. When it comes to peer responding, I have two objectives. First, I want the students to respond in a supportive and encouraging manner so that as writers they feel comfortable enough to take risks and chances in their work, to explore different forms, and to experiment with different rhetorical strategies. Writers grow and develop by expanding and pushing the boundaries of their writing, and they need a space that provides them the freedom to take risks and to fail. Second, I want peer responses to be effective in terms of revision by providing comments that do not correct but rather offer descriptive reactions to the text, questions that enable the writer to think about the piece in a new way, and options for revision.

Part of the struggle with peer workshops is that students come into the writing class having had limited experience with revision and feedback. Many students tend to consider their drafts as finished and have difficulty seeing revision as anything beyond editing for surface errors (Spear 24). Students also have limited experience as responders. They tend to see feedback as criticism or evaluation and their job as a responder as one of fixing and correcting the text (Spear 131). Students also tend to want to preserve the harmony in their group and in their class (Spear 25) and are hesitant to judge, feeling they do not have the authority to do so (Elbow and Belanoff 507). The intersection of all these factors results in student responses in peer workshops that alternate between two types. They either praise a draft they see as done—"I like it"; "This is good"—and circle typos and surface grammar errors, or they harshly criticize, tearing to shreds a draft they consider inadequate.

Spear, Elbow and Belanoff, and Bishop, as well as others, offer a variety of ways to establish and enact peer responding in the classroom. The particular exercise I describe here is meant to be used in conjunction with these and other methods of teaching peer response. It serves as a type of background exercise, one that helps lay the groundwork for others by making visible to students the types of responses that encourage revision and those that do not. This exercise enables students to recognize the importance of being specific as well as the importance of focusing on the text rather than making judgments about the writer.

I have also found this exercise helpful in enabling students to work through texts of published writers. Students tend to read and respond to published texts and student texts differently. I have found that students tend to be less generous with published texts, quick to harshly criticize a published writer they do not understand or agree with. Their harsh criticism and attacks on the writer prevent them from moving forward into understanding the text. When this happens, I have found it helpful to refer back to this exercise, to remind students not only to separate the writer from the text, but also to respond to the published writer as they would to one of their peers. If I ask them to respond to the published writer in the same way they have been working through their peer groups—by separating the writer from the text, by describing what they see in the text, and by asking questions—they have a way into the text, a way to begin to understand what the writer is saying.

Description of Activity

I have used this exercise in all kinds of undergraduate writing courses, including lower- and upper-division composition and creative writing. I have also found this exercise useful in courses and workshops that prepare new teachers for the writing classroom. I do the following exercise early in the semester, before we begin any kind of peer workshopping. Generally, the exercise and the discussion it leads into take an entire class period.

First I take the students through the following steps:

1. List three comments/responses you have ever received on a piece of writing.

2. List three comments/responses that if you ever received on a piece of writing you would be so discouraged you would never write

again. Be creative. These may or may not be comments you have ever actually received. Hopefully they are not.

3. List three comments/responses that if you ever received on a piece of writing you would be so encouraged you would keep writing forever. Again, be creative. And again, these may or may not be comments you have actually received. Hopefully they are.

4. Look over all the comments/responses on your list and rank them in terms of their effectiveness for revision—1 being the most effective for revision, 9 being the least.

Each of these steps raises different issues concerning the kinds of responses that can be given on a piece of writing. As a way to prompt a discussion on these issues, as a class we begin looking at the comments/responses the students have listed in each step of the exercise. Beginning with the first step, I ask each student to read one comment from his or her list out loud. I then ask if they see any similarities among the comments and if they can make any specific generalizations about them; this leads us into a discussion about the issues that emerge.

As we move through and discuss each step of the exercise, the following issues generally surface.

Responses/Comments Received on a Piece of Writing. The issues raised here generally have to do with what instructors' comments mean. Students usually list responses they have received in the past but are never quite sure what they mean exactly. Many students list things such as "awk." and "trans." and confess they have never known what these abbreviations stand for. We also discuss that although they may know what the teacher means by these kinds of comments, they are generally at a loss as to how to "fix" and/or "correct" the problem. As many students point out, if they had known the sentence was awkward sounding, they would not have written it that way. Students also list comments such as "nice" or "good" and discuss how they are never quite sure how to read these comments. As the discussion progresses, the students begin to see the need to be specific in their own comments and responses. If, for example, a sentence is "awk.," it is helpful to the writer to suggest how to rewrite the sentence.

Students also begin to see that one-word comments in the margin give writers very little information about the effectiveness of their piece.

Responses/Comments That Discourage. As we go around the room reading these comments out loud, students quickly see that comments such as "This looks like it was written by a first grader" and "My dog can write better than you" focus on and attack the writer and say little about the writing itself. Students also see that these comments are hurtful and highlight what is wrong with the writer rather than discussing what is going on in the text. This leads to a discussion on the importance of separating the writer from the text and staying focused on the piece itself. The students also begin to see that these comments are meant to be hurtful rather than encourage any type of revision.

Responses/Comments That Encourage. Although these comments tend to be full of praise (e.g., "You are a talented writer") and encouraging (e.g., "This should be published"), students quickly see that these comments also focus on the writer rather than on the writing. Students begin to understand that these are dead-end comments, comments that do not help or enable revision. The students acknowledge that they like to hear these kinds of comments and that there are points during the drafting process when they need to be encouraged in order to continue to write. They also acknowledge, however, that these types of responses do not provide them with any information or a sense of direction to help them revise their piece. This generally leads us into a discussion of the last step of the exercise.

Ranking in Terms of Effectiveness for Revision. In terms of effectiveness for revision, students rank responses such as "This is good" and "I like it" and "This stinks" near the bottom of their list. Students acknowledge that they want to be encouraged to keep writing, but they also need direction and guidance to help them revise. Generally, the discussion focuses on the value of descriptive and specific responses. Responses that describe what is happening in a piece, that raise questions about the issues or points in the piece, that explain how something is or is not working, and that suggest ways the piece could be developed are all effective comments because they give writers information about their writing.

Although the focus of this exercise is on the students in the role of responders, it is during this section of the exercise that the discussion begins to shift to how students use and interpret the feedback they receive. As we work our way through each step of the exercise, they begin to realize which kinds of responses they can discard and which kinds of comments they want to consider. Students realize, for example, that comments that do not deal with their writing can be discarded. They also realize there may be times when they need to ask their responder for more information. Students begin to see that if a responder tells them he or she likes something in the essay, it is helpful to know why the responder liked it. By recognizing the type of responses they need in order to revise their texts, students will enter their peer groups ready to take responsibility for their own feedback.

Some Reflections

I have found this exercise to be successful regardless of the specific teaching context. The issues that emerge always lead into a productive discussion on responding and the various ways in which feedback can be used. When student resistance occurs, it is usually at the second step, "Responses/Comments That Discourage." I have had students claim that *nothing* could ever prevent them from writing. As one student told me, "You would have to chop off my arms to keep me from writing!" These types of responses usually occur with two sorts of students: honors students and creative writing students who strongly identify themselves as writers. Their resistance can be traced to two factors: confidence and a sense of audience. Honors students and self-identified creative writers come into the writing classroom with a high level of confidence in their abilities. Generally, they are students who have in the past been recognized and rewarded as "good" writers. They already have a strong sense of their abilities and feel it would take more than one harsh comment to silence them from writing.

Although both groups of students have high confidence levels, their sense of audience differs and leads to two very different and interesting discussions. The creative writing students who strongly identify themselves as writers do not see themselves as writing for an audience. They tend to subscribe to a more romantic notion of writing and writers. They believe that all their writing comes from within, from some deep-down burning desire to express something. They see writing as something they *must do,* with little regard for audience. They write for themselves, and if they are misunderstood by their audience, they see that as a sign of genius. As one student told me when I explained that neither I nor anyone in his group could understand his essay, "No one understood James Joyce either." With the creative writers, this activity leads to a discussion about the importance of audience, centering on the following questions: Can you ever be completely free from audience? Can you ever write with a complete disregard for audience, particularly if you want to be published?

Whereas the creative writers strongly identify as writers and are completely invested in their words, the honors students tend toward the opposite reaction. Although they do not identify themselves as writers, they have a strong sense of writing for their audience—the teacher. Past experiences in the classroom have taught them that a successful piece of writing does what the teacher (audience) wants. They feel they could never be silenced or prevented from writing because they would just do what the audience demanded. This leads into an interesting discussion on how we identify audiences and what strategies we use to identify what audiences want to hear. This also, however, leads into a discussion concerning how to use feedback and how to be personally invested in our own writing.

When I have used this activity in teacher preparation courses, the results are different still. Although new teachers offer little resistance to the idea that comments can discourage writers, their discussion tends to focus on the ways *they* have been silenced and/or blocked from writing in the past. Teachers tend to list comments they have received, comments they were troubled by and/or that prevented them from writing. The discussion tends to focus on how they dealt with these comments, understood them, and worked through them in order to continue writing. This type of discussion often highlights new strategies we can offer our students to help them work through their own periods of being blocked.

Conclusion

Teachers generally accept the idea that responding to writing is something we need to teach our students. Responding to texts is not only a skill students need to develop but also an ongoing process in their development as writers. This exercise is one of the beginning steps in that process. I have found it useful to continually refer to this exercise throughout the semester as we work through other activities related to peer workshopping and as a way to remind students how we want to respond to texts. Since students tend to have limited experience as responders, they usually see themselves on the receiving end of responding. During the exercise, I find I must continually reinforce the new role of responder they will be assuming and make the connections for them between the issues we are discussing in class and their new role. This also provides opportunities to model responses I think are effective for revision.

For teachers, this exercise is useful for our own development as responders to writing. It enables us to check the effectiveness of our own comments and responses with the people who are reading and using our comments to revise their work. Periodically, some of my own responses and comments come back to haunt me as they surface in the class discussion and students rank them low on their list of effectiveness and/or discuss how they do not understand what they mean. In one class session, for example, a student included "This is fine" on his list of comments received. He began discussing how he was never sure how to read this comment. To him, *fine* was a word someone used when they could not think of anything better to say. Someone else in the class thought that the comment "This is fine" was a response a teacher gave when she did not really like the piece and that it was a nice way of saying, "This essay is really not very good." During this discussion, I began to realize this was a comment I had used frequently on papers and that although to me the comment "This is fine" was a way to begin responding and literally meant, "This is fine" or "This is good," the students were not reading it that way. I realized that since this was generally the first sentence of my response, the writers were reading the rest of my comments thinking their essays on the whole were not very good. As a result of this discussion, I stopped using "This is fine" as a way to begin my response.

As teachers we sometimes fall into a routine of responding, using the same stock phrases and saying the same kinds of things to every text. This exercise serves to make our routine visible to us and, through the class discussion, enables us to find alternative ways of responding. If done early in the semester, this exercise also enables us to gear our responses to the particular class we are teaching.

Works Cited

Bishop, Wendy. 1990. *Released into Language: Options for Teaching Creative Writing*. Urbana, IL: National Council of Teachers of English.

Elbow, Peter, and Pat Belanoff. 2000. *A Community of Writers: A Workshop Course in Writing*. 3rd ed. Boston: McGraw Hill.

Spear, Karen I. 1988. *Sharing Writing: Peer Response Groups in English Classes*. Portsmouth, NH: Boynton/Cook.

CHAPTER TWENTY-ONE

Critical Reading and Response: Experimenting with Anonymity in Draft Workshops

J. PAUL JOHNSON
Winona State University

The student body of Winona State University in Minnesota, a four-year undergraduate/master's-level institution delivering liberal arts, teaching, technical, and preprofessional programs, comprises primarily first-generation students who see college as job training. First-year students come to campus with a wide range of critical reading and writing abilities. Some, of course, were raised in literacy-rich environments and progressed through reading- and writing-intensive college preparatory courses; others had little more than the occasional interaction with the joys and demands of reading and writing. Nearly all, though, are subject to the prevailing cultural condition known as Minnesota Nice, which requires politeness in all exchanges, even at the expense of honesty or critique. As a result, students see their introductory college composition course as a place to hone skills and meet friends—not as a site of contested ideologies and certainly not as a workshop for conducting critical readings of their colleagues' writing. Despite those assumptions and expectations, like many instructors I expect students to critique their colleagues' arguments with both honesty and rigor. Here I wish to make a case for using the condition of anonymity as one means of encouraging accuracy and minimizing the social risks of student responses.

Some instructors of composition have expressed frustration with the lack of sophistication and rigor in peer response (e.g., Beaven 1977). But for the most part, the literature in the field suggests that the critical reading of colleagues' work is a crucial component of writing pedagogy. The effectiveness of peer response groups has been reported frequently (from Hillocks's 1986 metanalysis to Gere's 1987 *Writing Groups* to a series of studies cited in Nystrand and Brandt's "Response to Writing as a Context for Learning to Write" [1989]), and, if one can judge from its prominence in best-selling rhetorics, peer response is common in the classroom. Certainly, as Ede and Lunsford (1985) suggest, using peer response groups is an "effective way to introduce students to collaborative or group writing" (123). But even more important, the peer response activity I discuss here—*a directed draft workshop*—is one well grounded in contemporary composition theory: more focused than mere peer review, the draft workshop reinforces the social constructedness of writing. It provides student writers with diverse readers, reminding them that conventions, expectations, and support must inform successful writing.

In all peer-response activities, I expect my students to read one another's work carefully and critically, assess and evaluate the writer's approach, articulate possible alternatives, and, when the class content focuses on stylistic concerns, suggest experiments with the writer's prose. It took me a long time to learn to read students' work well, however, and I can't expect my first-year college students—who may be asked to read one another's work critically for the first time in their academic careers—to critique effortlessly and purposefully without guidance. Simply put, successful peer response requires preparation and practice.

The workshop assignment for students is simple: (1) log on to the course Web site, (2) post drafts for others' critique, (3) write and post (using pseudonyms) critiques of two colleagues' drafts, and (4) read and reflect on the comments received. Yet the activity takes place in a richer context of discourse than that brief description allows. Again, to be able to craft purposeful critiques, students must be taught and guided in the practice. I've found that anonymous critique yields consistently thoughtful—and trusted—response.

Well in advance of each workshop, I guide students in a whole class activity through a rigorous critique of at least one draft (either from my own files or from a current student volunteer). Each student writes out a set of notes in response to ten questions about the writer's work, questions that range from their affective response to more narrowly posed concerns about the piece's organization, cues, focus, style, evidence/detail, and rhetorical appeals. What I aim for here is careful *evaluation* in the sense Peter Elbow (1993) uses the word: not a simple "good" or "bad" but critical distinctions about the work's features (194). I focus primarily on the writer's intent, rhetoric, and evidence, and I require considerable response in full-sentence discourse (as opposed to mere "yes," "no," or "good"); furthermore, in these sessions I link the concerns of the class to the analysis of the draft and allow the writer to contribute at least one or two questions of his or her own making.

Devoting an entire class period to such a "practice court" session helps accomplish a number of objectives. First, students have the opportunity to practice the critique without pressure. These class sessions often raise difficult questions about "best phrasings" for their concerns. (For instance, when the reader finds all the evidence in an argument anecdotal, what should one say? Simply that?) Second, the devotion of class time helps underscore the importance of the work; in other words, given the emphasis in class, students are less likely to devalue the workshop itself as something peripheral to their own concerns. Third, the session allows me to acknowledge the complexity of writing purposeful critiques while providing a model of response that is critical yet polite, evaluative yet purposeful. To assume that any group of students will know how to do so without guidance or preparation is foolhardy, and the practice helps students prepare for the work of the workshop itself.

Once students are practiced in the craft of critique, and once they have completed drafts of their own to post, they are ready for the workshop. One can arrange the system of who responds to whom in any number of ways, but I prefer a simple draw of straws, partly to preserve the condition of anonymity in students' response. Students post their drafts under their own names—so that they are obligated to provide a good-faith critique—but the critiques are posted under pseudonyms that I provide students. Each student keeps a pseudonym, an "alter ego," for the duration of the course; only the student and I know the pseudonym.

Although one might question the validity of critiques written under such unusual circumstances, the use of pseudonyms proves

particularly useful in a number of ways. In particular, the pseudonyms allow my students to write their critiques "more objec-
tively," as my students say, as they are less concerned with building
or maintaining social relationships and more concerned with simply providing an accurate critique. Why not, one might then
wonder, simply have students post without names at all? Without some way of knowing who wrote which critique, it would be
impossible to credit individual students for their purposeful participation in the workshop; more important, it would be impossible to critique individual students' efforts. But the pseudonyms
seem to have other effects as well: writing under a name encourages some consistency in their response, as well as providing an
identity for the writers to respond to if and when they have questions about some portion of the critique. The workshop forum
allows the writer to reply to the respondent and the respondent,
again, to the writer.

After the workshop has been completed, it's important to
guide students in interpreting the critiques as well. I typically set
aside class time for assessing the results. During this session, I'll
assess the content and quality of the responses, displaying some
particularly strong (and, if necessary, some notoriously poor) critiques. Students address problems specific to their individual
projects, summarizing the critiques of their writing and creating
an "action plan" for their revisions; finally, when they submit
those revisions, they reflect on the value of the workshops. For
students, then, the workshop is an activity carefully woven into
the fabric of the course and their own writing. More often than
not, students credit the workshop critiques with providing a clear
sense of how their work is read. Even if the activity yields little
change in the presentation version of the paper itself, the critical
thinking workout of writing and considering responses is itself
invaluable.

A rich thread of scholarship—in particular, Anson's *Writing
and Response* (1989) and Straub and Lunsford's *Twelve Readers
Reading* (1995)—exists to inform practice in responding to student writing. Unfortunately, just as an instructor's response can
be determined by any number of contextual factors (Anson, 1999;
White, 1998), peer response too can be sidetracked by all kinds
of phenomena tangential to the writing itself: grade anxieties,

social relationships, undue competitiveness, and so forth. More than anything else, I've seen students work at being (Minnesota) nice in their workshops—consoling, encouraging, cheerleading their colleagues rather than critiquing their writing, no matter the state of the work in progress. When that happens, student writers miss out on what a good workshop can provide them. Well-written response not only provides the writer with a broader perspective on his or her own piece, one that demonstrates how the same argument or narrative might be reshaped, rethought, or retooled, but it also introduces the respondent to a wider range of responses to the project assignment, in the process sharpening critical thinking skills and honing the ability to read others' work critically and well. The draft workshop can become some of the course's most important work.

At its best, an anonymous draft workshop, guided and executed carefully, will focus critiques on the logic and rhetoric of the writers' work. Nearly to a person, my students tell me that their anonymity proves helpful when writing their responses. "I wasn't worried about what they thought about me or whether they liked what I had to say," says one; "I know I was more critical than I would have been if the workshops weren't anonymous," says another. The following excerpted post, from "Mary Morrison," suggests the focus of the critiques. Rather than merely encouraging or consoling, the critique provides a close, critical reading of the writer's work.

Re: Analysis
From: Mary Morrison
Date: 12/7/99
Time: 6:06:46 PM
Remote Name: 199.17.159.18

Comments

1. After reading your analysis, I agree that sexual harassment in schools is widely overlooked. However, I disagree that what is sexual harassment is completely determined by the "victim." There is an actual line separating what is and isn't sexual harassment, and everybody should be aware of

it, so as not to be too quick to prosecute the offender. The most authoritative statement is the survey taken by the American Association of University Women Educational Foundation, because it shows how widespread the problem is, and how such a great number of kids are affected. Any other reader would probably agree with me. The least authoritative statement is definitely when you disagree with Nan Stein, because you show how authoritative Stein is, give a quote, and then disagree with the quote without giving any evidence supporting your disagreement. Readers would find that least authoritative also, because the opposing side to your argument is presented with more evidence than your side.

2. The fact that the subject exists is supported well, but the fact that it is worth consideration is very shaky. You should get rid of the two sources that actually go against what you are trying to argue, 'cause they don't help at all. Also, it would be very good to show the effects that sexual harassment has on the students—this would show its worth. You provide examples, which makes it interesting, but more facts and statistics would be more convincing. To start the analysis, I would put the "pants pulling" incident from Our Guys at the beginning.

3. From what I understand, you are writing about how sexual harassment is common in many schools, and widely overlooked. The thesis is "Sexual harassment in schools is anything but a forgotten crime. However, it is one of the most widely accepted and overlooked crimes that is plaguing school systems across the United States." What seems weird is that you state it as being widely accepted—sure, people might not do much about the problem, but I don't think it is ACCEPTED, and you don't give any proof that it is accepted. I would delete that word. I think the thesis should be given its own paragraph with other sentences supporting it—that would tell the readers what, exactly, you are analyzing. *(Ed. note: Points 4–9 of the critique are deleted for space considerations.)*

I won't suggest that this critique couldn't have been written without the condition of anonymity. In fact, readers might be surprised by its matter-of-factness, its focus on the writer's claims and evidence. The comments don't display any features that loudly announce their anonymous nature—in fact, few do. But, in essence, that's exactly what I'd hoped for in conditioning the anonymity: that student responses would be focused entirely on the writer's work and not on the various social relationships at play.

As important, the anonymity proves particularly helpful not only for students critiquing the writers' work, but also, and especially, as the writers themselves read the critiques: "I wasn't able to dislike the readers for their comments; I just focused on their ideas and tried to use them to make my papers better," says one student. In fact, the anonymity nearly forced writers to consider the critiques more carefully: "Because I didn't know who wrote the critique, I couldn't just think 'Oh, it's him, he doesn't know what he's talking about,' or 'Oh, she's so smart, I better do everything she suggests.' [The anonymity] made me think more about what the critiques were saying and whether or not I should take their advice," says another.

Because it is certainly possible to imagine implementing a pseudonymous exchange of papers in the classroom followed by written comments, Luddites and technophobes might wonder why such a workshop should be conducted online. After all, although most college students in the twenty-first century have come to view Internet access as a basic right (not unlike library privileges), not all instructors have the technical prowess or institutional support to create an interactive forum. Other instructors' institutions may not be in the midst of a sweeping "universal access" technology initiative, as mine currently is, but there are nonetheless a few advantages to conducting the workshop online for any instructor to consider. First, the public nature of the forum tends to discourage most halfhearted efforts: lackluster posts are on display, next to the strongest of efforts, plainly visible to students and instructor alike. Second, the workshop is accessible to students from a number of locations at home and across campus, a feature that seems to appeal to most students today. And last, the electronic text composed and posted by students has a clear virtue: samples of students' work from the workshop can be displayed, either by printing out transparencies, copying and pasting, or using a Web browser for projection in class. Showing samples of thoughtful critiques or complex dilemmas helps reinforce the value of students' efforts.

For those instructors who value and wish to teach critical response in an oral setting, not unlike the creative writers' model or the exchange idealized in the 1988 Wordshop Productions video *Student Writing Groups: Demonstrating the Process,* working so hard to create and maintain anonymity in written student response may seem counterintuitive. The mere condition of anonymity, even if carefully constructed and protected, is no panacea for a poorly motivated student, a poorly designed assignment, or a poorly orchestrated workshop. In general, the better students are taught to read one another's work, and the more apparent the rewards of their work, the more likely they are to read and respond to one another purposefully. So whether or not the workshop is conducted anonymously, the activity is still subject to the same kinds of concerns as any response to student writing, which we know to be determined by an array of contextual factors. It's even possible that the condition of anonymity itself might precipitate an undue focus on the respondent's identity that wouldn't appear in a face-to-face workshop (although that hasn't been the case in my experience).

Anonymity, then, is hardly protection from all that might misdirect peer review. But even the editorial practices of our field's best journals depend on blind review to ensure an impartial, multiperspectival critique. Whatever one might lose in terms of oral, face-to-face communication, the advantages seem clear, especially when considering that critical reading is something we must *teach,* not merely *expect,* in the composition classroom. Indeed, avoiding the distractions of interpersonal relationships and irrelevant commentary; having a record of what was said; being able to follow up on questions or concerns; providing practice in writing; and focusing student work on the logic and rhetoric of writing—and in a complex and purposeful rhetorical situation at that—go a long way toward helping students learn the kinds of critical reading strategies we envision when we design our courses and curricula.

Works Cited

Anson, Chris, ed. 1989. *Writing and Response: Theory, Practice, and Research*. Urbana, IL: National Council of Teachers of English.

————. 1999. "Reflective Reading: Developing Thoughtful Ways to Respond to Students' Writing." Pp. 302–24 in *Evaluating Writing: The Role of Teachers' Knowledge about Text, Learning, and Culture*, ed. Charles R. Cooper and Lee Odell. Urbana, IL: National Council of Teachers of English.

Beaven, Mary H. 1977. "Individualized Goal Setting, Self-Evaluation, and Peer Evaluation." Pp. 135–56 in *Evaluating Writing: Describing, Measuring, Judging*, edited by Charles R. Cooper and Lee Odell. Urbana, IL: National Council of Teachers of English.

Ede, Lisa, and Andrea Lunsford. 1985. "Let Them Write—Together." *English Quarterly* 18: 119–27.

Elbow, Peter. 1993. "Ranking, Evaluating, and Liking: Sorting Out Three Forms of Judgment." *College English* 55: 187–206.

Gere, Anne Ruggles. 1987. *Writing Groups: History, Theory, and Implications*. Carbondale: Southern Illinois University Press.

Hillocks, George Jr. 1986. *Research on Written Composition: New Directions for Teaching*. Urbana, IL: National Council of Teachers of English.

Nystrand, Martin, and Deborah Brandt. 1989. "Response to Writing as a Context for Learning to Write." Pp. 209–30 in *Writing and Response: Theory, Practice, and Research,* ed. Chris M. Anson. Urbana, IL: National Council of Teachers of English.

Straub, Richard, and Ronald Lunsford. 1995. *Twelve Readers Reading: Responding to College Student Writing*. Cresskill, NJ: Hampton Press.

White, Edward M. 1998. *Teaching and Assessing Writing: Recent Advances in Understanding, Evaluating, and Improving Student Performance*. 2nd ed. Portland, ME: Calendar Islands.

Wordshop Productions. 1988. *Student Writing Groups: Demonstrating the Process* [videocassette]. Tacoma, WA: Wordshop.

CHAPTER TWENTY-TWO

Steal This Assignment: The Radical Revision

WENDY BISHOP

Florida State University

Recently, an anonymous reviewer of a well-known composition journal pointed out that most editors were wary of providing their readership with examples of heroic teaching stories of the "try it: it works" variety. When I talk about radical revision, I tell just that type of story because I believe that every time we enter writing classrooms we want them to "work." And anyway, I'm not the hero of this tale—the radical revision assignment is; it's a "something old, something new, something borrowed, something blue" kind of endeavor and one that I have used regularly, in every class, every year, for some time now. By elaborating on what it is and how it works, I'm writing to urge you to try it too.

In fact, this assignment has been borrowed and adapted more often than any other teaching assignment I've designed in a fairly full teaching life. I realized this when I discovered the degree to which it had spread through a writing program after I used it in a graduate-level writing teacher education course. The radical revision so quickly made its way into new teachers' courses that I began explicitly to present it to others as something worth trying, something bigger than the sum of its parts (see Korn [1997] for a discussion of how she adapted the assignment). I believe the radical revision was adopted by teachers—those coming from our literature, creative writing, and composition tracks at Florida State University—because any large-scale writing program constrains both teachers and writers, and they naturally struggle with and against those constraints. The radical revision assignment provides a location for doing this productively.

Of necessity, a large writing program must create some form of common curriculum (usually by outlining program goals and then suggesting common textbooks and assignments). When a program like ours—comprising over one hundred GTAs and adjuncts teaching over two hundred sections of first-year writing each term—works to develop continuity, a certain homogenization takes place. And that's reasonable: the writing program director and staff should be able to describe and explain the curriculum to upper administrators, new teachers should have support and guidance as they begin teaching, and students comparing notes about classes they have enrolled in should feel that roughly the same sort of work is required of them, section by section.

At the same time, these teachers and their students are varied and individual; at best, they are writers and teachers of writers in the act of forming smaller, productive writing communities within the larger program community. They need to examine and understand conventions *and* they need space to challenge constraints. The radical revision assignment allows for—in fact insists on— exploration but does so while respecting the backbone of program work: essay writing as usual. I think the radical revision has been adopted so readily and regularly by teachers because it is an investigative exercise that enlarges the status quo.

Here's how the radical revision assignment works, more or less. For the final paper of the term, I ask writers in my classrooms (first-year through graduate) to take an earlier class essay (or story or poem) and revise that text by their choice of a variety of means (which we discuss) to the point that the new, revised text is so different from the original that it may be near failing. In order to investigate revision as a generative process, writers are encouraged to take their text and systematically stretch it to the limit, to push the composing envelope, to challenge their writing to come apart at the seams (but then again, maybe not; maybe to truly re-vision it in a way that produces work that is much more interesting and engaging in this new incarnation). Then, the author writes the story of what he or she learned during this revision process, and this story takes the form of a meta-essay (letter or narrative) that accompanies the student's end-of-term presentation to peers of the radical revision project (text and/or performance).

The exercise includes something old (some trace of the original text); something new (the revision direction—a new genre, media, on- or off-paper format, concept, etc.); something borrowed (the exercise itself represents a borrowing, an amalgam of my own stylistic investigations leavened with work on grammars of style [Weathers 1990]; provocative revision [Fulwiler 1992]; feminist revision [Bridwell-Bowles 1992]; rhetorical analysis [Davis 2000]; and multigenre writing [Davis and Shadle 2000; Johnson and Moneysmith 2001; Romano 1995]); and something blue, in the sense of creating in the author a sense of melancholy appreciation for the challenges of innovation on that occasion when the original text seems preferable to the revision.

Radical revision is both an assignment and a teaching and learning location. It succeeds because it is fun: just saying the words wakes up a few students. It allows rule following and rule breaking to make more sense because the assignment requires that writing conventions be placed in dialogue with experimental pressures on those conventions. It teaches writing as a writer experiences it. Most of us realize that practicing writers thrive on the tensions created by trying to predict *and* to challenge readers' expectations. The radical revision assignment enacts that realization, explores it.

Enough claims. Here's a review of the assignment sequence I currently follow. Together as a class, we list fifty ways to radically revise on the board, borrowing—after I share some terms in handouts—from Winston Weathers's (1990) grammars A and B (crots, labyrinthine sentences, collage and montage) and from Lillian Bridwell-Bowles's (1992) diverse discourses (personal/emotional writing, breaking the boundaries of textual space, language play, and so on). Additional group brainstorming results in lists that usually look something like this:

> change point of view or time of day
>
> talk from another character's point of view
>
> interweave types of texts

go off the text by using other media (painting and collage)

insert photographs and illustrations

write on shoes or clothes

create bumper stickers

collaborate, sing a song together, etc.

We define radical as *radical for the writer*. Once, for instance, I was convinced that writing a five-paragraph theme would prove radical and challenging to a student. It did. And it did for me too when I followed him and tried the experiment for myself (see Olsen et al. 1999). Radical, remember, equals personally defined: outrageous to complicated, simple to scary to satisfying, failing to frustrating to generating (leading some portfolio-invested writers to "radically revise" additional earlier papers [even papers from other classes], and leading a writer with a developing writer's identity to self-promise to work on a recalcitrant text over the summer, to really get it right). Next, writers outline the project, asking, What is my self-challenge? Which paper will I revise? What is my time line? (that is, what are the demands of the project, including the learning curve for changing media, conducting further research, and so on?).

After reviewing the course schedule, writers set up a personal drafting time line (I begin discussions on the project two-thirds of the way into the term). Drafts and/or progress reports are brought to class at least twice. Group members brainstorm ways to enhance the project and ways to proceed in order to discover possible problems. Students are encouraged to keep asking one another, What is the thread of connection to your original text? What do you expect to learn as a writer about writing in the course of this project? On the last day of class, as final portfolios are turned in (along with the narrative essay on the radical revision project), writers share their radical revisions in any way they choose. Each class member is given five minutes.

What do the products of this assignment look like? They are varied and difficult to reproduce in a limited space, but I can give a sense of them. After reading about grammar B, John wrote his second paper, an experimental meditation on spaces that provide him with unusual sanctuaries (part of a city storm drain, an abandoned silo, a rural bridge over the Sopchoppy River, and an opening in the base of a huge cypress tree). Influenced by Weathers's (1990) discussion, John incorporated rough line drawings in his essay and used crots (space-separated prose segments) and fragments effectively. The day we responded to John's essay draft, our workshop was transformed: arguments arose over the verities of English grammar, but most of us praised the piece (a later revision won a department writing award). John's draft became a touchstone for discussions throughout the rest of the term. Here is a section from the rough draft, which was also illustrated with a line drawing:

> Downtown, there is a narrow corridor—a crack in reality—a rat tunnel. It is a space that leads to nowhere, and back out. It is tight and compromising; a P.V.C. pipe, slippery from the trickle of sludge running through and around it, is difficult footing. I think of walking on a warm, dank vein. Tingles of adrenaline surge along my spinal cord. I inhale the stench, sweetly fecal. There is a faded, crumpled, cigarette pack—some broken glass. This is not virgin space. The corridor opens to a chamber, ten feet by six feet, there is room to stretch and sit down.

Matthew's radical revision of his initial "How I Write" essay turned into a song titled "Keep Me Moving Along." Here's the opening of Matthew's original essay "The Natural Pretension of Writing":

> Pay attention to me! You think I write for my health? Well, maybe I do write for myself, but I mainly write for you. Whoever you are: Mr. disgruntled teenager, Little Miss dreamer. I have a lot of things to say. I might not be Will Shakespeare or Virginia Woolf, but that doesn't matter. I write so that I can release some energy and get other people to listen to my thoughts.

Here's the beginning of the song:

Keep Me Moving Along (lyric sheet)

Well I've to get on back to my baby
I've been gone and she's been worrying on
I been stuck in my bedroom
and these feelings make me write this song
    Chorus:
Feelings
Feelings
These feelings keep me moving along
(followed by five more stanzas).

These very brief excerpts also don't capture our initial discussion about Matthew's essay (many classmates urged him to write a more honest, less pretentious draft) nor Matthew's final class performance, in which he sang the song while accompanying himself on acoustic guitar, getting the entire class to sing along and also providing me with a tape and lyric sheet—a multimedia performance. Matthew: talking, singing, performing, exploring.

Clearly, radical revisions are more and less successful as standalone products, but they are almost universally successful as writer-invested investigations about composing. They represent carnival plus the day after: celebration tempered with analysis. Because the assignment represents a reflective practice, it is safe from the "doesn't this mean anything goes?" critique. Anything doesn't go. Something goes and then that something is studied, evaluated, and learned from. This happens because these revisions generally take place near the end of a term during which writing students have been composing together in a workshop environment to improve all student drafts. It works at this point in the term because we've also created a climate of trust by sharing papers and drafts and because we've already explored revision exercises that have something in common with radical revision. That is, *revision has been emphasized as a way to create more meaning in a text.*

For instance, after students complete their first full draft of the term and receive some form of peer response, I ask them to write either a fat draft or a memory draft for that paper before the next class. For a fat draft, they're required to double the size of their draft (good for those who haven't yet generated enough text to play with it productively). For a memory draft, I ask writers to read a text, set it aside, and write a new text of approximately the same length. The memory draft allows salient points to come to the surface and receive more attention. Both revision exercises give a hint of what is to come in the radical revision assignment (see Ostrom, Bishop, and Haake 2001).

End-of-term placement of the radical revision is important because it allows a writer to choose earlier work to revise; that is, I encourage them to choose a paper they have some distance from. In a normal term, we write four or five papers. Since I assign the topic of the first paper—a literacy autobiography—some students are willing to dismantle this paper more readily than they are a paper topic of their own choosing or a paper they've finished so recently they feel it's in flux. This might keep the radical changes they are about to make from being and feeling as radical as they do when using an early—retired—paper. Using an early paper can make the process less painful for the overinvested-in-final-text-as-final-text student and more visible for the new-to-or-resistant-to-ideas-of-revision student.

Overall, the radical revision is productive for writers because it allows for the pairing of the experiment with a narration of the experiment, which allows this sort of risky writing to take place in a nonevaluative space (necessary for the student) and also for the learning to be evaluated by means of the accompanying writer's narrative (necessary for the student and the teacher). No risk; no learning. But if we think our risks (or mistakes) will be graded, we'll notch them down from risky attempts to reasonable attempts. And most writing insights don't occur in the land of reasonable attempts. Teachers, too, don't want to evaluate or grade difficult products, yet they learn from helping their students learn from such products. I *can* evaluate or grade the narrative of a first-year writing dance student who sets sentences from her literacy autobiography to music in a voice-over and then performs the dance of that autobiography for the entire class in the university gym. I don't want to rank the dance: I want to talk about its composition with other writers.

I was going to end with some more do's and don'ts; a discussion of what can fail and what can work; a last exhortation or two. But I'll resist and leave you instead with the list of works cited, which may provide you with ideas for elaborating on the basic assignment I've shared here. Now it's your turn. Steal the radical revision. Make it yours.

Works Cited

Bridwell-Bowles, Lillian. 1992. "Discourse and Diversity: Experimental Writing within the Academy." *College Composition and Communication* 43: 349–68.

Davis, Robert, and Mark Shadle. 2000. "'Building a Mystery': Alternative Research Writing and the Academic Act of Seeking." *College Composition and Communication* 51: 417–46.

Fulwiler, Toby. 1992. "Provocative Revision." *The Writing Center Journal* 12: 190–204.

Johnson, Cheryl L., and Jayne A. Moneysmith. 2001. "Multigenre Research: Inquiring Voices." Pp. 178–92 in *The Subject Is Research: Processes and Practices,* ed. Wendy Bishop and Pavel Zemliansky. Portsmouth, NH: Boynton/Cook.

Korn, Kim Haimes. 1997. "Distorting the Mirror: Radical Revision and Writers' Shifting Perspectives." Pp. 88–96 in *Elements of Alternate Style: Essays on Writing and Revision,* ed. Wendy Bishop. Portsmouth, NH: Boynton/Cook.

Olsen, Scott W., Dawn Marano, Douglas Carlson, and Wendy Bishop. 1999. *When We Say We're Home: A Quartet of Place and Memory.* Salt Lake City: University of Utah Press.

Ostrom, Hans, Wendy Bishop, and Katherine Haake. 2001. "The Fat Draft and the Memory Draft: When Energy Runs Out." Pp. 156–58 in *Metro: Journeys in Writing Creatively.* New York: Longman.

Romano, Tom. 1995. "The Multigenre Research Paper: Melding Fact, Interpretation, and Imagination." Pp. 109–30 in *Writing with Passion: Life Stories, Multiple Genres.* Portsmouth, NH: Boynton/Cook.

Weathers, Winston. 1990. "Grammars of Style: New Options in Composition." Pp. 200–214 in *Rhetoric and Composition: A Sourcebook for Teachers and Writers,* ed. Richard L. Graves. 3rd ed. Portsmouth, NH: Boynton/Cook.

CHAPTER TWENTY-THREE

Getting Textual: Teaching Students to Proofread and Edit

BRIAN HUOT

University of Louisville

Donald Murray once said that the greatest compliment you can give a writer is to edit her or his text. I begin with this concept because, while this essay focuses on teaching students to proofread and edit, it should be understood from the beginning that students need to learn how to polish their prose within a rich understanding of the process of writing. Before proofreading and editing, students should have already written and rewritten, invented, had their texts responded to, and if possible "re-seen" what it is they want to say and how they want to say it. I say all of this not because most writing teachers haven't already heard it, but because it's an important principle to remember as students, disciplinary faculty, administrators, politicians, testers, and parents often see good writing as that which approximates the prestige dialect of American Edited English. There is, then, a fairly constant pressure on the writing teacher to emphasize correctness. This essay is intended to help teachers focus this pressure in productive ways for their composition students. The practices I describe have been adapted from many sources, some within the field of composition, some from language arts and teacher education, and some from ESL classrooms. Over the last twenty years, I have used all of these with varying degrees of success, depending on individual students and contexts.

In addition to my assumptions about the need to contextualize any instruction on language conventions, I should share a few other assumptions that guide me as a writing teacher and in writing about proofreading and editing. First of all, as Joseph Williams (1981), Elaine Lees (1987), Bruce Horner (1992), Min-Zhan

Lu (1994), Charles Coleman (1997), and many others have demonstrated, error in student writing is a complex issue. Marilyn Sternglass (1997) showed us in the up to six years she followed some CUNY basic writers that students whose home and community dialects and literacies are far removed from the dialects and literacies favored in colleges and universities can take some time to be able to produce "error-free prose." Another assumption I hold is that all language use is rule governed, so editing and proofreading are not about not being lazy or not making mistakes. As Charles Coleman (1997) points out, it can be counterproductive to talk to students about sentence boundaries or subject-verb agreement if their grammatical orientations do not include those ways of working with language. My final important assumption is that teaching students grammatical structures outside the context of their own writing is pointless. As Patrick Hartwell (1985) illustrated over fifteen years ago, there is no evidence that knowledge about grammar translates into the ability to write grammatically. A more recent study by Ellen Barton, Ellen Halter, Nancy McGee, and Lisa McNeilley (1998) demonstrates that teachers themselves have trouble deciding what they mean by an awkward sentence, and while it is possible to read the conclusions of their study as recommending the teaching of some language structures, it is difficult to ascertain which structures or how they should be taught.

On the other hand, many students lack even the slightest rudiments of a systematic approach to proofreading and editing. Ask most first-year college students what their system is for proofreading and editing, and they will either look at you with a puzzled expression or they will say something about glancing over their work after they finish writing. I believe that one of the reasons many students do not edit and proofread very well is because they have had little formal instruction. This is probably due to two main factors: first, grammar exercises and instruction and corrections of student writing often substitute for any attention to proofreading and editing; second, because current-traditional rhetoric often emphasized correctness over everything else, new approaches to teaching often failed to provide enough support to help students produce polished prose. On the upside, because students have so little experience and instruction in proofreading and editing, it is often possible to help them make big strides with a little real attention to learning how to proofread and edit their writing systematically.

As I detail a set of practices for helping students "get textual" and learn how to proofread and edit their own texts, I proceed from practices that are less interventive to those that require the instructor to work one on one with a particular student. My reasoning is that activities involving an entire classroom may allow many students to learn how to proofread and edit their texts. If certain students do not catch on, then an instructor can go on to more focused activities that require working specifically with particular students. These one-on-one procedures are also appropriate for tutorial or writing center conferences and don't necessarily require that students work with their composition teacher.

Getting Textual

Write It Out

Many times students exhibit error in their writing because they have not written much prior to the months in which they enroll in a writing course. Students often don't write much during the summer, and many high school courses focus on writing in the earlier part of the year, so it's possible that first-year writing students working on their initial assignment in a first-year writing course are producing prose for the first time in several months. In my writing classes, I have students write regularly for three different purposes. One, students write responses (usually a half-page if typed) for each reading assignment. This kind of assignment encourages students to do their homework, and, unlike quizzes, responses give students much-needed practice in writing. Two, students write a set number of pages in a journal each week. Three, students work on formal writing assignments that go through multiple drafts and peer review. I find that having students write so much in an introductory writing class often allows them to write themselves out of many problems they may initially have with language conventions. A few years ago I taught a section of first-year writing in which three or four students who might normally have been placed into a developmental writing course were slotted into my section with students who had been determined ready for first-year college writing. To this day, I am not sure who the mainstreamed students were, though if I had to guess, I would assume one of them was a student whose first few journal entries and reactions were especially weak in terms of language conventions. By the end of the semester, however, her work was indistinguishable from the writing of several other students in the course. She had written herself out of the problems that distinguished her writing from others in the class. So the first thing I do to help students learn to proofread and edit is nothing at all, except provide them with an opportunity to practice their writing. I know this may sound like harebrained advice, and I certainly thought so the first time I heard it, but I have found over the years that it is a waste of time to pounce on errors students make early in the semester because there is a good possibility they will no longer make those errors if we have them write a lot and leave them alone.

Responding with Correctness

Joy Kreeft Peyton and Jana Staton (1993) were involved in a series of research studies of native and second-language users, supported by the Center for Applied Linguistics in the 1980s, in which they looked at dialogue journals, a procedure in which the teacher and student conduct a conversation on paper. One of the features they observed was that instead of correcting the students' problems with language conventions, the teacher would respond in a note to the student using similar language but following the conventions of American Edited English. The student might say, for example, "Me and my friend went to the movies and shared a large popcorn." To which the teacher would respond, "When my friend and I go to the movies, we always get butter on our popcorn. What about you?" I have adapted this technique in responding to my students in a variety of contexts, and it appears to work quite well. As I said earlier, I don't usually do anything when I encounter students' problems with language conventions early in the semester, but after a while, if I continue to see that a student is struggling, I'll begin to reply to her or him,

being careful to use the same language convention more appropriately in my responses, usually out in the margin next to the
student's text. Oftentimes, students seem to pick up on the appropriate form and need no other help. I remember a student
who used to write "have went" for "have gone." We were well
into the middle of the semester, and he was still doing it. I decided that every time I saw this in his writing, I would model
"have gone." By the end of the semester, he seemed to have gotten it, and I no longer saw "have went." You can take my word
that this actually works well or you can check out Kreeft Peyton
and Staton's (1993) book, in which they claim that students who
receive such responses end up producing prose with fewer errors
than those who receive traditional grammar instruction, even if
English is the student's second language.

Talking and Nudging

In his 1980 Braddock Award–winning essay "The Study of Error," David Bartholomae describes working with a writer who
produced a text full of problems with approximating the language conventions of academic discourse. When Bartholomae's
student read his essay, he articulated far fewer errors than did his
written text. Of course, this is not news for any of us who have
worked with students whose texts appear much more problematic than their readings of their texts. Years ago, when I worked
at an open admissions school and taught basic writing and pre–
basic writing classes, it was not uncommon for me to have an
entire class of students whose ACT verbal scores were in the single
digits. In this context, I first developed the procedure in which
students worked in pairs and read their texts aloud for each other.
The listening student not only heard the oral version but also
silently read along with the author. Each time the author devi-
ated from the text, the listening student nudged the author to
make her or him go back to the spot in the text where she or he
had read something different from what was written.

Bartholomae theorizes that students often have a more highly
developed notion of oral language than they do of the written
code. This activity helps students understand that they know much
more than they think they know about producing error-free prose

and that with help they can learn to identify the problems in their texts and offer alternatives that work better. This activity also illustrates that writers who have trouble producing acceptable academic prose don't necessarily need to be taught the rules, but perhaps they need some help like a nudge in recognizing that they don't always produce the language conventions they actually do know. Noam Chomsky (1965) introduced the twin concepts of competence and performance to explain this phenomenon. At any rate, having students read their writing for each other, reminding each other when their reading deviates from their texts, is a good way to help students become more aware of what they write and how to learn to proofread their own work. This is also a useful practice because it allows a whole class of students to work with one another on proofreading and editing without having to depend on the teacher. I first used this technique when I taught a pre–basic writing center course for students who needed additional help in passing basic writing. It seemed to work especially well for these students, though I did have one incident of two football players bouncing off each other's chests, since the nudging part seemed so familiar to them.

The Editorial Board

I found this idea in Dan Kirby and Tom Liner's classic text for secondary school teachers, *Inside Out: Developmental Strategies for Teaching Writing* (1988). Kirby and Liner suggest setting up an editorial board to edit and proofread student writing. Their suggestions include grouping some of the best proofreaders and editors with some of the least proficient, since it is a great learning experience to be on the board. An editorial board can be used in several different ways, depending on your classroom and the way in which the course is organized. If students are producing a set of formal papers they must take through the entire writing process, then it might be appropriate to set up an editorial board for each paper. If evaluation occurs only at the end of a course using portfolios, then perhaps there could be an entire class session set up for one or more editorial boards. For those classes employing a workshop approach in which students choose topics and work at their own pace, then perhaps the editorial board could be invoked as needed. Classes that organize students into groups that produce zines or other publications could act as their own editorial boards or switch writing with other groups. I have used editorial boards in all of these ways and find that they work well, giving students with less knowledge about language conventions a strong context within to learn.

However a writing course is organized, there are ways to structure editorial boards. They not only are flexible, but they also furnish students with autonomy and real reasons for focusing on language conventions. Several years ago a friend of mine worked on writing with middle school students from the I Have a Dream Program in which selected students are promised a full ride in college if they complete high school graduation and college admission requirements. The task facing these middle school students was to produce on computer (this was in the late 1980s) a newsletter that could be shared with a German *gymnasium* class. The initial version of the newsletter contained many lapses from American Edited English, which the middle schoolers initially said was fine with them. Once the students realized that their instructor planned to send the newsletter just as it was to Germany, however, students volunteered an ad hoc editorial board so that "kids in Germany wouldn't think kids in Indianapolis are stupid." As this story illustrates, the editorial board is a good way to help students organize their efforts to learn proofreading and editing.

Working with Individuals

So far most of the procedures I have suggested involve working with students in groups within the context of responding to student writing or in the course of having students practice their way out of the need for extensive proofreading and editing. It's important to note that what I next suggest should be used only once the other methods have proved unsuccessful. Although the methods I propose have been quite successful even with students who have learning disabilities and need to produce error-free prose for proficiency examinations, it may be that it will take some writers years to be able to successfully proofread and edit their own texts. It's important to explore other avenues first because working individually with students is labor-intensive for both instructor and student. Such attention also detracts from time that could be spent on other aspects of a student's writing, so it's important to make sure that individual attention is necessary. Writing center and other tutorial contexts are perfect environments for working with students individually on their proofreading and editing.

The first step involves having students compile an inventory of the language convention problems most frequently found in their texts. Sometimes this is something students can do on their own, and sometimes it's necessary for the instructor or tutor to help the student. Once the instructor or tutor has a good sense of what the student's problems are, then it is possible to prioritize what language conventions are most important. Remember, one of the main things instruction in proofreading and editing should give the student is a systematic approach to proofreading and editing. One problem with more traditional approaches to correctness is that students are often inadvertently given the message that they have to work on everything at once.

Once the teacher and student have prioritized the list, the instructor should ask the student why she made the choices she did in the text. The instructor should help the student with a nonjargon, no-frills version of how to correct the specific problem. If a student is having a problem with sentence boundaries, for example, the instructor should find out what the student thinks a sentence is made up of and how the student would correctly punctuate it. Sometimes it is enough to make the student aware that each time a subject and verb appear, certain steps must be followed: "Once you note a subject and verb combination, you should either (1) place a period, (2) insert a comma with *and, but, for, so,* or *yet,* or (3) place a semicolon with an optional *however, therefore, moreover,* or *nonetheless.*" Of course, I am simplifying here; it is impossible for me to write exactly what a specific student will need to know, since this can only come from an examination of the student's text and explanation of what she or he now does.

Once a student has compiled a list of the language conventions he most needs to focus on, he should be instructed to read his paper once all the way through for each of the proofreading and editing problems he wants to focus on. Although it's probably okay to focus on four or five, at the most, I suggest limiting the number as much as possible because it is time-consuming and taxing for a student to read his paper each time for each problem. Focusing on one or two problems not only makes it easier for students, but it also allows them to make more rapid progress. Once students see that they can indeed proofread and edit their own writing, they are motivated to continue the laborious effort required to produce correct prose. One of my greatest successes in using this method came when I was tutoring a student in a writing center to pass the university's writing competency exam. This student had failed the test four times. He was dyslexic and could have petitioned to be given a venue other than the timed essay to demonstrate his proficiency as a writer. But he thought he was smart enough to pass the exam like everyone else. I agreed with him, and we worked on a number of practice exams for which he used his list in timed conditions; eventually he was able to complete all of his composing process, including his proofreading and editing, in the allotted time. He passed the exam on his next try.

Conclusion

The practices and activities described here and the theories that inform them should be helpful for teachers and students working on proofreading and editing. Certainly, no other aspect of learning to write is as stressful and debilitating for students and teachers. While some of what I propose might seem easy or simplistic, all of these activities take much effort from both students and teachers. It's also important to remember that, like writing itself, proofreading and editing is a process that takes time, effort, feedback, and patience. All one has to do is recall the pervasiveness of errors in published texts to understand what a complex task it is to ask students to produce several errorless papers in a single semester. On the other hand, I have seen students who had trouble producing a single comprehensible, literate message learn to write intelligent and insightful prose. You and your students should find much value in these ideas and in the practices they engender.

Works Cited

Bartholomae, David. 1980. "The Study of Error." *College Composition and Communication* 31: 253–69.

Barton, Ellen, Ellen Halter, Nancy McGee, and Lisa McNeilley. 1998. "The Awkward Problem of Awkward Sentences." *Written Communication* 15: 69–98.

Chomsky, Noam. 1965. *Aspects of the Theory of Syntax.* Cambridge, MA: MIT Press.

Coleman, Charles. 1997. "Our Students Write with Accents." *College Composition and Communication* 48: 486–500.

Hartwell, Patrick. 1985. "Grammar, Grammars, and the Teaching of Grammar." *College English* 47: 105–27.

Horner, Bruce. 1992. "Rethinking the 'Sociality' of Error: Teaching Editing as Negotiation." *Rhetoric Review* 11: 172-99.

Kirby, Dan, and Tom Liner, with Ruth Vinz. 1988. *Inside Out: Developmental Strategies for Teaching Writing.* 2nd ed. Portsmouth, NH: Boynton/Cook.

Lees, Elaine. 1987. "Proofreading as Reading, Errors as Embarrassments." Pp. 216–30 in *A Sourcebook for Basic Writing Teachers,* ed. Theresa Enos. New York: Random House.

Lu, Min-Zhan. 1994. "Professing Multiculturalism: The Politics of Style in the Contact Zone." *College Composition and Communication* 45: 442–58.

Peyton, Joy Kreeft, and Jana Staton. 1993. *Dialogue Journals in the Multilingual Classroom: Building Language Fluency and Writing Skills through Written Interaction.* Norwood, NJ: Ablex.

Sternglass, Marilyn. 1997. *Time to Know Them: A Longitudinal Study of Writing and Learning at the College Level.* Mahwah, NJ: Lawrence Erlbaum.

Williams, Joseph. 1981. "The Phenomenology of Error." *College Composition and Communication* 32: 152–68.

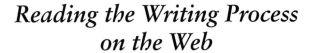

CHAPTER TWENTY-FOUR

Reading the Writing Process on the Web

JANICE MCINTIRE-STRASBURG
Saint Louis University

In his discussion of the limitations of process theory, Gary Olson (1999) stresses that the most integral of these limitations is that "process theorists assume that we can somehow make statements about the process that would apply to all or most writing situations" (7). The limitation then is an essentialist one—the assumption that one writing process exists and can be codified into a single set of "rules" instructors can impart to their students, thereby offering them the magical key that will open the door to better writing. The magic key is what our students want, and on some level it is also what we as writing instructors want. This narrower application of process, however, oversimplifies the complex cognitive work we know as writing and shortchanges our students' development as writers and thinkers. Generalizing process across situations marginalizes process theory's most promising pedagogical implications as espoused by James Moffett and Peter Elbow: the parallel processes of writing and the personal development of writers as empowered thinkers and speakers (Couture 1999, 34). As a worst case, such generalizing reduces Montaigne's definition of the essay as exploration to a boilerplate conception of personal expression. None of us really wants the five-paragraph essay, but without careful structuring, a course in writing that emphasizes process can achieve just that sort of reductionism.

This problem resonates in my experience as a teacher of first-year composition at Saint Louis University. SLU is a Roman Catholic, Jesuit university of about ten thousand students. The profile of first-year students indicates that 33 percent of our students come from the top 10 percent of their high school graduating class, and that 91 percent of them were at least in the top 50 percent. Statistically, SLU students might be classified as the "best and brightest" of high school graduates. Yet many of these "good" students arrive at the university as inexperienced writers unable to look reflexively at their writing, assess it, or articulate their own personal process of writing. Like most/all of my colleagues, I stress process in my first-year composition courses, offering the students ample opportunities and strategies for prewriting, drafting, and revision. Because of my emphasis, and because they have been taught various versions of "writing process" throughout their schooling, my students are often unwilling to identify their own writing process as anything different from "the" textbook process. One of my better writing students once sheepishly confided that she always wrote her essays the night before they were due. She seemed embarrassed by the fact that she was not following the prescribed process. When I suggested to her that although she sat down to write the night before, perhaps she had been thinking about the paper and planning it in her head all week, it was as if a lightbulb exploded over her head. She replaced her fear that she wasn't following the correct process with the knowledge that she had her own process; it just wasn't the one boxed off and numbered in the text.

That student's relief in being able to articulate a process for herself is one of the reasons I ask my students to write a one-page "process essay" at the close of each assignment during the semester. I ask them to assess their writing process for that particular assignment; and with the assumption that hindsight is 20/20, I ask them to tell me what particular problems they encountered, how they solved them, what worked well for them, and what they might do differently if they had the assignment to do over again. The object of this exercise is to force the students to think self-reflexively about their own individual processes of writing. Early in the semester, students typically resist this assignment. The braver ones accuse me of giving them busywork; the less brave respond in a minimal paragraph to the effect that "I didn't do anything special, I just wrote it." But as the semester wears on and they see that I am serious, most students slowly begin to use this writing space as a place to think on paper, analyzing their particular strengths and weaknesses as writers, and to recognize that each assignment poses different problems and demands, different strategies for writing and revising.

I chose this approach to reflect James Moffett's concern in *Teaching the Universe of Discourse* (1968) that writing reflects a writer's personal development, generates thought, and enables agency. Each student takes control of her or his own writing by recognizing and engaging with the individual process and making it work for him or her. It also attunes students to their own idiosyncratic "juju" of writing, which Peter Elbow (1981) calls "the magical view of language" (358). The fact that they need absolute quiet or blasting rock 'n roll; a comfortable chair, a library kiosk, or the great outdoors; pencil and pad or computer console to summon up the combination of language that generates powerful writing—these physio-mental processes that take place inside them enable them to grow as writers.

Within this context, I choose reading assignments that highlight writing as "thinking on paper." Students read Donald Murray's (1999) "The Maker's Eye," incorporating his idea of the "zero draft." The first draft, what Murray calls the zero draft, rather than being the finished product, is merely the starting point—something to work with. I follow this up with Kurt Vonnegut's (1999) "How to Write with Style" and Maxine Hairston's (1997) "What Happens When People Write," both of which stress considerations of audience in composing and revising writing. Both readings showcase the fact that no one writes in a vacuum and that the best writers revise with the audience's needs, desires, and tastes in mind. Coupling the readings with peer response sessions, students come to the (often jarring) realization that what they've said on paper can convey an entirely different (and often wholly unintended) message to a group of readers.

I've set an elaborate stage here because my overall approach to writing is integral to the capstone assignment for my first-year writers. At the end of the semester, they have compiled a number of writing assignments of varying lengths and purposes. They have written one- to two-page responses to their reading assignments (about eighteen total), three four- to six-page research essays on three different general topics (which vary by semester), and peer responses (both given and received), in addition to their process essays for all major assignments. I ask them to cull these writing assignments and put together a Web portfolio. Specifically, the collection should summarize their entry-level writing process; demonstrate changes they have incorporated over the semester to improve their writing; assess their current achievements, highlighting problem areas that they recognize as still needing work; and, finally, suggest some strategies for improving these areas in future writing projects. They are encouraged to include rough drafts as well as "finished" products and to include peer/instructor responses where applicable in their assessments.

The Web portfolio is a modification of the traditional portfolio of student work, but the hypertext medium offers some decided advantages over the hard-copy version. The first is that the nature of hypertext as a medium of expression repositions the student as writer and reader; the nonlinear properties of hypertextual narrative broaden the mode of expression available. Creating this "new" writing situation encourages them to look at writing from a fresh perspective, one that must take into account entirely different reading strategies and organizations. Theoretically, the reading of hypertext is endlessly recursive, continually building a structure and then modifying it as readers navigate varying paths (Douglas 1994, 161). In this sense, it mirrors the recursiveness of the writing process, with each revision generating changes in thought and expression. Hypertext also places an additional burden on the writer to create a clear, concise organizational "path" through the pages. While the general organizational strategies for writing hypertext are not so different from good writing in a printed format, the construction of electronic "pages" that are clear and self-contained are more easily recognizable to students precisely because of their visual nature.

Another important aspect of the Web portfolio is that considerations of audience are more obviously essential to successful Web writing. John Morkes and Jakob Nielsen draw three main content-oriented conclusions from their work in hypertext design and reading. First, users of the Web do not read a Web page per se. They scan the text, trying to pick out sentences or parts of sentences that will give them the information they need. Second, they prefer the text to be short and to the point, so writers need to hone and winnow, emphasizing word choices that are concrete, vivid, and precise. And finally, readers detest anything on a Web page that seems like "marketing fluff" or smacks of overly hyped language (1997, 1; see also Nielsen 1997a, 1997b). Thus, writers for the Web cannot afford to fall back on those long-winded and overgeneralized phrases that less experienced writers use while trying to decide what they really want to say.

Finally, the flexibility of the hypertext portfolio allows for a multiplicity of expression that is absent (at least in our students' minds) in traditional text. By incorporating elements of image, sound, graphics, and color, students literally build concrete expressions of personality and voice into their texts. The "published" document has a finished, professional look, and the document's availability on the Web allows all members of the class to view it and offer feedback. This opportunity for a wider audience has been key for my students in opening their work to critique from the class as a whole, rather than depending on me as the instructor to pass judgment on the final version. Although peer responding sessions and group projects give them a glimpse of varying reader responses to their work, I find that they still tend to fall back on my reactions as more central to revising strategies. In general, they distrust the reactions of fellow students, privileging "teacher's comments" only. With the Web project, students seem to get a clearer sense that their peers are the final arbiters of effectiveness: the evaluation is no longer a private one between instructor and student. Instead, students tend to see the Web as a space outside the traditional academic world, and they feel more confident in their ability to "write for" this medium.

A Web project of this nature is necessarily complicated, and its success or failure is dependent on the focus of the course as a whole. It involves creating a Web document with some depth, a clear idea of purpose, and careful attention to the mechanics of organization and outlining to obtain the desired effect. Assessing themselves as writers and researchers is a difficult task for students. Unless they can become adept at self-conscious assessment of their writing, they will not have the necessary perspective for cohesive purpose. Successful completion of this assignment demands an awareness of the underpinnings of their writing process

—identification of what they are doing right (and wrong)—and the ability to invent strategies to capitalize on their strengths as writers while minimizing or eliminating weaknesses.

The homepage itself offers students a firsthand look at the benefits of outlining and organization. The index page should demonstrate a clear controlling purpose and be organized with an eye to guiding readers quickly and efficiently through the document. Related topics need to be linked in a cohesive manner for ease of navigation, and the page should also include a summary of the writer's conclusions that take into account all of the individual Web links, interlinking where necessary to supply readers with additional navigational tools for reference. In short, the homepage should contain all of the same kinds of information, coherence, and documentation in the form of links to particular essays students have written as any well-conceived traditional essay. The object of the writing is the same, but the medium forces the writer to look at the actual construction in novel ways.

This project requires some technological expertise on the part of both students and instructor. Creating a detailed Web page demands either a knowledge of HTML coding, access to Web publishing software, or access to one of the newer word processors. Rather than try to teach my students HTML, I opt to use FrontPage, Microsoft's Web publisher. Its format is nearly identical to Word, and thus students who are fairly adept at using any word-processing program need only minimal instruction to use it. Since I run a Macintosh lab, my version is 1.0, a bit less elaborate than the newest version, but certainly adequate for our needs. The project, from start to uploaded finish, takes about three weeks. The students spend the first two weeks planning and writing and the last week critiquing, revising, and uploading to the WebCT course I set up at the beginning of the semester. The WebCT course tool allows them to publish their work but avoids privacy issues since only members of the class have access to the pages.

The advantages become almost immediately obvious as the students use their ability to add backgrounds, graphics, and images to customize their portfolios. One student in my class created a jungle safari theme and carried it through the pages of the document as a symbolic representation of her journey through

the semester. Another chose a brick wall background to emphasize his attempt throughout his writing to build a solid foundation for each essay. One chose a circus ringmaster image, and yet
another capitalized on his penchant for self-deprecating humor
by creating "The Will Wide Web Proudly Presents . . . The Do's
and Don'ts of Writing Essays," using his own experiences as a
caution to other first-year composition students. In each case,
the student had the opportunity to personalize her or his project
to reflect personality and voice in novel ways. The project encouraged them to "metaphorize" their experience and allowed
them to demonstrate their individual imaginations and creativity.

Students' critiques during the peer response week demonstrate a clear understanding of the principle strengths of Web
writing. Typical comments praise individual creative efforts while
still identifying problem areas such as an insufficient number or
idiosyncratic placement of navigational links, an important problem in organizational cohesion that transfers directly to
transitioning in more traditional print essays. Many use the Web
pages of others to recognize shortcomings in their own pages,
such as, "Your return links made your page much easier to read;
I should revise my pages to include those." In addition, although
one or two of my students had written personal homepages before the course, none had attempted Web writing as elaborate as
the assignment calls for. Since this kind of writing project is new
to all of them, everyone begins at ground zero; as a result, I see
more and better critical review than is typical in first-year composition peer responding.

A project of this nature can only work as the culmination of
an overall semester-long commitment on the part of both instructor and students to exploring writing as an individual process
unique to each student and writing situation. It also involves some
technological challenges; however, where the burden of technology threatens to overtake the emphasis on writing, I shift that
burden to myself as the instructor to minimize student frustrations. These problems are few, though; most have to do with the
mechanics of uploading. I believe that what my students gain in
terms of insight into their writing and its effect on readers more
than compensates for a few mechanical difficulties that are relatively easy to overcome. I have constructed my own Web portfolio

along with students, focusing it on my controlling purpose for the course, which they also critique and compare with what they believed they have accomplished.

Our "final examination" for the semester is to view the Web pages as a whole and discuss our achievements, shortcomings, and plans for future writing projects. In addition to whatever specific changes my students make to improve their writing, they gain a coherent vision of themselves as writers and a plan for future development beyond their first-year writing experience.

Works Cited

Couture, Barbara. 1999. "Modeling and Emulating: Rethinking Agency in the Writing Process." Pp. 30–48 in *Post-Process Theory: Beyond the Writing-Process Paradigm,* ed. Thomas Kent. Carbondale: Southern Illinois University Press.

Douglas, J. Yellowlees. 1994. "How Do I Stop This Thing? Closure and Indeterminacy in Interactive Narratives." Pp. 159–88 in *Hyper/Text/Theory,* ed. George P. Landow. Baltimore: Johns Hopkins University Press.

Elbow, Peter. 1981. *Writing with Power: Techniques for Mastering the Writing Process.* New York: Oxford University Press.

Hairston, Maxine. 1997. "What Happens When People Write." Pp. 39–44 in *Language Awareness: Essays for College Writers,* ed. Paul A. Eschholz, Alfred F. Rosa, and Virginia P. Clark. 7th ed. New York: St. Martin's Press.

Moffett, James. 1968. *Teaching the Universe of Discourse.* Boston: Houghton.

Morkes, John, and Jakob Nielsen. 1997. "Concise, SCANNABLE, and Objective: How to Write for the Web." Online. Accessed 2 February 2000. <http://www.useit.com/papers/webwriting/writing.html.>

Murray, Donald A. 1999. "The Maker's Eye: Revising Your Own Manuscript." Pp. 76–80 in *The Pocket Reader,* ed. David Munger. New York: Addison Wesley Longman.

Nielsen, Jakob. 1997. "How Users Read on the Web." Online. Accessed 2 February 2000. <http://www.useit.com/alertbox/9710a.html.>

————. 1997. "Top Ten Mistakes of Web Management." Online. Accessed 2 February 2000. <http://www.useit.com/alertbox/9706b.html>.

Olson, Gary A. 1999. "Toward a Post-Process Composition: Abandoning the Rhetoric of Assertion." Pp. 7–15 in *Post-Process Theory: Beyond the Writing-Process Paradigm*, ed. Thomas Kent. Carbondale: Southern Illinois University Press.

Vonnegut, Kurt. 1999. "How to Write with Style." Pp. 137–40 in *The Pocket Reader*, ed. David Munger. New York: Addison Wesley Longman.

Teacher Response and Assessment

CHAPTER TWENTY-FIVE

Taking Out the Guesswork: Using Checklists in the Composition Classroom

LEE NICKOSON-MASSEY
University of Illinois at Urbana-Champaign

Teaching Context

I have taught first-year composition for the last three years in the Academic Writing Program (AWP) at the University of Illinois at Urbana-Champaign. AWP is a program designed specifically for first-year students who need additional attention to their writing. The AWP classroom is designed to promote close interaction between students and instructors and therefore is capped at sixteen students. The University of Illinois is a Research I institution with a student population of approximately 37,000 (28,000 undergraduates and 9,000 graduate students). Over 90 percent of the university's student population are Illinois residents, most of whom live in the Chicago suburbs.

The majority of my students are likely to come from either Chicago's inner city, one of Illinois's many small rural communities, or one of many foreign countries in which English is not the primary language. And as the university offers over 150 programs of study, the students I encounter represent a wide range of educational experiences and interests. Significantly, although they may come from very different communities and have very different academic experiences and goals, my students articulate the same feelings of insecurity about their abilities as writers.

I structure every course I teach around portfolios in an effort to create a space in which writing is approached as a process and attention to revision is privileged. I try to be as explicit as possible when I introduce each assignment; I make sure to thoughtfully review with the class not only the instructions for the assignment, but also the purpose for and my expectations of the assignment. These practices may seem obvious concerns for any instructor, but I have found that, especially with new and/or developing writers, making goals, requirements, and expectations public is central to promoting a learning environment in which students feel (more) certain of the multiple subject positions we ask them to occupy. Lisa Delpit (1988) adeptly articulates the importance of making accessible the criteria by which we evaluate our students when she argues that members of a given culture "transmit information to co-members" and that if one is not "already a participant in the culture of power, being told explicitly the rules of that culture makes acquiring power easier" (282). I believe this concept to be at the center of learning.

In an effort to create a space in which students actively participate in the making of knowledge, I require students to continually draft and revisit (revise) between five to seven three-page essays throughout the semester before submitting their writing portfolio for a final grade at the close of the semester. Students understand that the portfolio grade counts for 60 percent of their final course grades (with daily assignments and participation constituting the remaining 40 percent).

Approach: Implementing Collaboratively Produced Checklists

Assessing writing—the task of assigning a letter grade to our students' writing—is often the most overwhelming and frightening task we as instructors are asked to perform. I use the verb *perform* here intentionally, because when we assess, I think, we often feel least like ourselves. We are actors, playing the role of the teacher who knows exactly what "good" writing is—knows how to teach it, identify it, and respond to students' writing with steadfast rigor. While most of us receive training in many areas of course design and assignment development and feel as though we are perhaps better prepared teachers as a result, the teachers with whom I work (from new graduate student instructors to tenured professors) continue to describe feelings of isolation, confusion, and even despair when talking about assessment practices. How do we grade student writing in ways that are constructive, consistent, fair, and meaningful to students?

This question evokes another, equally challenging problem we face as college writing instructors. We must try to respond to student writing in such a way that students both understand and appreciate what we are saying to them so that they have an idea of how they might revise their work in light of our comments and those of others. In doing so, since assessment is no longer universally held to be an exclusively top-down, teacher-to-student practice, we must simultaneously create an environment in which students respond to and assess one another's writing meaningfully. I have tried, with some success, to meet this challenge by including in my pedagogy explicit attention to assessment vocabulary and practices in the form of a semester-long sequence of activities, the culmination of which is a collaboratively designed checklist that students draft (by first brainstorming by themselves, then working in small groups, and, last, working as a class); implement (when responding to subsequent peer revision drafts); critically reflect on (in their final reflective introduction to the portfolio); and revise into a final portfolio checklist—a set of criteria, or standards, used to assess their writing. The students know that I will then use their checklist to evaluate the portfolios at the close of the semester.

Our work begins the first day of class with a discussion of the students' thoughts on and experiences with writing and writing assessment. Students repeatedly express frustration over seemingly arbitrary grades and unhelpful, incomprehensible, or even, at times, hurtful comments. I then ask them to list what they perceive to be their strengths as writers, and I write their responses on the board. The class meeting ends with students drafting a statement of goals they would like to achieve over the course of the semester, focusing on particular things about their writing they would like to improve. Students unfailingly write of their need to improve spelling, grammar, and punctuation; following that are comments about a need to learn how to organize and develop their essays. A few students in each class will also narrate problems with "getting started" or "ending." My goal for this activity is simply to begin a critical conversation about the vocabulary we use when we talk about writing, as well as about what constitutes "good" writing.

We resume this conversation often throughout the semester. At the time their first drafts are due (usually at the end of the second week of the semester), I distribute copies of a checklist I use as a complement to the marginalia and end comments I provide in response to student drafts. (See Appendix A for a copy of the response checklist.) The checklist is based on the concerns I generally find myself highlighting when responding to student essays. Class time is devoted to discussing the various points listed on the checklist and the place each criterion inhabits on the hierarchy of standards listed. Students usually ask a few general questions about the response checklist on reviewing it but do not posit many queries about the significance of the particular points listed. Students have asked, for example, how closely I follow the checklist, but they usually do not question what is listed. They appear to accept the checklist as it is.

Both the students and I then use the response checklist as a standard to guide comments until the twelfth week of the semester, when we turn our attention to assembling and revising the portfolios. By this time, students have drafted several essays, received multiple peer and teacher comments, and become intimately familiar with the checklist. Before they begin final revision work for their portfolio, I ask the students to use their experiences with the checklist to reflect on its effectiveness. This is an opportunity for the class to introduce revisions to the checklist before engaging in end-of-the-semester peer response and revision and before submitting the portfolio for a grade. This activity does more than provide students with the opportunity to reflect on their strengths as writers and to have those strengths reflected on the checklist. It is also the point when students start to realize the slipperiness and depth of terms such as *clarity, audience awareness,* and *voice.* That is, while the language of the checklist typically does not change that much, what students understand that language to mean has; their comments and questions illustrate a much more complex understanding of the terminology associated with writing assessment. This is what I believe makes the process worthwhile: students have taken on the responsibility of being accountable for the standards by which they will be assessed.

I introduce the collaboratively drafted, student-generated checklist by asking the students to review the lists of what they had initially said determined "good" writing. I then ask students to draft a "working" checklist for the following class meeting. I divide students into small groups the next time we meet and ask them to use the individual checklists each has drafted to develop one checklist for the group. Each group then writes their checklist on the board, and, as a class, we talk through all of them, discussing the merits, implications, and possible disadvantages of each point. Eventually (often after a series of debates), the students create a new checklist, one that I then critique and ultimately agree is an effective means of assessment. (See Appendix B for a sample collaboratively drafted student checklist.) Interestingly, I have never had to require any additions to or revisions of the final collaboratively drafted checklist. In fact, I have found that students do not want their checklist seen as "easier" or "less professional" than one an instructor would provide, and they work hard to create a checklist they feel is tough yet fair. Though the student-drafted checklists consistently contain fewer subdivisions than the response draft I distribute earlier in the semester, each still includes attention to the same general content and format concerns that I present them with earlier.

What begins as explicit attention to assessment ends as a fundamental contribution to the broad classroom goal of "learning to write." I have come to agree with the notion that assessment does not have to be thought of as an experience distinct from a student's learning experience. Learning does not have to end so that assessment can begin: assessment can instead become a valuable component of a student's learning process (Huot 1996, 550). And, as a result of the students' engagement with assessment vocabulary and standards, I find that my own confidence that I know what I am assessing (and that students know what I am assessing) is sound, and the idea of assigning final grades seems much less arbitrary.

Theoretical Rationale

The term *assessment,* as I use it here, denotes a process-based dialogue between the writer and herself or himself, the writer's peers, and the instructor in which the participants articulate a well-supported critique of a given text. Assessment practices may be formal or informal, and assessment information can be gleaned without tests. Assessment does not always include comparing or ranking students, or assigning a fixed letter grade to a text (Ruth and Murphy 1988).

Incorporating explicit attention to assessment practices into the teaching of writing presents assessment as an invitation to response dialogue rather than as an evaluative or punitive measure that can actually hinder a student's performance. Grant Wiggins (1994) argues that testing encourages students to think only of and write only for the test, whereas assessing writing (if done properly) encourages the writer to consider her or his work in larger contexts. Wiggins's critique of testing makes explicit the need for students to feel invested in the writing we ask them to produce. Wiggins further argues that teachers must conceive of assessment as something that should "improve" rather than "audit" performance. Teachers, then, need to explore ways in which assessment may "do the best job of teaching students about how writing works" (129). By foregrounding assessment as part of the writing process, students learn to practice assessment methods—self, peer, and instructor response—as a means of further developing their writing skills. By teaching students the vocabulary of assessment, having them participate in the formation of classroom assessment criteria, and developing the questions they ask when discussing their own work or that of their peers, the teacher encourages students to perform assessment practices they feel are most effective. By engaging in discussions with students about assessment and having them write reflective pieces on the responses they both give and receive as members of the writing class, the teacher establishes a classroom in which learning about assessment practices is integrated into the students' learning experience.

We know that feedback often plays an essential role in the writing process. Critical feedback offers writers the opportunity to revisit their work, to enter into a conversation with another person about it. And while I agree with Peter Elbow's claim that multiple-trait scoring gives students "substantial" feedback and that that feedback can be helpful to students (1996, 132), I believe that currently we do not make the most effective use of the benefits such response comments provide. Introducing assessment methods (i.e., vocabulary, criteria, and hierarchy of criteria) early in the semester as part of the writing process allows students to participate in assessment practices themselves. And by practicing methods of assessment themselves, students gain a better understanding of (1) the criteria by which their work will be assessed and (2) how they can further develop their writing to meet those criteria.

Appendix A

Essay Response Checklist

The following aspects of this paper tend to detract from its effectiveness. Please note that the aspects are listed in roughly descending order of importance: thus the elements listed first here have probably affected the grade more heavily than the elements at the end of the list. See also the marginal comments I've written on the paper for specific suggestions or notes. Note also: I may not mark all errors; after I have marked several errors of one kind, I will often stop marking them.

If you were to revise this paper, I would suggest working on the following elements:

___ Amount of support:
    ___ adding more quotations from the text(s) being examined in order to demonstrate the arguments
    ___ adding more research (if assignment calls for research)

___ Use of outside material:
    ___ reducing "dumped" quotes
    ___ improving grammar when incorporating quotations into sentences
    ___ fair identification of source material (quotes or paraphrase)

___ Clarity of content
___ Amount of analysis

___ Focus (thesis) of essay
___ Thesis statement
___ Depth of content

___ Length of paper, by adding either more sections or more detail to existing sections

___ Opening paragraph
___ Concluding paragraph

___ Organization (structure) of paper
___ Effectiveness of paragraph structures
___ Transitions between ideas or between paragraphs

___ Style-varying lengths and patterns of sentences
___ Style-varying methods of incorporating quotations into sentences
___ Reducing "clutter" or "fat" in sentences
___ Incorporating more precise/clear wording or sentences
___ Incorporating fresh word choices

___ Grammar. Specifically: ___comma splices; ___fragments; ___subject-verb agreement; ___pronoun agreement; ___mixed or illogical constructions; ___dangling modifiers; ___faulty parallelism; ___fused (run-on) sentences; ___other:

___ Mechanics. Specifically: ___commas; ___semicolons and/or colons; ___ apostrophe errors; ___spelling; ___quotation marks; ___other:

___ Documentation: Specifically: ___Works Cited; ___in-text citations; —correct form/placement/punctuation

Appendix B

Collaboratively Drafted Portfolio Checklist

♦ *Revision:* Author's work shows reflection on ideas posed by (1) peers, (2) teacher, and (3) the author him/herself.

♦ *Goal:* Author's goal is clearly stated and subsequently met.

♦ *Audience:* Author's audience is clear. Discussion is written for that audience.

♦ *Development:* Author develops his/her ideas well (clearly). Author provides support for his/her ideas through sources appropriate to the paper:

___ documented sources

___ personal experience

___ interviews

◆ *Organization:* Author's ideas "flow" easily. The author includes a thesis statement in which s/he introduces the topic of the discussion and states his/her purpose for writing the essay. Author writes strong, coherent introduction and conclusion paragraphs that complement each other. Title accurately reflects the content of the essay.

◆ *Style:* Author uses an appropriate tone and level of formality. The author is thoughtful about word choice—no "made-up" words. Author uses proper grammar, spelling, and punctuation. Author follows MLA guidelines.

Works Cited

Delpit, Lisa. 1988. "The Silenced Dialogue: Power and Pedagogy in Educating Other People's Children." *Harvard Educational Review* 58: 280–98.

Elbow, Peter. 1996. "Writing Assessment: Do It Better, Do It Less." Pp. 120–34 in *Assessment of Writing: Politics, Policies, Practices,* ed. Edward M. White, William D. Lutz, and Sandra Kamusikiri. New York: Modern Language Association.

Huot, Brian. 1996. "Toward a New Theory of Writing Assessment." *College Composition and Communication* 47: 549–66.

Ruth, Leo, and Sandra Murphy. 1988. *Designing Writing Tasks for the Assessment of Writing.* Norwood, NJ: Ablex.

Wiggins, Grant. 1994. "The Constant Danger of Sacrificing Validity to Reliability: Making Writing Assessment Serve Writers." *Assessing Writing* 1: 129–39.

CHAPTER TWENTY-SIX

Awakening the Writer's Identity through Conferences

KATE FREELAND

Indiana University–Purdue University Fort Wayne

Afte four years of *teaching* basic writing at a four-year, community-based university, I gave up. I quit teaching. I abandoned my authoritative, traditional blackboard pedagogy and began using writing conferences to redefine myself as a collaborative writer working in a community of writers: basic student writers. The result is revealed in the words of one student writer in last semester's evaluations: "I got to know other writers and did not feel ashamed if I made mistakes that all writers make. Mostly, I enjoyed having Ms. Freeland as my writing friend."

Now each semester I teach less and my students learn more. I cancel ten or more class days to provide time for approximately five fifteen- to twenty-minute conferences. As a result of this one-on-one time, my students are no longer victims of "bleeding drafts" that immobilize them through lack of confidence and dread of writing. Over the last four semesters, I have come to love my job, and my students are generally surprised by their writing potential—and that they don't hate to write.

Since graduate school, I had used conferences with my first-year composition classes. Names such as Janet Emig, Thomas Carnicelli, Peter Elbow, and Donald Murray were headliners in my graduate rhetoric and composition courses, so I knew that writing conferences should be an aspect of my pedagogy for basic writing courses. When I prepared my first syllabus, I obediently scheduled several conferences each semester: the first early as a get-to-know-you effort and a few others sprinkled later throughout the semester to go over my comments on a draft of

an essay. Unfortunately, for the majority of their writing assignments, these basic writing students, who were for the most part
inexperienced in both study skills and writing, were expected to
navigate alone through my generous feedback to their drafts. They
would then rewrite based on my written comments, trying des-
perately to get the paper up to my standards, and return the final
effort to me for a grade. Clearly, the concept of the writing conference had been lost on me.

In the few conferences I did schedule, my basic writing students were cordially invited to sit down in cozy proximity to me
in my office with a mauled draft on the desk between us. Then I
would begin. First, I *told* the student what I thought the strengths
of the paper were—often a standard generalization about an interesting topic or a contrived "I like the way you catch the reader's
attention." Then came the "But." The remainder of the fifteen-
minute conference centered on a detailed "going over" of problems that *I* felt the student needed to work on. The student, eyes
shifting back and forth from the draft to me, sat silent, nodding
when appropriate.

In the interest of self-evaluation, I even asked students to tell
me in their journal writing how they felt about the conference
experience. The diligent students responded that they were grateful
for the abundant feedback, and, in turn, their revisions mirrored
my ideas, and the final product was graded accordingly. A few
outspoken students who generally did not do well in my class
made comments like "Ms. Freeland made me see what a bad
writer I am and how hard I will have to work to pass this course."
Even more telling, however, was the attrition in my basic writing
classes. Every semester I would lose or fail approximately one-
third or more of my basic first-year students. Of course, I attrib-
uted this loss to my high standards and rationalized that if these
students couldn't take the pressure, they probably didn't belong
in college. My formal student evaluations were generally high
among those who survived the class, because I was "a good teacher
who told us how to make our papers better." *familiar*

After a few years, however, I realized there was no joy on
either side of the desk. I was forcing students to make rote changes
in their drafts that had no meaning to them as writers, whereas

sitting for hours writing prescriptive, mostly negative comments on student drafts exhausted me.

I knew I had to rethink my approach to teaching writing and how basic writing students learned to become writers. Those writing process theorists and practitioners I had studied in graduate school came 'round to haunt me—not from textbooks, but from my own unproductive teaching practices.[I needed to create in my conferences a climate that allowed students to learn based on their own observations of their writing.]Rather than telling them where their writing needed work through copious, handwritten comments,[I wanted students to *discover*, through a genuine sense of audience need and writer purpose, what worked and what did not in their writing.] Peter Elbow in *Embracing Contraries* (1986) affirms that the writer has the right to ground his behavior on his own experiences, "to embark on his own voyage of change, development, and growth as to what is right for him" (69).

Evaluative, teacher-centered conferences were having a negative effect on my students' perceptions of themselves as writers, resulting in frustration and high attrition in my classes. So I set out to redefine my role from authoritative teacher to collaborative reader and to design writing conferences that affirm the student's identity as "writer," thus placing control of the writing process where it belongs: in the hands of the writer.

To establish a collaborative, reader-writer relationship in writing conferences, I made three basic adjustments in my pedagogy: (1) I changed the way I respond orally to students' work to impart a collaborative rather than an authoritative relationship; (2) I have students write reflectively both before the conference, to set their own agenda, and after, to establish personal writing goals; and 3) I changed the way I assess students' work, moving from traditional grading to portfolio assessment so that writing conferences were about writing, not grades. As a result of these adjustments, I have seen over the last three semesters a marked change in student motivation, as well as lower attrition and higher grades.

Setting up a nonthreatening learning environment in a writing conference requires the use of collaborative language, which shifts the students' self-perception from mere students to the position of writer, and the use of nonevaluative responses to students' work, which allows the students to make decisions about the needs of their readers and their own purposes for writing.

Changing the way we think often requires changing the way we speak. I began referring to basic writing students as "writers" both in the classroom and in the conference because anyone who is creating a written document is a writer, no matter the scope of the work or the experience of the creator. When discussing writing strategies or concerns about a student's work, for example, I refer to myself as the "reader" (Clark 1988, 128). As a student writer and I are going over a draft and I hear a portion that is not written clearly, I will say, "As a reader, I get confused here." When examining possible solutions, I will say, "As a writer, it seems you have several choices." Through this collaborative language, the student understands that "good" writing begins with identifying purpose and the reader's needs. A multitude of drafts soaked in my authoritative comments might *inform* students that this is true, but they only truly *learn* by discovering that, as writers, they are capable of making decisions about their own work.

Overwhelming students with "constructive feedback" on drafts, whether verbal or written, provides them with new information but no new skills (Taylor 1993, 24). Therefore, I also changed the way I respond to student writing. Because as a writing teacher I have extensive experience in solving writing problems, I sometimes find myself slipping into the authoritative role of teacher and dominating the conversation. To maintain a collaborative environment, I use Beverly Clark's conferencing strategies of asking open-ended questions, being silent, and mirroring (1988, 124).

Using nonevaluative, open-ended questions in dialoguing with basic writing students about their writing is a strategy that affirms a collaborative relationship in the writing conference. Nonevaluative questions, which neither praise nor criticize, draw out the writer's meaning (Murray 1988, 236). Instead of telling students what they are doing wrong and how they should fix the problem, I begin by assuming that the writer knows the work better than I do (Connors and Glenn 1999, 57). I ask questions such as, "Is this what you want to say?" or "How can you revise this sentence to make it easier to read?" or "As a writer, you have several choices—which do you think conveys your meaning to your reader?" When my students answer open-ended, nonevaluative questions, they hear in their own language, based on their experience as readers and listeners, what their reader needs or wants from the text.

I try to remain silent while the student writer thinks of a response, even if the silence goes on for an uncomfortable amount of time. I may *think* I know the best answer, but I must give the writer time to work out his or her meaning and purpose. Once the writer has spoken and I have listened, I often summarize, or mirror, what was said in an effort to reassure both of us that we understand the ideas. I might say, for example, "What I'm hearing is that you want the reader to see that having more classroom aides is the most important aspect of successfully mainstreaming disabled students. Okay. Do you think your thesis conveys this message?"

Of course, it is never my intent to frustrate the basic writing student by not providing any suggestions when the writer simply cannot move forward on his or her own. A writing conference is often a balancing act between spontaneity and pedagogy (Black 1998, 25). When a student draws a blank, I offer simple directive suggestions that model my own writing experience ("I would try . . ."), but I always leave the writing decision to the student.

Another crucial element in establishing a collaborative reader-writer relationship with my basic writing students in the writing conference is having them gain ownership of their writing process through reflective writing. The students' reflective writing not only provides me with information that guides our conferences, but also engages the writers in a form of assessment that maximizes learning; the students are forced to identify what they have done and what they can do (Camp and Levine 1991, 200). I finally realized that if students can't ask the question, they probably are not ready for the answer; so I ask them to bring to the conference a written reflection about their work—its strengths and weaknesses, and questions that they as writers would like to focus on in the conference. This exercise puts the students in control of their own writing processes and sets the agenda for the conference (Walker 1992, 72). I have found, however, that early in the semester basic writing students often don't know enough to ask specific questions about their work, or they will ask general questions such as, "Is my paper interesting?" and "Does my paper flow?" When a student arrives at the conference with no questions or vague ones, <u>we begin the conference by</u> <u>reading the paper aloud</u> (Clark 1988, 129). Although basic writing students may lack writing experience, they have been *listening* all their lives and are usually capable of identifying unclear statements, choppy syntax, or illogical organization. In other words, students adopt the role of intelligent reader for a few moments while listening to the sound of their own words. As the writer reads, he or she discovers, as a reader, some of the problems with the content and language of the text. It is my job to add vocabulary or "writer talk" to these concerns (e.g., structure, syntax, transition, etc.) and, little by little, the writer learns to read critically and to use this new vocabulary to dialogue about the work.

Even this vague question about "flow" can initiate a productive conference. I first ask the student, "Can you show me where you attempted to use language and/or structure to help the reader 'transition' from one idea to the next?" If the student cannot specify any particular words or strategies, we turn to the handbook or textbook and examine the information on transitions and coherence. After this minilesson, we go back to the student's work and find places where a transition is needed. Our inquiry leads the writer to discover meaning and the audience's need for logical organization. The student leaves with plenty to work on for the next revision.

But before the student writer walks out of the conference, I ask him or her to jot down either on the draft or a separate piece of paper what we learned in the conference and goals for revision. Those notes will become a reflective journal or letter that assesses the revised work. The postconference reflective journal encourages the students to narrate, analyze, and evaluate their own writing and thus connect this assessment to their own learning (Yancey 1998, 146). Student writers become responsible for reading their own work critically, reflecting on its strengths and weaknesses, and discussing possible revision strategies while fortifying their writing vocabulary. This reflective journal serves to expedite my response or the responses of other readers such as peer groups and can also be used to set the agenda for a subsequent conference.

Reflective writing not only gives the basic writing students ownership of their work in the one-on-one writing conference, but its benefits also spill over into peer groups in the classroom. After several conferences with me, I find that students begin to emulate this writing conference model in their peer groups. By the middle of the semester, as I listen to groups interact, it is with great satisfaction that I hear writers talking about writing. As Roger Garrison (1999) states so well, "The primary job of a teacher is to do himself out of a job as quickly and efficiently as he can" (358). Reflective writing teaches student writers to evaluate their own work, which makes my job as facilitator much less stressful. I agree with Elbow (1986) that we haven't taught the student how to do something unless she can determine on her own whether she has done it (167).

As writing conferences became the primary tool in my writing pedagogy, assigning a grade to drafts or to each individual project seemed to undermine the students' ownership of the writing process and the collaborative relationship I was striving to advance. I was compelled to rethink my mode of assessment and move away from traditional grading practices to portfolio assessment. Portfolio assessment allows students to use their expanding knowledge of writing to revise all of their writing throughout the semester. The student writer chooses selections from a revised body of work—the result of many writing conferences and much revision—to present for final evaluation and a course grade. By deferring grades until the end of the term, I am able to foster a "writing environment" in my conferences, maintaining my role as reader/collaborator (Sommers 1991, 156). Yes, ultimately, the writing must be evaluated, but the final grade represents a body of work written over the course of a semester rather than a compilation of individual, terminal grades that each assignment earned, including those written early in the semester when the writer had little experience or knowledge.

Students' responses to portfolio assessment are mixed at the beginning of the semester, although usually a few had experienced this kind of assessment in high school and are immediately comfortable with the concept. A carefully presented introduction to the concept and process of portfolio assessment in the early days of the course usually allays the fears of those who are initially uncomfortable with the idea of not receiving grades on each assignment. I have found, however, that once we begin the conferencing, reflective writing, and revision pattern, the question of grades rarely comes up. The course becomes about writing and writers, and the notion of grades seems unnatural.

Undeniably, due to lack of maturity or confidence, some basic writers need the accountability that grades provide; therefore, I do midsemester writing conferences for which the students must prepare a portfolio of their work so far. At this point, I tell students who either want to know or are in danger of failing what grade they are earning. But because students are allowed multiple revisions, those who are revising to meet the criteria for the assignment know where they stand based on our discussion in conferences and carefully worded "clues" written on drafts. I will write, for example, "Your work on adding transitions to create coherence is effective. As a reader, I'm still anticipating more support for your final point on parents' reactions to the new 'zero tolerance' policy." Or, "I'm satisfied that this project meets all the criteria for the assignment. If you are satisfied, why don't you put it aside for final polishing later and work on your informative project." In other words, I continue to encourage the student to revise but not to the point of frustration. Even though it can be argued that "real writers" are never satisfied with a product, I think basic writers can become overwhelmed and discouraged if they are asked to rewrite indefinitely on a project, sometimes feeling pressure to work on several projects at the same time.

So what happens when the day of reckoning comes and the course grade must become the subject of our conference? The student and I negotiate the grade for the course during an exit conference. At this terminal point in the semester, the student's writing for the course is finished, and she presents a body of written work that demonstrates her accomplishments in the class. The reflective writing for this final portfolio consists of a cover letter and a self-evaluation sheet, which lists the criteria for the course. The student writer measures his work against the criteria for the course, which has been a continual source of discussion throughout the semester, and, in the cover letter, explains why, based on evidence in the portfolio, he has earned a particular grade. Before the conference, I review both the portfolio contents and the cover letter and write a brief assessment of the student's work based on the criteria sheet. At the conference, we negotiate the grade. Since the grade is based on hard evidence, portfolio grade disagreements are rare. I have encountered only two out of ninety-one basic writing students with whom I could not amicably reach a consensus. When that happens, I assign a grade that I feel reflects the standards of the course and the university.

As each semester passes, I am more convinced by the positive atmosphere of my classroom and the success of my basic student writers that the writing conference is pedagogy at its best because it is pedagogy at its least. Writing conferences are now the foundation of all my 100- and 200-level writing classes. All writers, regardless of experience, need to talk through their ideas and concerns to identify their purpose and direction. In Lewis Carroll's *Alice in Wonderland* (1960), Alice asks the Cheshire Cat, "Would you tell me, please, which way I ought to go from here?" The Cat replies, "That depends a good deal on where you want to get to." Writing conferences work this way. In a writer-rich collaborative environment, I no longer have to *teach* writing; I merely participate as an experienced fellow traveler as my students, through "writer talk," written reflection, and self-evaluation, find their way—not only as writers, but also as intelligent readers and thinkers.

Works Cited

Black, Laurel Johnson. 1998. *Between Talk and Teaching*. Logan: Utah State University Press.

Camp, Roberta, and Denise Stavis Levine. 1991. "Portfolios Evolving: Background and Variations in Sixth- through Twelfth-Grade Classrooms." Pp. 194–205 in *Portfolios: Process and Product*, ed. Pat Belanoff and Marcia Dickson. Portsmouth, NH: Boynton/Cook.

Carroll, Lewis. 1960. *The Annotated Alice:* Alice's Adventures in Wonderland *and* Through the Looking Glass. Anno. Martin Gardner. New York: N. Potter.

Clark, Beverly Lyon. 1988. *Talking about Writing: A Guide for Tutor and Teacher Conferences*. Ann Arbor: University of Michigan Press.

Connors, Robert J., and Cheryl Glenn, eds. 1999. *The New St. Martin's Guide to Teaching Writing*. Boston: Bedford/St. Martin's.

Elbow, Peter. 1986. *Embracing Contraries: Explorations in Learning and Teaching*. New York: Oxford University Press.

Garrison, Roger H. 1999. "One-to-One: Tutorial Instruction in Freshman Composition." Pp. 357–79 in *The New St. Martin's Guide to Teaching Writing*, ed. Robert Connors and Cheryl Glenn. Boston: Bedford/St. Martin's.

Murray, Donald M. 1988. "The Listening Eye: Reflections on the Writing Conference." Pp. 232–37 in *The Writing Teacher's Sourcebook*, ed. Gary Tate and Edward P. J. Corbett. 2nd ed. New York: Oxford University Press.

Sommers, Jeffrey. 1991. "Bringing Practice in Line with Theory." Pp. 153–64 in *Portfolios: Process and Product*, ed. Pat Belanoff and Marcia Dickson. Portsmouth, NH: Boynton/Cook.

Taylor, David. 1993. "A Counseling Approach to Writing Conferences." Pp. 24–33 in *Dynamics of the Writing Conference: Social and Cognitive Interaction*, ed. Thomas Flynn and Mary King. Urbana, IL: National Council of Teachers of English.

Walker, Carolyn. 1992. "Teacher Dominance in the Writing Conference." *Journal of Teaching Writing* 11: 65–87.

Yancey, Kathleen Blake. 1998. *Reflection in the Writing Classroom*. Logan: Utah State University Press.

CHAPTER TWENTY-SEVEN

Building Relationships through Written Dialogue

CARL GERRIETS WITH JENNIFER LOWE
Century College

Century College is a two-year community and technical college located in one of the northeast suburbs of the Twin
Cities. Century is part of the state system and is the result of a
state-mandated merger five years ago of Lakewood Community
College and Northeast Metro Technical College. The students of
Century College are diverse. Some are in a technical program
seeking specific job training for a particular career; others are
taking general courses for transfer to any of a number of state or
private four-year schools in the area. Slightly more than half of
the students are female; most of the students are white, though
the numbers of minority Americans and particularly international
students are growing. In my classes, I have had students from
Brazil, Bosnia, France, Ethiopia, Jordan, Kenya, and Sri Lanka.
Asian American students, especially Hmong, are a common sight
in the halls, but they often exist in their own subgroup, not fully
accepted into the white mainstream. Many of the students at
Century are part-time students, and most work in addition to
going to school. Our students range from working- to upper-
middle-class in background, and several are first-generation college students.

From my perspective, the common feature of all these diverse students is that they are in some way marginal in the college world. Often the best-prepared students I see academically
are the students who are still in high school and taking college
classes at state expense through the Postsecondary Enrollment
Options program. Although most of these students are from

wealthy white suburbs and have strong educational backgrounds, they face at Century social demands for maturity and responsibility they may not be sure they can handle. Other students at Century aren't sure they have the grades, the money, the commitment, or the ability to succeed in the academic world. Some are sure they can't, so they are seeking a technical degree, and these students often resent the general education courses they are required to take. Along with traditional-age high school graduates seeking technical education or affordable general education classes, we see working professionals seeking to improve their professional skills or pursuing a degree, single parents trying to improve their ability to take care of their children, and retirees looking for a new challenge or being pushed into school by their children.

To reach this diverse group of students, I need to establish a conversation with each student and build on it throughout our time together. The specific practice I feel most confident about in my writing classes is the ongoing dialogue between me and each student, a dialogue that takes place in their cover letters for their drafts and my responses. My best teaching occurs in this dialogue, and through it I build stronger relationships with my students.

One student I've built a strong relationship with is Jennifer Lowe. She's taken three writing classes from me, so we've exchanged a lot of paper. Jennifer agreed to help me with this project by writing about her experiences. We traded questions and answers and even wrote a draft of this article entirely as a dialogue. I've included some of Jennifer's comments along with my observations in order to give a student's perspective on written dialogue and its effects on teacher-student relationships.

Here's a brief look at this practice: Every draft a student gives me for comment must be accompanied by a cover letter. These cover letters (which I used to call reflective memos, as many teachers still do) are informal notes to the reader explaining what the writer thinks about the draft.[1] My comments on the draft then take the form of a letter of reply, which almost always begins by responding to the comments made in the student's cover letter. I keep a copy of all my responses in the student's file so that I can refer back to them in the future to watch for progress and build

on what has gone before. When students compile their final portfolios, they are accompanied by cover letters in which the students evaluate their own work over the semester.

Depending on the kind of writing assignments I am using, I
may provide specific instructions for a particular cover letter ("Tell
me whether you like this revision or the original draft better") or
just a general sheet of instructions suggesting topics students might
want to address ("What's your favorite part of this piece so far?";
"What frustrations did you encounter?"). A frequent difficulty is
getting the students to approach the cover letters seriously yet
informally. When students don't take the cover letters seriously, I
get cover letters that sound like this:

> Dear reader:
> This is my first draft. I think it is pretty good, but I had some
> trouble with it. What do you think?

So I tell the students that cover letters are important and should
be taken seriously. Although I seldom give firm length requirements on papers, I sometimes do with cover letters to demonstrate that they must be thorough. Inevitably, some students then
start to consider the cover letters more formally than they should,
and they worry over commas and where to put the date, or even
fail to turn in a draft because they're afraid the cover letter isn't
good enough. So I strive to make clear, through my instructions
and samples, that a good cover letter is thorough but informal. I
encourage the students to be thoughtful, specific, and honest.

Once students give me a draft, the cover letter is central to
my reading and my response. I read the cover letter first and last,
and my response is directed first to what the cover letter says. I
try to answer all the questions raised by the cover letter along
with any other concerns I might have. Whenever possible, I start
out by agreeing with the student's comments, especially positive
ones. This approach is valuable for alleviating fears, but also for
building a conversation and thus a relationship. With one hundred or more students a semester, I have limited ability even in
conferences to make a strong personal connection with each student, especially when so many of these students are overworked
and rarely on campus. In their cover letters, I get to hear about

the actual struggles of writing as they happen. In my responses, I can struggle alongside the student.

I handle responses with one eye toward practicality and one eye toward building relationships that will help each student. My responses are typed for two reasons: I type 80 wpm and so am more efficient at the keyboard, and my students can actually read what I have to say. Typing also allows me to easily keep a copy of my comments so that I can quickly glance through a student's file with each new draft and be reminded of what we were working on in the past. I even retain comments from previous classes when students might take another class from me. With an eye toward the relationship I am trying to build with the student, I take the advice of my wife to always select a readable and "friendly" font, something that looks more like a friendly letter than a textbook. The note is hand-signed "Carl" (as my students know me), and I put it right behind the student's cover letter so that it looks like a reply.

When Jennifer got her first response from me, it surprised her:

> I will never forget it because of how scared I was when I saw it. Usually the only time that a teacher takes time to write to students personally is when they did something awful. I began to read it and I remember you told me that it was a great start. This lifted the weight off of my shoulders. I was nervous enough to actually have you read it, and with you starting the letter with a compliment it gave me the courage to do the next draft. My mom knew that I was nervous about turning this paper in to you, so after I got the response note I had to show her. She was also shocked that a college teacher would take time to write all of his students personal notes like that one.

I notice that by telling Jennifer she was off to a great start, I got our relationship off to one too. Both Jennifer and her mother are struck by the personal nature of the response, which also indicates that this exercise serves to build a relationship.

In the interest of building a relationship, probably the most important element of my responses is what is *not* included. I never grade individual pieces of writing. I have experimented with a variety of portfolio and contract approaches and am now working with a combination of the two; whatever grading scheme I choose, it always allows me to comment on a piece of writing without grading it. The harshest grade-related comment a student will ever read in my response is "If you want this to be a finished piece, you'll have to keep revising to address [whatever issues]." Initially, this approach can cause confusion and even frustration among those students who have not encountered such an approach before (Jennifer said that initially "it drove me nuts" although now "it doesn't really bother me"), and a small number of my students never stop arguing with me about it. Despite this minority opposition, I remain convinced that this decision is crucial to my ability to use my responses to really teach and to build relationships. Because my comments are not tied directly to a grade, my students are more likely to read what I have said rather than just lumping my comments into a grade category. Also, I am freed from holding back in my comments. I always sympathize with my students, and I wince for them when I know the grade won't be to their liking. If there is no grade, however, I can assess freely without wincing.

Cover letters also help me to be freer and more honest in my responses. When I read in a cover letter that a student is extremely frustrated with a piece and recognizes several specific flaws, I know that what is needed from me is not critique (the student has already done that) but encouragement and coaching about how to deal with these flaws. If the same paper were accompanied instead by a cover letter saying, "This is the best piece I have ever written!," I would know that I need to provide some praise and applause before I move into suggestions that might allow the student to make the piece better yet. By meeting the students' needs in these ways, I earn their trust and learn more about what they need to accomplish in the course. Because the cover letters and responses work together as part of an ongoing dialogue, I seldom worry that a student won't understand my comments or that the student and I won't see the paper in the same light. In those cases where we do have widely divergent readings of a piece, the cover letter usually cues me to that, and my response usually takes the form of a call for conferencing: "I think we're really looking at this piece differently. We should probably get together and talk about your purpose for this piece and who you think the audience is." Such a response also reminds me what we're supposed to talk about when we finally get together. The conference then lets me build on the relationship already established in our written dialogue (and, of course, in classroom interactions).

As I write my responses, I try to take the ongoing relationship with the student into account. In responses to rough drafts, especially early in the semester when the relationship is still new, I tend to limit my comments to praising specific features and asking lots of questions intended to help the student consider other possibilities for the paper. My purpose in such comments is to appear to the student as an ally who is interested in and able to offer useful suggestions for writing, not as a tyrant or judge who wants to take over the writing. As I earn the students' trust and come to know their goals and personalities better, I can give more direct advice if it seems appropriate and if our relationship will support such a move. So when Shannon took a second composition class from me, I felt comfortable enough to write: "Some of what follows may be more 'pushy' than my usual comments, so I want to warn you about that up front. I'm doing this because I want to be very clear about what I see in this paper, and because I think our relationship is at a point where I can trust you to reject my advice if you don't like it." With a student such as Jennifer, who is an eager and aggressive reviser, I know that I can be much less directive and just help her to explore options. As she explained, "You don't tell me what to do and I like that. You ask questions about the characters, the story, and the point, which gets me to think." As a result, our relationship has reached a point at which Jennifer grants me special trust and really sees her cover letters as part of a written dialogue with me: "When I write you, I am expecting your ideas, and I try to let you know what help I need. I have found out that my peers can tell me if it makes sense with organization and style, but usually when I am stuck I come to you."

Rationale and Reflection

At a strictly commuter college like Century, many students are on campus only long enough to attend classes before rushing off to a part- or full-time job or to relieve the babysitter. With such busy, diverse students and so many students who consider themselves marginal in the academic world, building relationships with individual students is crucial for student success and retention. As I earn the students' trust, I become an ally rather than an obstacle preventing their success. As mentioned earlier, nearly all the students at Century are in some sense marginal in the academic world, and many are keenly aware of it. They need to know that someone in the academic world is on their side and believes they can succeed. They also need instruction in how to turn their strengths into academic success, but many of them will not accept such instruction from me as an authority figure; instead, they need to see me as a friend who corrects and exhorts them for their own good. My written dialogue with students allows me to connect with these students and make a difference in their academic lives.

At the heart of any pedagogy concerned with dialogue is the work of Paulo Freire, especially *Pedagogy of the Oppressed* (2000). In my efforts to understand Freire and apply his theories to my own classroom, I have been drawn repeatedly to the work of Ira Shor in books such as *Empowering Education* (1992) and *Critical Teaching and Everyday Life* (1980). Shor's books translate the sometimes abstract work of Freire into specific classroom activities and give examples of what dialogue means in actual practice. While my practices may not look exactly like the examples Shor gives, they are certainly in part an outgrowth of Shor's work. Like Shor, I seek to create a dialogue in which the student speaks first and has the opportunity to define where our dialogue will start. Other U.S. instructors who seek to apply Freire's ideas to their teaching have helped me understand the possibilities and benefits of dialogue in my own teaching. Linda Shaw Finlay and Valerie Faith, for example, remind me that "adults learn to read and write only when they are simultaneously learning the skill and reflecting on its personal and social significance" (1987, 81); so the cover letters my students write not only begin or continue our dialogue but also allow the students to do the reflection necessary for true learning.

I was encouraged to further my experimentation with dialogic or conversational responses to student writing by the suggestion of Anne Righton Malone and Barabara Tindall that such "ongoing conversations between teachers and students" (1997, 127) could serve as a way to reduce the pressures associated with grading and evaluation. Likewise, Brooke Horvath summarizes a variety of scholars who suggest that response to student writing must develop a relationship of trust and safety (1994, 212).

While all of this theoretical rationale is convincing and important to me, my practical experiences and the dialogues I have been involved in as both a teacher and a student remain more convincing and more important. I first implemented this approach because I saw it done and done effectively by my teachers and colleagues. I continue to do it because I see the benefits it brings in practice to the wide range of students I see every day, students who often enter my classroom with little or no confidence in themselves as writers or students. Through our dialogues and our relationships, I can challenge and encourage them to develop their skills, their knowledge, and their confidence.

Note

1. For more on reflective memos, see Jeffrey Sommers in this volume and elsewhere (1984, 1985) and Kathleen Blake Yancey (1998).

Works Cited

Finlay, Linda Shaw, and Valerie Faith. 1987. "Illiteracy and Alienation in American Colleges: Is Paulo Freire's Pedagogy Relevant?" Pp. 63–86 in *Freire for the Classroom: A Sourcebook for Liberatory Teaching,* ed. Ira Shor. Portsmouth, NH: Boynton/Cook.

Freire, Paulo. 2000. *Pedagogy of the Oppressed.* Rev. 30th anniversary ed. Trans. Myra Bergman Ramos. New York: Continuum.

Horvath, Brooke K. 1994. "The Components of Written Response: A Practical Synthesis of Current Views." Pp. 207–23 in *The Writing Teacher's Sourcebook,* ed. Gary Tate, Edward P. J. Corbett, and Nancy Myers. 3rd ed. New York: Oxford University Press.

Malone, Anne Righton, and Barbara Tindall. 1997. "Dear Teacher: Epistolary Conversations as the Site of Evaluation." Pp. 125–40 in

Grading in the Post-Process Classroom: From Theory to Practice, ed. Libby Allison, Lizbeth Bryant, and Maureen Hourigan. Portsmouth, NH: Boynton/Cook.

Shor, Ira. 1980. *Critical Teaching and Everyday Life.* Boston: South End.

———. 1992. *Empowering Education: Critical Teaching for Social Change.* Chicago: University of Chicago Press.

Sommers, Jeffrey. 1984. "Listening to Our Students: The Student-Teacher Memo." *Teaching English in the Two-Year College* 11: 29–34.

———. 1985. "Enlisting the Writer's Participation in the Evaluation Process." *Journal of Teaching Writing* 4: 95–103.

Yancey, Kathleen Blake. 1998. *Reflection in the Writing Classroom.* Logan: Utah State University Press.

CHAPTER TWENTY-EIGHT

A Comprehensive Plan to Respond to Student Writing

JEFF SOMMERS
Miami University Middletown

Teaching Context

My institution is a two-year open admissions branch campus affiliated with a four-year state university. The 1,600–2,000 students, whose average ACT score fluctuates in the 15 to 18 range, live within driving distance of our commuter campus in southwestern Ohio, situated halfway between Cincinnati and Dayton. The median age of our students is twenty-seven, somewhat more than half of them are female, and 85 percent hold jobs while attending college. Over 40 percent of the students are enrolled part time. While the overwhelming majority are white, some minority students are enrolled. Many students come from Appalachian backgrounds, with a majority being the first generation of college students in their families. I employ the strategies described here in Miami's first-year composition sequence, English 111 (College Composition) and English 112 (Composition and Literature), the two writing courses required of all Miami students. Each class enrolls up to twenty-three students, and I customarily teach three or four sections of composition each term.

Teaching Practice

What I describe here is an approach to responding to and grading student writing that consists of four components: writer's memos, tape-recorded response, early-middle-late grading, and portfolio assessment.

Writer's Memos. With every draft they submit, students are asked to complete a writer's memo, a brief reflective note to the instructor in which they write about their experiences in working on the writing project. Each memo poses four to five questions particular to the assignment, questions that focus on the challenges faced by the students, the decisions they have made, their self-assessment of their writing, and their primary concerns as they look ahead to revision. The memos are not graded, so students freewrite their responses. They also know, however, that their drafts will not be read until they have completed their memos. Revisions are also accompanied by a memo in which students describe the changes made in the paper, explain which of the instructor's suggestions were not used (and why), and pose more questions for the instructor to answer about the new draft. (See Appendix A for instructions provided to students for the first writer's memo assignment.)

Tape-Recorded Response. Students are required to submit a blank audiotape cassette with every draft submitted for comment. The instructor reads the writer's memo and draft and then responds on the audiotape. Each commentary generally runs five minutes. Comments consist of praise for successful aspects of the draft, questions about choices made and not made, suggestions for revision, and individualized tutoring focused on the student's progress in the course. The instructor keeps a written record in the form of three- to four-sentence summaries describing the gist of each comment. Students receive a handout on tips for using tape-recorded comments when they get back their first paper. (See Appendix B.)

Early-Middle-Late Grading. Each draft receives not only a set of comments but also a descriptive "grade." Rather than the usual A-B-C-D-F grading scale, the instructor uses a three-point scale: early, middle, late. These descriptors provide students with a sense of how far the draft has progressed toward being polished enough to publish in their final portfolio. (See Appendix C for the explanation I include in my syllabus.)

Portfolio Assessment. At the conclusion of the course, students make a selection of their writing for final assessment. The portfolio may be negotiated between the instructor and students, or the instructor may decide on its contents. Usually, the portfolio allows students to omit less-successful writing by requiring three polished pieces out of five assigned projects, for example, but the actual number of finished projects can vary. Students also complete an introductory reflective piece, which appears as the first item in the portfolio, usually in the form of a letter to the instructor. (See Appendix D for the instructions students receive about their introductory portfolio reflection.)

Rationale

The approaches I have described rest on several theoretical beliefs:

◆ Students need to be active participants in their own learning.

◆ Students can learn more about their own learning through reflection.

◆ Students need both formative and summative evaluations to improve as writers.

Students need to be active participants in their own learning: Paulo Freire (1990) used the term "the banking model" to describe a classroom in which students passively wait for learning to be delivered to them by their teachers. The thrust of composition instruction over the past quarter-century has been to transform the writing classroom from that passive model of learning into a classroom that nudges students toward assuming "agency" (Yancey 1998, 4) for their own learning. Asking students to write memos about their drafts positions them as having the first word about their own writing; the dialogue between student-writer and teacher-reader begins with the student's description of the writing experience and continues with the questions raised by the student in the memo. Although admittedly not as active as engaging in a one-to-one conference—not a viable alternative for an instructor with three classes and over sixty students—listening to the instructor's response on a tape cassette requires students to take an active interpretative role by taking notes on their own drafts of what they understand the instructor to be saying. Tape-recorded response is more extensive than written response (two minutes of comments equal one full double-spaced typewritten page of written comments), giving students more detailed reader response with which to work. The early-middle-late grading approach assumes that each draft is in progress and that the student will be actively revising it in order to move it along to a final, finished stage. But because some drafts will not be revised in a portfolio system, students must make choices about which projects to complete. The combination of these strategies encourages, even requires, students to take an active role as writers, listeners, and thinkers in the composition course.

Students can learn more about their own learning through reflection: When composition instruction shifted its focus from the final products of writing to the process by which those products were composed, the need for students to become more self-aware increased. It was no longer enough to complete a writing task; students were expected to learn more about how—and why—they had completed the writing task in the way that they did. Susan Miller (1982), for example, has called for a "post-rewriting" stage of the composing process, which suggests she is convinced of the value of metacognition (182). Engaging in metacognition, or thinking about their own thinking, provides students with opportunities to learn more about the answers to those questions "How?" and "Why?" Such reflection, Sharon Pianko (1979) argues, often distinguishes "able and not so able" writers from one another (277). The writer's memo is a reflective piece of writing that asks students to step back from the completed draft and explore what they experienced in completing it, moving them toward becoming more able writers. The portfolio also requires reflection in the form of the introductory letter.

Students need both formative and summative evaluations to improve as writers: According to Louise Wetherbee Phelps (1989), theories underlying teaching practices evolve toward greater depth

(49), in response, no doubt, to continued theorizing about the nature of composing processes. Thus, she criticizes response that treats a student text as "self-contained and complete in itself" (50). Instructors need a more advanced form of response; they need to intervene during the composing process if students are to become more accomplished writers. Restricting response to grades issued after a project is completed does not facilitate learning about the writing process; if the writing is complete, then the comments are summative and cannot assist the student in forming a revised draft. While there is a time and place for such summative response—which grading the final portfolio provides—such response can also prove to be a "major stumbling block" to effective learning (Burnham 1986, 125). Instructors need strategies that help students break out of the pervasive socialization into a grading system that makes them unable to figure out how to succeed without being graded every step of the way (Kohn 1993).

Thus, there is a place in composition classes for formative responses, responses that can influence the writing process in action. The writer's memo has such influence by providing the student with a site from which to ask questions of the instructor; the instructor's responses can assist the student in deciding how to revise the draft. Taped response, which is more closely akin to a one-on-one conference than to written comments, provides instructors with a venue in which they can share their responses to the developing draft in detail; it is far easier for an instructor to provide a running commentary on how the draft has affected him or her when using an audiotape than when using a keyboard. That kind of comment is formative rather than summative because it opens up the possibilities of revision rather than closing down the project as completed. Such response, Peter Elbow (1997) argues, can assist both students and teachers in seeing the complexity of a text in all its "multivalent implications" because the conversation moves away from the "limiting, one-dimensional lens of good versus bad" (18). The early-middle-late grading system emphasizes that the work is in progress; the descriptors have rhetorical weight in that they mean what they say. Compare that to the traditional letter grades, through which each letter is a symbol that says nothing about the process of the work toward completion; letter grades merely affix a final value to a draft, a value, as some have argued, that is rather illusory anyway in its subjectivity and contextual nature (see Milton, Pollio, and Eison 1986).

Finally, the portfolio is both formative and summative in that during the term, the portfolio assessment approach provides the students with an opportunity for choice and revision; at the conclusion of the course, it provides a vehicle for the student to obtain a summative evaluation of the work she or he has chosen.

Conclusion

While these four components of response work effectively together, they also all can work effectively individually, depending on the instructor's objectives and goals for the writing class. They work particularly well with the diverse student body at my campus. Many of my students have come to college with the hope that they can develop more successful study habits than they had in earlier school experiences. Many of the students have been away from school for a long time, and many of them have been unsuccessful in earlier attempts at college. The familiar methods of response (assign a project, collect it, write comments on it, assign it a grade) have not proved particularly successful for a number of my students. They usually welcome the alternatives described here because the alternatives provide a fresh start and because they invite the students themselves to be more active and reflective learners.

Appendix A

Writer's Memo Assignment #1

As part of each writing assignment this semester, you'll need to compose a memo responding to several questions about how you wrote your paper. You can answer each question in separate paragraphs or in the form of a single long paragraph. But plan on writing a full page in answer to my questions. View the memo as a conversation. Remember that I don't grade the memos, so you can freewrite your answers. Be sure to complete your memo when you finish your first draft, and provide your peer group members with copies.

Writer's memos are very helpful to readers of your drafts because they give some insight into what you were trying to accomplish, what you feel good about in the draft, where you're experiencing problems.

Writer's memos provide you with a regular opportunity to engage in *metacognition*, which means "thinking about your thinking." When we think about how we think, we learn more about what we know how to do and more about areas we need to improve upon. I take these memos seriously; I hope you will also. I urge you to save your memos since they may help you later in revising your papers and in preparing your portfolio.

The Memo Questions:

1. Which part of your paper is the most successful or best part? Why?

2. Were there ideas, examples, stories that are not in your draft that you considered including? If so, why did you leave them out? How would it affect your draft if they were included?

3. How would you describe the Ideal Reader for your paper? What would that reader "get out of" your draft? In other words, what's your purpose in writing this draft?

4a. (Before the workshop) What problems does your draft still have? What three questions do you have for your peer group to consider as they read the draft and memo at home? (Bring the questions with you to the workshop.)

4b. (After the workshop) What problems does your draft still have? What should I try to help you with as I comment on the draft?"

Appendix B

How to Use Tape-Recorded Comments

1. Find a quiet place to listen without interruptions. Try to listen to the comments as soon as possible after receiving your folder back.

2. Listen to the tape straight through without pausing.

3. Listen again to the tape with your draft and memo in front of you. Note: If your tape doesn't work for some reason, bring it to class along with your paper so I can try again.

4. Pause the tape to write down notes of things you want to remember or discuss with me, either in my office or in your weekly letters. Jot your notes right on the draft, at the appropriate points in the text if possible.

Note: I don't plan to write you a "prescription" that lists exactly what to say in your revision. I also don't plan to point out every single thing I see in every draft because that can be overwhelming.

5. Listen carefully for positive comments—they will be there! I hope you will feel good about your draft and want to revise it. (I always find more things to suggest, however!)

6. Think about the suggestions and questions you've heard. Freewrite for five minutes about your reactions—ideas that occur to you, questions you might have for me, plans for revision. These notes will be helpful when you do revise or when you come to see me.

7. Leave your tape set at the conclusion of my comments so that I can record the next set of comments when you hand in the tape again.

8. Make an appointment to see me to discuss the comments if you don't understand them or you don't agree with them or you're angered by them.*

9. Finally, revise your draft and resubmit it for more comments. Is revision necessary in this course? Only if you want your written work to earn you a higher grade!

*On the tapes I try to be positive, enthusiastic, honest, and tactful. Most of us are very sensitive about our writing, however, and often anything less than total praise can be upsetting. Sometimes we get upset because we're hearing things that we already knew but were trying to deny, and sometimes anxiety makes us hear things in the wrong way. If you're upset, wait a couple of days and listen again to see if you still feel the same. If you do, then come see me.

Appendix C

Early-Middle-Late Grading

How do I grade student drafts? When you hand in your first drafts, I'll make comments and suggestions for revisions and will label your draft with either an "E" (early draft), "M" (middle draft), or "L" (late draft). My comments will try to guide you toward making useful and effective revisions, and you may submit a revised version of any of your papers whenever you choose, as many times as you choose.

- ◆ An "E" means that your draft seems to be an early one—one that could benefit from some rethinking and reseeing.

- ◆ An "M" means that your draft appears to be in the middle stages of the writing process. This draft has some solid and interesting ideas, but it could benefit from some revision and editing in order to prepare it for presentation.

◆ An "L" means that your draft is close to being a "presentation draft"—a draft that is ready to be presented in your portfolio. This draft probably needs some polishing and editing.

◆ Note that "E," "M," and "L" do not represent traditional grades; they are not comments on the quality of the writing. They are designed to let you know how much more revising each paper needs.

Appendix D

Instructions for Students' Introductory Portfolio Letter

Please write me a letter to introduce your final portfolio. The point of writing this letter is to help me better understand how I should read your portfolio. Try answering one or more of these questions:

◆ What do you know about your own writing that you didn't know before?

◆ How is your writing different now than it was when you began this course?

◆ How has your writing process changed over the course of the term?

◆ If you were to choose one piece of work that represents your best effort, which one would it be? Why is it a significant effort?

◆ What connections are there between the pieces in your portfolio?

◆ What surprises you about the pieces you have included in this portfolio? Why?

◆ What do you want your reader to learn about you from reading your portfolio? How would the reader learn that from the portfolio?

◆ What does your work in the portfolio say about you? Why? How?

◆ What things can you show me in your portfolio about your learning that I would otherwise not know about?

How can you go about writing this letter? If you took the time to write substantial writer's memos, you'll probably find them rather useful in beginning to think about this assignment. I'd recommend that you begin by looking over all of your English 111 written work: drafts, revisions, memos, weekly letters, journal entries. See what you can learn about your own experience.

This is one of the most important writing assignments of the term because by writing this letter you'll learn more about your experience in English 111 as well as teach me something about your portfolio as I begin to read it. The entire portfolio receives a grade, so this letter is as important as any of the other three pieces you include in the portfolio. Don't write a one-page, 15-minute draft; it will hurt the overall evaluation of the portfolio.

Remember that even in this letter, showing is more powerful than telling. I expect to see specific references to your other writing: quotations from other papers, memos, journal entries; stories about specific choices you made; comparisons of specific aspects of your work; and so forth.

Works Cited

Burnham, Christopher C. 1986. "Portfolio Evaluation: Room to Breathe and Grow." Pp. 125–37 in *Training the New Teacher of College Composition,* ed. Charles W. Bridges. Urbana, IL: National Council of Teachers of English.

Elbow, Peter. 1997. "Taking Time Out from Grading and Evaluating While Working in a Conventional System." *Assessing Writing* 4: 5–28.

Freire, Paulo. 1990. *Pedagogy of the Oppressed.* Trans. Myra Bergman Ramos. New York: Continuum.

Kohn, Alfie. 1993. *Punished by Rewards: The Trouble with Gold Stars, Incentive Plans, A's, Praise, and Other Bribes.* Boston: Houghton Mifflin.

Miller, Susan. 1982. "How Writers Evaluate Their Own Writing." *College Composition and Communication* 33: 176–83.

Milton, Ohmer, Howard R. Pollio, and James A. Eison. 1986. *Making Sense of College Grades.* San Francisco: Jossey-Bass.

Phelps, Louise Wetherbee. 1989. "Images of Student Writing: The Deep Structure of Teacher Response." Pp. 37–67 in *Writing and Response:*

Theory, Practice, and Research, ed. Chris M. Anson. Urbana, IL: National Council of Teachers of English.

Pianko, Sharon. 1979. "Reflection: A Critical Component of the Composing Process." *College Composition and Communication* 30: 275–78.

Yancey, Kathleen Blake. 1998. *Reflection in the Writing Classroom.* Logan: Utah State University Press.

CHAPTER TWENTY-NINE

Why Use Portfolios?
One Teacher's Response

STEVEN P. SMITH
North Bullitt High School

> By definition a portfolio is a purposeful selection of student work
> that exhibits a student's efforts and achievements. (Kentucky
> Department of Education, 1999)

This definition is found under the Philosophical Guidelines section in the first chapter of the *Kentucky Writing Portfolio Teacher's Handbook*: "Guidelines for the Generation of Student Work for Writing Portfolios." On a first reading, a teacher might have no problem with such a short, seemingly simple definition. Some readers could see the statement (in bold type in the source) as a liberating voice placing the assessment process in the hands of students. This freedom to write is further emphasized in the same section: "Since students must have total ownership of their writing, any intervention from teachers, peers, and/or others should enhance rather than remove or diminish the ownership and should be offered in the spirit of helping students reassess their own work" (2). Of course, the guidelines are based on the assumption that the intervention of the Kentucky Department of Education always enhances student ownership and is always based on "best practice." This state intervention began in 1990 with the passage of the Kentucky Education Reform Act (KERA).

Since the inception of KERA in 1990, portfolios have been required of Kentucky students in the fourth, seventh, and twelfth grades in order to assess the progress of each school's writing program. The assessment results are returned in the form of a writing index score, which is 14 percent of a school's total accountability index. This accountability index is used to determine whether a school is to be rewarded or sanctioned. Consequently, schools are expected to reach certain quantifiable goals during every biennial assessment cycle, which consists of scores from both years. If a school fails to improve, it can receive sanctions from the state. This kind of high-stakes, large-scale assessment places a great deal of pressure on teachers, students, and parents to perform during those assessment years. As if this is not pressure enough, many schools, including mine, have enacted policies that require portfolio completion for graduation. One can imagine the reputation portfolios have acquired among interested parties in Kentucky's public schools—a reputation that has led to the prevalence of phrases like "the dreaded *P* word" to refer to the process. Furthermore, many schools also require "practice portfolios" for the ninth, tenth, and eleventh grades. My department has enacted a policy of practice portfolios for students, but the stakes are not nearly as high, especially for the school, so the pressure is not as high. So, yes, I can provide a sound rationale for using portfolios: I have to do it.

But even if my department decided that portfolios at the twelfth grade were enough, I would still make portfolios a central part of my curriculum, which leads me back to the question, Why? For me, the answer is a simple one: portfolios facilitate student growth in writing more than any other practice I have used over the last twenty-four years of teaching English. This growth is fostered through students learning to self-assess their writing, which requires that they learn the higher-level, metacognitive skill of reflection. This portfolio self-assessment entails what Kathleen Yancey (1992) has described as a three-stage process: collection, reflection, and selection. Some teachers may ask why students cannot learn the same self-assessment through the traditional practice of a teacher assigning a single writing project, encouraging development through the writing process (hopefully), and then collecting the assignment in order to evaluate it. Perhaps some student reflection and self-assessment are necessary when using this method as well, but the time frame is much shorter, usually just a few weeks for each writing assignment, before the class moves on to the next one. The portfolio process, at least in my classes, requires a yearlong time frame, which allows for student writers to grow and their writings to develop. These writings begin for my students in writing projects that last anywhere from a few weeks to an entire year, in some cases. A portfolio in my ninth-grade classes has the opportunity to grow over the entire academic year, the writing on any individual selection never truly being finished until the final portfolio is handed in at the end of the year. I find that this difference liberates students from the heavy hand of teacher grading as well as from the time pressure of having to get a piece to "work" in just a few class periods. Instead of assessing a single piece of writing, say a poem or an essay, a student compiling a portfolio of her or his writing has the opportunity to reflect over multiple writing pieces in various forms to different audiences and for various purposes.

The portfolio also works very well for the particular students I teach, most of whom are working class, will be the first in their families to attend college, and have rarely been encouraged to make connections between education and an improved life. I teach in a "white flight" school that was born of court-ordered busing in Louisville, Kentucky, in 1974. In 1975, North Bullitt High School opened its doors to about 1,000 white students who moved across the Jefferson and Bullitt County line so they would not have to attend schools in Jefferson County outside of their white neighborhoods and not have to go to school with increasing numbers of African American children. To this day, North Bullitt is 99.5 percent white, mostly lower-middle- to middle-working-class families. Last year's graduating class of around two hundred sent fewer than forty students to four-year institutions of higher learning. We sent about twice that number to community colleges, but still less than 50 percent go on to pursue higher education in any form, including technical/vocational schools. My students' ways of looking at the world are very cut-and-dried, black-and-white (dare I say narrow?), even entrenched.

This cycle is hard to break, and I have had more luck helping students work individually from their notebooks toward finished pieces of writing than from mass-assigned topics. Many of the most entrenched students would prefer the mass-assigned topics because they do feel more like "school," because they are "safer," and because these students have learned how to play the game to get a passing grade. This makes the teaching of writing a difficult and often frustrating task. I keep reminding myself to present writing as positively as possible so that students can see how it can improve the quality of their lives in ways that may or not be connected with getting a good job down the road. Toward this end, I try to make their writer's notebook the space in which they can take liberties with their thoughts and lives, and I tend to stay away from formal assignments *because* they feel too much like school. So although the portfolio is required by the state for seniors and by my school for the other grades, my approach allows me to reach my students and help them see the value of writing.

How do my students use portfolios to do all the things I claim they do? Perhaps the best way to explain the process is to use Yancey's three-stage model of collection, selection, and reflection. Please bear in mind, however, that neither Yancey nor I see this model as a linear process but as a recursive one, not unlike the writing process.

Collecting the Writing

During the first week of school, I pass out brand-new manila folders to all of my students and ask them to leave the inside of both covers blank. They are free to decorate the outside anyway they wish as long as it is appropriate for an academic community and has their name written legibly on the top. The inside covers are reserved for two things: writing criteria and possible topics to cover during the year. This folder is not the portfolio but a working folder we use to begin our collection of prewriting, down drafts, revisions, revision plans, conference notes, PQS (praise/question/suggest) forms, and updrafts. By the end of the first week of school, students have papers in these folders, usually prewriting lists, clusters, wordpools, or observational sketches. These folders are kept in a filing cabinet from which students can pull them as needed. At the end of each grading period (six weeks in our situation), students pull these folders and use their contents to construct a portfolio. Each six weeks the requirements for the portfolio get a little more demanding since students should have more writing from which to select and since their writing skills should be improving with practice. Students are given a list of requirements based on what we have been writing, studying, and practicing during our writing workshop (see the appendix). This approach does several things: (1) it allows students more time to develop quality writing, (2) it allows them to apply the criteria we have been learning as we read and write in different genres, and (3) it allows students to see their own level of achievement, and it reinforces the writing process. By the end of the first semester, students typically have collected 60–100 pages of writing. Some of this writing undergoes substantial revision as students continue to work on favorite writings throughout the semester and the year, by the end of which they often have accumulated 120–200 pages of writing in the working folder. This collection is just one part of the portfolio process in my classes, but it's an essential one because students need to reflect on the effectiveness of their writing in terms of their audiences and purposes and learn how to select quality writing from writing that does not quite get the job done, for whatever reason.

Selecting the Writing for the Portfolio

The selection process begins early in the year, as well. Sometime during the first couple of weeks of school, after we have read and discussed several essays, a few poems, and a story or two, I ask students to go home and write down a list of what they think good writing should exhibit or do. The next day students bring in their lists, and someone in class writes down their ideas on the chalkboard. We discuss each criterion nominated. Some are listed more than once and duly noted on the board. This process often takes more than one class period, but I am willing to give it as much time as necessary so that students begin to "own" the criteria. Once the standards are agreed on, we recopy them on poster board and post them in a prominent place in the room. Students also write them inside their notebooks so they have access to them at all times. These criteria are important in the portfolio process because the qualities of effective writing that students generate are used throughout the year for self-assessment. Students sift through their working folders looking for selections for their portfolio based on how well each piece performs according to these criteria. Every six weeks I target specific criteria for minilesson topics in our workshop. If students have designated "interesting beginnings" as one of the qualities of effective writing, for example, I will teach strategies for developing question leads, quotation leads, anecdotal leads, and so forth. In this way, assessment and learning go hand in hand, and the assessment has come from the inside instead of the outside. Students are more likely to accept the necessity of writing well when they have played a vital role in determining how high the bar is going to be set and what it is going to be made of. As a matter of fact, as the year progresses we revisit the criteria and reflect on their continued viability within our community. Usually, the criteria are strengthened as a result of our ongoing reading, writing, and discussing of various professional and student texts. When the criteria are revised, they are changed on the posters, in the folders, and in my lesson plans. The students come to see the value of reflection and revision if the changes really occur.

While I could rely solely on the writing criteria set by the Kentucky Writing Program, I find that my students benefit from being involved in developing, discussing, and assessing their own criteria. Also, while the state standards are valid to a large degree, they do not take into account particular teaching contexts. I teach in the same school and the same room every year, but the students change every year and every period of the day within a year. The students' community-based standards seem more valid and more in tune with their particular interests and abilities. Fortunately, the state's criteria are broad enough to serve as an umbrella under which the specific criteria that students generate can fit. If, for example, my class says that "interesting" is a quality of effective writing, that criterion can fit under the state's mandate for attention to audience. If my students say that good writing needs to "flow," they are illustrating an awareness of the state's emphasis on appropriate organization.

Student Reflection

If one stage of the portfolio process is more important than any other, it would be the student reflection on the criteria in order to select writing for the portfolio. They do this every six weeks so that they develop a practice of reflection and selection within the parameters of the standards we have set. The more they look at the qualities of effective writing and the more they read and re-read their own writing, the more internalized the criteria are likely to become. This reflection takes written form in a cover letter to the reader of the portfolio. This reader may be another student, a parent, the teacher, or a student in another class or even another school, depending on the time of year. I try to mix up the readers of portfolios so that students get practice in writing to other audiences and so that my position as "grade giver" is further decentered. Students know from the beginning that I will read the final portfolio of each semester for grade purposes but that the first-semester grade is based largely on process effort and not on final quality. They know that the final grade for their year of writing will be the ultimate summative grade of the portfolio.

I deemphasize grades so much because I have found that all real revision and reflection come to an abrupt halt when a final grade is placed on any piece of writing or an entire portfolio. I stress to my students that all interim grades throughout the year are merely progress reports of their general effort in class, not of the quality of their writing, which can always be improved on. If they wish, students can revisit in the last six weeks a piece that was completed in the first six weeks. Some do; others do not. Not all writing assignments, not all forms, click with all writers. They learn that the standards we have set are more important than genre; form follows function. And the writing in their portfolios takes many different forms from student to student. One student might have a portfolio with several poems and only one essay. Another might have a portfolio full of editorials and one short story. Genres vary from student to student, as do their topics, their purposes, and their audiences. This variety is another reason that portfolios make a more logical choice for my teaching. They support the diversity of thought and language I have come to value as a reader and a writer.

It may sound like a god-awful mess, but the standards in each class (and they do vary some from class to class) give the portfolio process a structure for both students and teacher. Nowhere is this structure seen more clearly than in the letter to the reader mentioned earlier. Throughout each six-week period, I keep track of those criteria I have covered in minilessons and those the class has covered in seminar discussions. I try to keep these to a workable number so that students can focus on improving those specific skills. When it is time to write the cover letter, I give them a list of framing questions pulled from this list I have been keeping. It goes something like this:

> Set the standard/criterion/quality.
>
> Teach the standard/criterion/quality.
>
> Practice the standard/criterion/quality.
>
> Reflect on the performance of the standard/criterion/quality.

The cover letter can be very revealing with respect to a student's growth within these parameters, especially when the portfolio is read in tandem with the letter. These letters are also helpful when I begin to conference with each student. If a student has written in the letter that she had trouble organizing an essay she selected, I can read the essay especially for its degree of organizational success. If the student was incorrect in her evaluation, I can show her where she organized well, but most of the time students are right about what they can do well and what they need help with. Using the letter as a conference tool has helped me focus my reading of the portfolios (which otherwise can become a time-intensive ordeal) and focus my responses during conferences so that students can develop a realistic plan for the coming term and the writing we are going to do.

Final Reflection

If I have made it sound as though portfolios will solve all problems with grading student writing, I apologize. This practice has evolved over the ten years I have been using portfolios, both state-required and teacher-and-student-devised. If I have learned anything from using portfolios, it is the power of reflection, especially within a certain context. By generating for themselves the qualities of effective writing, my students develop a critical way of reading, a new lens. This lens is very different from the one that told them that what they had written was good because "I liked it." That lens does not lead to willing revision and writing that will stand up to scrutiny by a demanding reader. What's more, the "I like it" lens never sharpens its focus because it rarely meets the grindstone of specific standards, or does so only by chance. I am willing to give my students time to develop their writing, but I am not willing to leave that development up to chance.

Learning to see the power of reflection has also helped me revise my teaching. I still change some element of the portfolio process every year. This coming year will see my biggest change in some time. I plan to abandon the working folder in favor of a writer's notebook, in which students will collect not only their own writing but also handouts on the individual minilessons, copies of readings, observations, and so forth. This is a small change, but a change nonetheless. As with my students' writing, which benefits from reflection and selection, I find my portfolio approach benefits from these same activities as I reflect and revise my approach, trying something new, evaluating it, tweaking it, to best meet the needs of my student writers.

Appendix

Portfolio Requirements

Requirements for First Six Weeks Portfolio/English I (Ninth Grade)

1. Select your best piece of writing from the past six weeks from the following writings:

   ◆ Reading responses

   ◆ Freewrites

   ◆ Observations

   ◆ Personal literacy history drafts

   ◆ Interviews on personal literacy history

2. Include all prewriting and revisions and peer responses.

3. Include a reflective memo in which you discuss your growth as a writer during the past six weeks.

Requirements for Second Six Weeks Portfolio

1. Select your two best pieces of writing from the past six weeks from the following writings:

   ◆ Reading responses

   ◆ Freewrites

   ◆ Observations

   ◆ Poetry immersion (up to three poems or 100 lines)

   ◆ Personal literacy history (if revised again during second six weeks)

2. Include all prewriting and revisions and peer responses.

3. Include a reflective memo in which you discuss your growth as a writer during the past twelve weeks.

Requirements for Third Six Weeks (1st Semester) Portfolio

1. Select your three best pieces of writing from the past six weeks from the following writings:

   ◆ Reading responses

   ◆ Freewrites

   ◆ Observations

   ◆ Character sketch

   ◆ Poetry immersion (up to three poems or 100 lines)

   ◆ Personal literacy history (if revised again during second six weeks)

2. Include all prewriting and revisions and peer responses.

3. Include a reflective memo in which you discuss your growth as a writer during the past eighteen weeks.

Works Cited

Kentucky Department of Education. 1999. *The Kentucky Writing Portfolio Teacher's Handbook*. Frankfort: Kentucky Department of Education.

Yancey, Kathleen Blake. 1992. "Portfolios in the Writing Classroom: A Final Reflection." Pp. 102–16 in *Portfolios in the Writing Classroom*, ed. Kathleen Blake Yancey. Urbana, IL: National Council of Teachers of English.

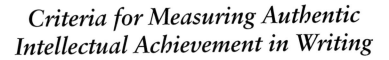

CHAPTER THIRTY

Criteria for Measuring Authentic Intellectual Achievement in Writing

KENDRA SISSERSON
University of Chicago

CARMEN K. MANNING
University of Chicago

ANNIE KNEPLER
University of Illinois at Chicago

DAVID A. JOLLIFFE
DePaul University

Two of the challenging tasks that English language arts teachers face each day are to design assignments that are meaningful, demanding, and appropriate for their students and to coach students through the creation of compositions that respond to the invitation the assignment offers. Adding to the responsibility are current reform agendas calling for more challenging academic work for all U.S. students, implicitly charging teachers with the task of improving the intellectual quality of students' work. These calls for reform are bolstered by research providing evidence that when teachers give assignments that demand higher intellectual effort, students generally produce better work (Newmann, Lopez, and Bryk 1998).

The rubric discussed in this chapter originally appeared in Kendra Sisserson, Carmen K. Manning, Annie Knepler, and David A. Jolliffe, "Authentic Intellectual Achievement in Writing," *English Journal* 91.6 (July 2002), pp. 63–69.

We have spent the past four years developing a set of criteria (see the appendix) by which to examine what we call authentic intellectual achievement (AIA) (see Newmann & Assoc. [1996] for a history of the construct) in the writing assignments that teachers prepare and the student work these assignments call forth. These criteria are appropriate for informing writing instruction in grades K–12 and have been examined, discussed, and employed by teachers across the country, most extensively in Chicago public schools (CPS).[1]

The rubric evaluates the extent to which writing assignments ask students to construct knowledge, elaborate, and relate their writing to their own lives, and examines the extent to which students demonstrate these skills in their writing. While we see our criteria as valuable tools for helping teachers assess their assignments and their students' work, another useful feature is their power to motivate and guide conversations among teachers who want to ensure that they are helping their students do meaningful work in English language arts. The following rubric evolved from such conversations, from our classroom experiences, and from our understanding of AIA; we urge groups of teachers to perhaps use our criteria as a starting point but to develop their own context-appropriate rubrics through similar processes.

The Components of the Rubric

Construction of Knowledge

This criterion evaluates the degree to which teachers' assignments call for and student work demonstrates interpretation, analysis, synthesis, or evaluation of information. Assignments that emphasize construction of knowledge ask students to move beyond simple reproduction of information they have read, listened to, or viewed. An assignment that asks students to recount what they learned from a book on Mexico, for example, does not call for students to construct knowledge to the same degree as an assignment asking students to compare a Mexican village to their own neighborhood. In turn, student work should demonstrate that the writer has produced reasonably original material and has not merely repeated information she or he has read or heard.

A student who retells the plot of Richard Wright's *Black Boy* is primarily reproducing information, whereas a student who examines the story to write about the effects of racism on a young boy in the South must interpret and analyze the story to do so.

The terms *interpretation, analysis, synthesis,* and *evaluation* capture a full range of cognitive processes; an assignment or piece of work needs only to target one of these cognitive skills to demonstrate construction of knowledge. These processes do not function separately, nor do we see them as existing in a hierarchical relationship in which analysis, for example, represents a higher cognitive function than evaluation. (In this way, we differ significantly from Bloom's taxonomy [Bloom 1956].) The boundaries between these skills are fluid rather than distinct, and most of the time people apply more than one skill at a time. Comparing two political candidates, for example, may involve analyzing their platforms, interpreting their slogans and speeches, synthesizing information from various sources, and evaluating them as leaders.

Elaborated Written Communication

This criterion measures the extent to which students elaborate, which by our definition requires that the writing both state an original point and support it with evidence. The original point may be a conclusion, a generalization, or an argument; the evidence may be examples, details, illustrations, or reasons. There must be a coherent, logical connection between the generalization and its support.

We stress that elaborated writing must include both generalizations and support. In schoolwork, students are commonly asked to do one or the other: they are asked to watch a movie, look at a picture, or read a text and then make a conclusion about it, *or* they are given a generalization and asked to supply supporting reasons, facts, or details. In the common parlance of the classroom, elaboration often means adding details (a definition supported by many state writing assessment rubrics), and much of the writing students produce in school is in the form of fill-in-the-blank exercises or short answers to open-response questions. Yet even when students are given longer assignments, such as complete essays, all too often they are given the outline—a prompt that suggests a conclusion, for instance, or a set of details to examine for commonalities—and asked to complete the picture. We suggest that cognitive work is enhanced when students are called on to supply both halves of the equation: to make an argument, draw a conclusion, or suggest a generalization *and* to substantiate this through extended writing. Students may be asked, for example, to make an evaluation about a character and provide appropriate evidence from the story to support that evaluation. Or, in narrative writing, in addition to telling what happened, students may be asked to draw a conclusion about an event and to ensure that the narration supports the conclusion.

Connection to Students' Lives

With this criterion, we argue that the process of making meaning is strengthened when an assignment has some inherent relevance, when the student feels a significant connection with the assignment and its outcome. The spirit of this criterion is to facilitate an interaction between what students accomplish in the classroom and their lives at home, at work, on the playground, or on the sports field.

This criterion calls us to question what constitutes "authentic" activity. Students are often asked to complete "authentic" tasks such as writing letters, business reports, or journals. Yet writing a letter to a customer service representative asking for a refund on a defective product is not, in our view, an authentic assignment unless the product, the defect, and the customer service department are part of the student's life. A more authentic assignment would ask students to devise their own letters to real people concerning problems that are actually of concern to them.

Grammar, Usage, Mechanics, and Vocabulary (GUMV)

One goal of teaching writing is to help students develop control over their writing: to help them anticipate their audience and choose appropriate language. In order to do this, students have to master certain skills and conventions that allow their thoughts to be communicated clearly. Proficiency in GUMV represents a student's mastery of language.

How the Rubric Was Developed

The authors and Fred Newmann originally designed the criteria at the University of Chicago to examine the intellectual quality of schoolwork in Chicago's schools as part of an evaluation of the Annenberg reform initiative in CPS. Each summer of the five-year evaluation, a team of CPS schoolteachers was trained to use these criteria to evaluate thousands of teachers' writing assignments and students' written work collected from schools across the district. These scoring sessions provoked conversations among teachers about the intellectual demands their own assignments did or did not place on their students. Our first task as conversation leaders was to clarify the terminology of the criteria, which for many teachers provided a unique opportunity to examine what we as teachers mean when we use common parlance. We discovered, for example, that teachers often mean different things when we use terms such as *authentic* or *elaborate*.

In these conversations, we discussed what scoring high or low in each criterion might suggest and when it would be appropriate to give an assignment that would not score high on the criteria; we also stressed that assigning a score based on a criterion was not equivalent to grading, which we view as a more holistic and total act. For many teachers in the group, these conversations provided a unique and significant opportunity to evaluate student writing and, in particular, writing assignments with a peer group using a universal language and common criteria. Several teachers in the group took the criteria back to their schools to initiate similar conversations among faculty members. Others reported starting similar but age-appropriate conversations with students and using the criteria in student conferences as students were developing writing pieces.

These conversations prompted teachers to examine their own pedagogy and to experiment with ways they could elicit highly authentic, intellectually provocative work from their students. With input from these teachers, we translated the criteria into a rubric that illustrates a coherent vision of authentic intellectual quality in writing and writing instruction.

Theoretical Rationale

The theory of AIA in writing incorporates current thinking on constructivism, authenticity, and the writing process. Constructivism, perhaps best understood as a theory about learning that has given rise to theories about teaching (Cohen, McLaughlin, and Talbert 1993; Einbender and Wood 1995; Newmann and Associates 1996; Witte 1992), argues that students learn best when they acquire the strategies to actively construct new knowledge from interactions between what they already know and information they encounter in new social contexts. Over the last thirty years, the writing process movement has highlighted constructivist principles in writing instruction (see Grabe and Kaplan 1996).

Our scheme also draws on recent examinations of the relationship between authenticity and constructivism. The term *authentic* has been used synonymously with *performance* to suggest instructional activities that physically resemble real-world activities, which carries the danger of allowing student participation in activities to become an end in itself, without regard to the intellectual quality of those activities. In our view, this approach can give too much credence to the structure of an assignment at the expense of its substance. This may be particularly dangerous in the writing classroom, where the very act of writing may be seen as authenticating the writing assignment, or where the form of the writing may be seen as authentic even though the content is not as "cognitively authentic" as it could be.

Our use of the term *authentic* aligns us more closely with those who endeavor not to specify performance tasks but instead seek to describe the cognitive connections that authentic assignments promote (Wiggins 1998; Darling-Hammond, Ancess, and Falk 1995). Students may, for example, be asked to write a business letter. In our scheme, writing a letter asking for a refund on a defective product is not a truly authentic assignment unless the product and the defect are actually part of the student's life. Writing a letter to a city council asking for repair of the pothole on the bike path leading to school, on the other hand, could be authentic. To truly serve authentic purpose, we believe students should go through the processes of discerning how a citizen can effect change, to whom such a letter should go, and the most likely means of achieving a successful response to a real problem. We invite teachers to consider how journal writing, too, can be used as authentically as possible.

In this spirit, AIA envisions meaningful work in school as preparation for the future intellectual demands of productive employment, responsible citizenship, and successful management of personal affairs in society. When students are asked to construct new knowledge concerning a topic, issue, situation, or text that holds personal meaning for them, and to communicate this knowledge through extended writing, then they are preparing for the intellectual demands of adult society.

Appendix

Criteria for Examining Authentic Intellectual Achievement

Teachers' Assignments

Criterion 1: Construction of Knowledge

The assignment asks students to interpret, analyze, synthesize, or evaluate information in writing about a topic, rather than merely to reproduce information.

3 = The task's dominant expectation is for students to interpret, analyze, synthesize, or evaluate information, rather than merely to reproduce information.

2 = There is some expectation for students to interpret, analyze, synthesize, or evaluate information, rather than merely to reproduce information.

1 = There is very little or no expectation for students to interpret, analyze, synthesize, or evaluate information. The dominant expectation is that students will merely reproduce information gained by reading, listening, or observing.

Criterion 2: Elaborated Written Communication

The writing assignment asks students to draw conclusions or make generalizations or arguments AND support them through extended writing.

4 = Explicit call for generalization AND support. The writing assignment asks students to draw conclusions or make generalizations or arguments, AND to substantiate them with illustrations, details, or reasons.

3 = Call for generalization OR support. The writing assignment asks students either to draw conclusions or make generalizations or arguments, OR to offer illustrations, details, or reasons, but not both.

2 = Short-answer exercises. The assignment can be answered with only one or two sentences, clauses, or phrasal fragments that complete a thought.

1 = Fill-in-the-blank or multiple-choice exercises.

Criterion 3: Connection to Students' Lives

The writing assignment asks students to connect the topic to their lives.

3 = The writing assignment explicitly asks students to connect the topic to experiences, observations, feelings, or situations significant in their lives.

2 = The writing assignment offers the opportunity for students to connect the topic to experiences, observations, feelings, or situations significant in their lives, but does not explicitly call for them to do so.

1 = The writing assignment offers very minimal or no opportunity for students to connect the topic to experiences, observations, feelings, or situations significant in their lives.

Student Writing

Criterion 1: Construction of Knowledge

The writing demonstrates interpretation, analysis, synthesis, or evaluation in order to construct knowledge, rather than mere reproduction of information. The essential question is whether the writing demonstrates reasonably original thinking, rather than a restatement of some analysis previously given in a text or discussion.

4 = Substantial evidence of construction of knowledge. Almost all of the student's work shows interpretation, analysis, synthesis, or evaluation.

3 = Moderate evidence of construction of knowledge. A moderate portion of the student's work shows interpretation, analysis, synthesis, or evaluation.

2 = Some evidence of construction of knowledge. A small portion of the student's work shows interpretation, analysis, synthesis, or evaluation.

1 = No evidence of construction of knowledge. No portion of the student's work shows interpretation, analysis, synthesis, or evaluation; OR virtually all construction of knowledge is in error.

Criterion 2: Elaborated Written Communication

The writing draws conclusions or makes generalizations or arguments AND supports them with examples, illustrations, details, or reasons. Elaboration consists of two parts: a conclusion, generalization, or argument AND support for it, in the form of at least one example, illustration, detail, or reason. Elaboration is coherent when the support is appropriate for and consistent with the conclusions, generalizations, or arguments.

4 = Substantial evidence of elaboration. Almost all of the student's work comprises an elaborated, coherent account.

3 = Moderate evidence of elaboration. A moderate portion of the student's work comprises an elaborated, coherent account.

2 = Some evidence of elaboration. A small portion of the student's work comprises an elaborated, coherent account.

1 = No evidence of elaboration. No portion of the student's work comprises an elaborated, coherent account.

Criterion 3: Grammar, Usage, Mechanics, and Vocabulary

The writing demonstrates proficiencies with grammar, usage, mechanics, and vocabulary appropriate for the grade level so that the meaning of the writing is understandable to readers.

3 = The student writing offers a satisfactory demonstration of grammar, usage, mechanics, and vocabulary appropriate for the grade level. There may be some errors, but they present no problem for understanding the student's meaning.

2 = There are many errors in grammar, usage, mechanics, and/or vocabulary, OR the errors in grammar, usage, mechanics, and/or vocabulary make it difficult, but not impossible, to understand the student's meaning.

1 = The use of grammar, usage, mechanics, and/or vocabulary is so flawed that it is not possible to understand the student's meaning.

Note

1. The research informing this essay was supported by the Consortium on Chicago School Research with funding primarily by the Chicago Annenberg Challenge and by grants from the Spencer Foundation, the Joyce Foundation, and the John D. and Catherine T. MacArthur Foundation. This essay reflects the opinions of its authors and does not necessarily represent those of the Consortium on Chicago School Research or its funding agencies.

Works Cited

Bloom, Benjamin. 1956. *Taxonomy of Educational Objectives: The Classification of Educational Goals.* New York: Longmans, Green.

Cohen, David K., Milbrey Wallin McLaughlin, and Joan E. Talbert, eds. 1993. *Teaching for Understanding: Challenges for Policy and Practice.* San Francisco: Jossey-Bass.

Darling-Hammond, Linda, Jacqueline Ancess, and Beverly Falk. 1995. *Authentic Assessment in Action: Studies of Schools and Students at Work.* New York: Teachers College Press.

Einbender, Lynne, and Diane Wood. 1995. *An Authentic Journey: Teachers' Emergent Understandings about Authentic Assessment and Practice.* New York: Columbia University, Teachers College, National Center for Restructuring Education, Schools, and Teaching.

Grabe, William, and Robert B. Kaplan. 1996. *Theory and Practice of Writing: An Applied Linguistic Perspective.* New York: Longman.

Newmann, Fred M., and Associates. 1996. *Authentic Achievement: Restructuring Schools for Intellectual Quality.* San Francisco: Jossey-Bass.

Newmann, Fred M., Gudelia Lopez, and Tony S. Bryk. 1998. *The Quality of Intellectual Work in Chicago Schools: A Baseline Report.* Chicago: Consortium on Chicago School Research.

Wiggins, Grant. 1998. Letter to the editor: An Exchange of Views on "Semantics, Psychometrics, and Assessment Reform: A Close Look at 'Authentic' Assessments." *Educational Researcher* 27.6: 19–21.

Witte, Stephen P. 1992. "Text, Context, Intertext: Toward a Constructivist Semiotic of Writing." *Written Communication* 9: 237–308.

INDEX

EDITORS

Photo by Johnston Photography, Omaha, Nebraska

Cindy Moore is assistant professor of English at St. Cloud State University. In addition to directing the university's Composition Program, she teaches courses in writing and writing theory. Her research interests include composition theory and pedagogy, connections between creative writing and composition, mentoring, and faculty development. Essays reflecting these issues have appeared in such journals as *Dialogue, Feminist Teacher, Profession,* and *Readerly/Writerly Texts.* She is coeditor of *The Dissertation and the Discipline: Reinventing Composition Studies* (2002).

Peggy O'Neill, who began her teaching career as a public school English teacher, is assistant professor in the communication department at Loyola College, Maryland, where she teaches writing and directs the composition program. Her scholarship, which focuses on writing assessment and composition pedagogy, has appeared in journals such as *College Composition and Communication, Composition Studies,* and *Assessing Writing* as well as several edited collections. She also has co-edited another volume, *A Field of Dreams: Independent Writing Programs and the Future of Composition Studies* (2002).

CONTRIBUTORS

Margrethe Ahlschwede teaches writing at the University of Tennessee at Martin, where she also directs the West Tennessee Writing Project, a site of the National Writing Project, and helps facilitate Voice Lessons: The UT Martin Faculty Writing Project. Ahlschwede began her adult life in journalism, working for the Lincoln, Nebraska, newspapers, and then as an assistant editor with the Agricultural Extension Service at North Carolina State University. In the 1980s, she served two terms on the Lincoln City Council, an experience that is the backdrop for her citizen-advocacy stance in writing classes. She earned her Ph.D. from the University of Nebraska–Lincoln.

Wendy Bishop, Kellogg H. Hunt Professor of English at Florida State University, teaches composition, rhetoric, poetry, and essay writing. A former writing center director and writing program administrator, she studies writing classrooms, writes assignments with her students, and shares her evolving techniques in textbooks such as *Thirteen Ways of Looking for a Poem, The Subject Is Writing, Metro,* and the forthcoming *Writing Process Reader.*

Heather E. Bruce is assistant professor in the Department of English at the University of Montana. In addition to the first-year composition course described here, she teaches courses in English education. She has been a site director and teacher/consultant with the Utah Writing Project and will direct the Montana Writing Project. Prior to her doctoral work, Bruce taught English language arts at the middle school and high school levels for thirteen years.

Suellynn Duffey directed and taught in the basic writing program at Ohio State University for several years and is past president of the Conference on Basic Writing. As director of first-year writing at various institutions, she worked with novice teachers (through training and mentoring) as they began their careers, and she has frequently consulted with high school teachers on writing-related concerns. She has published in journals such as *College Composition and Communication* and *Rhetoric Review* and considers teaching to be at the heart of both her scholarly and administrative work.

Contributors

Kate Freeland holds a B.S. in education (1991) and an M.A. in English (1998) from Indiana University–Purdue University Fort Wayne. She has taught 100- and 200-level writing courses at IPFW for five years, working primarily with basic writers. She also consults with local English teachers (K–12) on writing pedagogy and assessment. Before beginning her college-level teaching career, she taught middle school language arts and high school English in both public and private schools.

Eve Gerken has taught English at Concordia Lutheran High School in Fort Wayne, Indiana, for seven years. She earned her undergraduate degree from Wittenberg University in Springfield, Ohio, and is presently finishing an M.A.T. in English at Indiana University–Purdue University Fort Wayne. Gerken has done additional graduate course work at the Bread Loaf School of English in Juneau, Alaska, through Middlebury College, and at Ball State University in Muncie, Indiana. She has shared her teaching experience and ideas in such journals as *Writing on the Edge* and NCTE's *Ideas Plus.*

Carl Gerriets reverse-commutes from the city (St. Paul, Minnesota) to work at Century College, sometimes on his mountain bike, thinking about topics such as the role of questions in critical thinking, what it means to practice a Christian pedagogy, and why *Star Trek: Deep Space Nine* never got the respect it deserved. He enjoys teaching at Century because he learns so much from his students, who are invariably generous, brave, strong, and very, very smart.

Janis E. Haswell is associate professor at Texas A&M University–Corpus Christi, where she teaches writing and British literature. Her scholarly interests include gender theory and gender studies, postcolonial theory, philosophies of place, and writing as a form of inquiry. In addition to articles in such journals as *College Composition and Communication, Journal of Teaching Writing, Rhetoric Review,* and *Studies in the Novel,* she has published monographs on Paul Scott's *Raj Quartet* and on the double-voiced verse of W. B. Yeats. Her book on Paul Scott's philosophy of place is forthcoming.

Brian Huot is professor in the English department at the University of Louisville, where he directs the composition program. He teaches first-year writing and the teaching of first-year writing every year. During the twenty-one years he has been a composition teacher, he has also taught at Lane College (a historically black institution in Jackson, Tennessee), the University of Northern Iowa, Syracuse University, and Indiana University–Purdue University Indianapolis (IUPUI).

J. Paul Johnson is associate professor and writing center director in the Department of English at Winona State University in Minnesota, where he teaches a variety of courses in language, literature, writing, and film. The Web site for the Fall 1999 English 111 course described herein can be found, with his other courses, at http://course1.winona.msus.edu/pjohnson.

David A. Jolliffe is professor of English and director of the first-year program at DePaul University. Jolliffe has taught at Wheeling Park High School, Bethany College, West Virginia University, the University of Texas at Austin, and the University of Illinois at Chicago. His new research examines how adolescents read elaborated, disjunctive prose.

Annie Knepler is a Ph.D. candidate and composition instructor at the University of Illinois at Chicago. Her current emphasis is on community-based literacy initiatives and urban education. She is also coeditor of *Crossing Cultures: Readings for Composition,* a multicultural anthology of essays, stories, and poems.

Catherine G. Latterell, assistant professor of English at Penn State Altoona, earned advanced degrees in rhetoric and technical communication from Michigan Technological University. She teaches courses in first-year composition and advanced writing and rhetoric, often asking students to examine the impact of technology on communication and their processes of problem solving. Her research interests combine composition theory and cultural theory to explore, among other things, issues in teaching with technology.

Jennifer Lowe began taking classes at Century College in the summer of 1999. She completed her A.S. degree in May 2002 and was immediately hired as a full-time employee by the Hazelden Foundation, where she works as the administrative assistant to the executive director of Regional Mental Health.

Carmen K. Manning is a Ph.D. candidate at the University of Chicago. Her current work focuses on K–12 literacy teachers' ability to reflect and the impact of ability on student achievement. She is a former high school English teacher who now teaches in the teacher education program at DePaul University.

Janice McIntire-Strasburg is assistant professor at Saint Louis University and director of the English department's computer-assisted instruction lab. She received her Ph.D. from the University of Nevada, Las Vegas, in 1998. She teaches first-year composition, Internet and media writing, hypertext design, and literature and is presently devising courses in teaching with technology and textual scholarship.

Margaret A. McLaughlin, associate professor of writing, has been teaching first-year writing classes at Georgia Southern University since 1990. She previously taught at several midwestern schools, including Spoon River College, Western Illinois University, Illinois State University, and Ohio University.

Dan Melzer is a doctoral candidate in the rhetoric and composition program at Florida State University. He teaches first-year writing and tutors in the reading/writing center.

Hildy Miller is director of writing and associate professor of English at Portland State University. She has taught a variety of graduate and undergraduate courses and conducted research on administrative issues, feminist theory, and theories of learning and writing. At her previous job at the University of Minnesota, she co-taught the writing service-learning course with Beverly Atkinson, English undergraduate adviser.

Mary M. Mulder received her M.A. in English language and literature from the University of Michigan in 1967 and began her teaching career at Camden County [community] College in New Jersey. She taught there for fourteen years and was the recipient of a midcareer fellowship at Princeton University in 1980. She has been teaching full time at Jefferson Community College since 1991. In 2000 she received a Ph.D. in rhetoric and composition from the University of Louisville.

Lee Nickoson-Massey, as visiting instructor in the academic writing program at the University of Illinois at Urbana-Champaign, teaches courses in developmental writing for first-year students. She has received several awards for her teaching, and her name appears on the *Incomplete List of Instructors Voted Outstanding by Their Students* at the University of Illinois. She received the Taimi Ranta Award for Outstanding Teaching by a Ph.D. Candidate and the Outstanding University Graduate Student Teaching Award at Illinois State University, where she is currently working to complete her dissertation in composition studies.

Annette Harris Powell is a doctoral candidate in rhetoric and composition at the University of Louisville. She has taught Introduction to College Writing and Intermediate College Writing for the past five years and has also taught Writing about Literature and Introduction to Pan-African literature. Her research interests include issues of access/agency and technology and theories of race, class, and literacy.

Mark Schaub taught for almost seven years at the American University in Cairo, Egypt, where he served as the writing program director. He has also taught at Wichita State University, Wichita Collegiate School, and Purdue University, where he received his Ph.D. in English. Schaub is presently assistant professor of writing at Grand Valley State University in Allendale, Michigan, where he teaches composition and professional writing.

David Seitz is assistant professor of English at Wright State University near Dayton, Ohio, where he teaches first-year writing; undergraduate courses in writing for popular publication, rhetorical theory, and cultural studies; and graduate courses in teaching composition, rhetoric, politics of literacy, and ethnographic research.

Kendra Sisserson is a Ph.D. candidate at the University of Chicago and a former high school English teacher. Her dissertation research looks at secondary writing instruction in Chicago public schools. She works for the University of California, San Diego, examining the impact of San Diego city schools' reform on literacy instruction.

Steven P. Smith has taught primarily ninth- and twelfth-grade English at North Bullitt High School since 1984. He taught seventh- and eighth-grade language arts at Lebanon Junction Elementary from 1978 to 1984, after having taught first-year composition as a teaching assistant at Western Kentucky University, where he earned his B.A. and M.A. in English. He has also been a member of the Louisville Writing Project since 1991. Smith has served as chair of the English department since 1990 and as his district's high school portfolio writing cluster leader since 1996. He has also been a part-time instructor in the composition program at the University of Louisville.

Jeff Sommers, professor of English at Miami University Middletown, teaches composition, children's literature, and American literature. He has published articles on composition and literature pedagogy, along with four composition textbooks. Winner of Miami University's Arts and Science Distinguished Educator Award in 1993, Sommers has taught graduate seminars on composition pedagogy for graduate assistants and K–12 teachers.

Katie Hupp Stahlnecker has taught at the University of Nebraska at Omaha for ten years, where she has held both part-time and temporary full-time positions. She has also taught part time and worked in the writing center at Creighton University in Omaha. Currently, she is pursuing a Ph.D. at the University of Nebraska–Lincoln.

Margaret M. Strain is assistant professor of English rhetoric and composition at the University of Dayton, where she teaches undergraduate and graduate courses in writing, the structure of English, composition theory, and research methods. Her scholarly interests include historiography in rhetoric and composition studies, oral narrative, and computers and writing. With James M. Boehnlein, she is editing *Principles and Practices: New Discourses for Advanced Writers.*

Tonya M. Stremlau is associate professor in the English department at Gallaudet University, where she has taught since 1996. She teaches (primarily writing) courses at all levels, from developmental through advanced. She received her doctorate in English from Louisiana State University in 1996.

P. L. Thomas completed his doctoral work at the University of South Carolina on the life of English educator Lou LaBrant. He has taught high school English for the past sixteen years, while often serving as adjunct instructor in English and graduate education at colleges in upstate South Carolina.

Stephen Wilhoit is associate professor of English at the University of Dayton, where he teaches graduate and undergraduate courses in composition, creative writing, and literature. He served as director of teaching assistant training for twelve years and as director of composition for three. In 1997 he was recognized as teacher of the year by the College of Arts and Sciences and now serves as a fellow in the Ryan C. Harris Learning-Teaching Center, coordinating Dayton's writing-in-the-disciplines program. Wilhoit has published several short stories, numerous articles and book chapters on TA education and writing pedagogy, and one composition textbook, *A Brief Guide to Writing from Readings.*

Peggy M. Woods, assistant director for teacher training for the writing program at the University of Massachusetts Amherst, teaches first-year writing and works with graduate students who teach within the program. As a fiction writer and compositionist, she has also taught creative writing and a range of upper-level composition courses.

Kathleen Blake Yancey is R. Roy Pearce Professor of English at Clemson University, where she teaches undergraduate and graduate students and directs the Roy and Marnie Pearce Center for Professional Communication. Author, editor, or coeditor of seven books, most of them addressing issues related to writing assessment, she co-founded the journal *Assessing Writing* and currently coedits *Journal of Writing Assessment.* President of the Council of Writing Program Administrators, Yancey is also assistant chair for the Conference on College Composition and Communication. Among her current projects she includes the development and implementation of the Clemson Digital Portfolio and an exploration into the role of delivery—from seminar to distance learning—in shaping college composition.

Pavel Zemliansky earned his Ph.D. at Florida State University and is now assistant professor in the writing program at James Madison University. Before becoming a writing teacher in the United States, he taught English as a foreign language in his native Ukraine and worked for the cultural section of the British Embassy. At the embassy, he designed and taught ESL methodology seminars to teachers of English as a foreign language at all levels. In addition to rhetoric and composition, his current pedagogical and research interests include ESL writing, linguistics, and creative nonfiction. Zemliansky is particularly interested in the rhetoric and pedagogy of the first-year research paper.

This book was typeset in Sabon by Electronic Imaging.
The typeface used on the cover was Cochin.
The book was printed on 50-lb. Husky Offset by IPC Communications.